Lawrence Frank

UNIVERSITY OF NEBRASKA PRESS: LINCOLN AND LONDON

Charles Dickens

and the Romantic Self

The paper in this book meets
the guidelines for permanence
and durability of the Committee
on Production Guidelines for
Book Longevity of the Council
on Library Resources.

Publication of this book was
aided by a grant from the
Andrew W. Mellon Foundation.

Library of Congress Cataloging
in Publication Data

Frank, Lawrence, 1933-
Charles Dickens and the
romantic self.
Includes bibliographical
references and index.
1. Dickens, Charles, 1812-1870–
Knowledge–Psychology.
2. Self in literature.
3. Psychoanalysis and literature.
4. Romanticism–England.
5. Fiction, Autobiographic.
I. Title.
PR4592.P74F7   1984
823'.8   84-3601
ISBN 0-8032-1965-2 (alk. paper)

To Austin Warren

Contents

Acknowledgments

This book had its beginning in a question posed by J. Hillis Miller of Yale University concerning the theoretical assumptions underlying my use of the works of Sigmund Freud in reading the novels of Charles Dickens. The Introduction and the chapters on *Dombey and Son* and *David Copperfield* are my attempts to explain and to justify the relevance of psychoanalytic insights to an understanding of Dickens's fictive world.

In completing the book, I enjoyed the support and the comments of colleagues at several universities. Charles Altieri, Malcolm Brown, Donald Kartiganer, and Robert Shulman of the University of Washington read early versions of much of the book and I have used their observations in my revisions. To Michael Magie, also of the University of Washington, I owe a particular debt for his observation that *Our Mutual Friend* provides a model of its own influence: his words appear in the Conclusion.

Chester Anderson, Michael Hancher, Gordon Hirsch, Martin Roth and Madelon Sprengnether of the University of Minnesota offered their comments and their sustaining friendship as I completed the manuscript. Ronald Schleifer of the University of Oklahoma was particularly helpful in guiding me to a fuller understanding of the implications of my Conclusion; its final form is a response to his observations.

Others have provided the support necessary to the completion of any project of this sort. I would like to mention specifically Avrom Fleishman of The Johns Hopkins University and G. Robert Stange of Tufts University.

One person deserves special acknowledgment. This book would not have been completed without the generous and unfailing encouragement of Austin Warren who has served—for me and for others fortunate enough to have come under his influence—as a model of the teacher and the literary critic. In his teaching and his writing, Austin Warren has exemplified the meaning of the word *vocation*. It is only fitting that I dedicate this book to him.

Charles Dickens and the Romantic Self

Introduction

Dickens, Freud, and the Romantic Self

In *The Order of Things,* Michel Foucault observes, "It is comforting . . .
and a source of profound relief to think that man is only a recent invention, a figure not yet two centuries old, a new wrinkle in our knowledge,
and that he will disappear again as soon as that knowledge has discovered a new form."[1] Foucault reminds us that forms of human knowledge
have a history and that conceptions of human nature undergo change,
leading to the possibility that there may be no human nature at all.

Within such a relativistic perspective, the sciences of a particular era not only offer an interpretation of the universe, they provide the world-view, the language, the figures of speech, by which human nature is conceived. Foucault is more than merely whimsical when he writes of man as a "recent invention, a figure not yet two centuries old": man as conceived or imagined within the last two centuries *is* a figure, a trope, constructed upon the sciences of the day. As these sciences become obsolete, through the vicissitudes of time, the ways in which men and women have habitually imagined themselves will prove to be obsolete too. As new forms of knowledge appear to supplant former truths, new forms of an elusive, if not illusory, human nature will inevitably emerge.

In this study of the Romantic Self in the later novels of Charles Dickens, I shall be exploring this recent invention, man, implicitly touching upon the "profound relief" Foucault feels as he anticipates the demise of a historical phenomenon that he perceives as burdensome. In part, Foucault is responding to the implications of the relativism he so forcefully promulgates. Human beings exist in time, they are finite creatures influenced by the physical bodies constituting a part of their being, by the modes of production shaping the societies they inhabit, and by the grammars and traditions of the languages they speak. Men and women become the subjective centers of the universe, with the status of their own subjectivity one of the most perplexing problems to be considered, but they are always influenced, if not determined, by "a life, a society, and a language that have a history" (pp. 372–73). In imagining the subjectivity of his heroes and heroines—and I am arguing for his profound concern with that subjectivity—Dickens avails himself of those romantic conceptions of the self emerging after, and in response to, the deconstructing skepticism of a David Hume and the recently triumphant science of life, biology.

The psychoanalytic perspective I shall employ in my discussion of Dickens's heroes and heroines exists in time and remains indebted not only to the biology, economics, and philology of the nineteenth century, but to those works of fiction, Dickens's novels among them, that Freud so avidly read throughout his life. The psychoanalytic critic must write with the awareness of what Frank Kermode, in *The Sense of an Ending,* describes as "an historical transition . . . from a literature which assumed that it was imitating an order to a literature which assumes that it has to create an order, unique and self-dependent."[2] This leads to Kermode's distinction between myth and fiction: "Myth operates within the diagrams of ritual, which presupposes total and adequate explanations of things as they are and were; it is a sequence of radically unchangeable gestures. Fictions are for finding things out, and they change as the needs of sense-making change. Myths are the agents of stability, fictions the agents of change. Myths call for absolute, fictions for conditional assent."[3] The sciences of the classical age as defined by Foucault and Kermode are myths, forms of knowledge once seen as "total and adequate explanations of things as they are and were." The sciences of the modern age are hypotheses or fictions, attempts to make sense out of the physical universe and the societies we inhabit. Science so conceived is always "science" in quotation marks, never able to assert its universal validity with the confidence of the eighteenth century, but always compelled to acknowledge its temporality: "When the fictions change, therefore, the world changes in step with them."[4]

In *Beyond the Pleasure Principle* Freud writes of his "being obliged to operate with the scientific terms, that is to say, with the figurative language" peculiar to depth psychology: "We could not otherwise describe the processes in question at all, and *indeed we could not have become aware of them*. The deficiencies in our description would probably vanish if we were already in a position to replace the psychological terms by physiological or chemical ones. It is *true that they too are only part of a figurative language;* but it is one with which we have long been familiar and which is perhaps a simpler one as well."[5] Freud's acute awareness of the sources of his language and its figurative status, through which he becomes aware of psychological processes, stands as a warning to everyone writing within the psychoanalytic tradition. The figurative language of psychology generates the psychoanalytic description of the mind and determines the phenomena it seeks to isolate and to describe. Psychoanalytic ideas, imbedded in the terminology of biology, of economics, and increasingly the terminology of linguistics, participate in the changes that the sciences and the language of a culture undergo. Every psychoanalytic critic is, of necessity, a neo-Freudian, writing within a tradition that must not become static, lest it harden into one of those myths of which Frank Kermode writes. In noting the "artificial structure of hypotheses," Freud sounds the call to the neo-Freudian endeavor of revision, a call echoing the warning of Nietzsche in *Beyond Good and Evil:* any philosophy "always creates the world in its own image; it cannot do otherwise."[6]

The relativism of Foucault and Kermode endorses the Nietzschean belief in that creation of the world where there are neither eternal laws to be discovered nor a human nature independent of the culture or the epoch in which an individual lives.[7] In the place of a human nature given to men and women independently of a cultural situation, there are instead acquired ways of imagining that nature and that changing idea of the self so indispensable to the ordering of their lives. Dickens and Freud write within the context of a romantic tradition that informs the assumptions by which Dickens imagines the careers of his characters and by which Freud attempts to understand the dilemmas of his patients. The psychoanalytic critic of a Dickens novel need not naïvely treat fictional characters as if they were real people. Freud's understanding of his patients—and their understanding of themselves—is indebted to the literary and the scientific traditions of the nineteenth century; his assumptions about the life of the self are akin to Dickens's. The ontological discontinuity between the characters in the pages of a Dickens novel and the patients discussed in Freud's case histories loses its apparent clarity. The literary artist and the physician of the mind necessarily avail themselves of romantic paradigms of the self. Freud's elaborate psychological speculations in *The Interpretation of Dreams* and elsewhere become a form of exegesis, a critical introduction to the literary world of the case histories.[8]

With the triumph of the biological perspective and the practice of anatomy, a new attitude toward the immediately perceivable or visible surface of things appears. According to Foucault, the aim of anatomy is to pierce the surface of an organism and to make visible "the primary organs, which are essential, central, hidden, and unreachable except by dissection—that is, by materially removing the coloured envelope formed by the secondary organs" (p. 268). Only through the examination of the hidden organs of an animal can their functions be determined, and only through the knowledge of an animal's function can its *telos*, or true nature, be understood: the animal "becomes the privileged form, with its hidden structures, its buried organs, so many invisible functions, and that distant force, at the foundation of its being, which keeps it alive" (p. 277). This is the project of biology, the quest for the distant force, to which Freud acknowledges his debt in *Beyond the Pleasure Principle*: "The uncertainty of our speculation has been greatly increased by the necessity for borrowing from the science of biology. Biology is truly a

land of unlimited possibilities" (*SE*, 18:60). The science of biology, and
the language it provides, creates uncertainty for Freud, but it also creates
the possibility of his discipline. Freud performs an anatomy of the psyche, moving always toward the invisible he seeks to make visible, the
distant force of the unconscious.

But one of the first to perform Foucault's "anatomic disarticulation"
of things is David Hume in his critique "Of Personal Identity." In his
attack upon the Cartesian cogito, Hume raises anew the nature of the
self and poses the problem to which romantic writers are to respond in a
variety of ways. For Hume disagrees with those philosophers "who
imagine we are every moment intimately conscious of what we call our
SELF; that we feel its existence and its continuance in existence; and are
certain, beyond the evidence of a demonstration, both of its perfect
identity and simplicity."[9] When he turns inward in an act of Cartesian
introspection, Hume does not perceive or intuit an entity, constant and
invariable, that has traditionally been called the Soul. Instead, he is
aware of sensations, feelings, and ideas in perpetual, if apparently or-
derly, flux: "When I enter most intimately into what I call *myself*, I always stumble on some particular perception or other. . . . I never can
catch *myself* at any time without a perception, and never can observe
anything but the perception" (p. 252). And yet we hold to the belief that
underlying these fluctuating states there is some *thing*, unchanging and
unified, that endures both in and through time. In an "action of the
imagination" we "feign some new and unintelligible principle, that connects the objects [of consciousness] together. . . . Thus we feign the
continu'd existence of the perceptions of our senses, to remove the interruption; and run into the notion of a *soul*, and *self*, and *substance*, to disguise the variation" (p. 254). We create the fiction of identity, the fiction
of a self persisting through the reality of change: "The identity, which
we ascribe to the mind of man, is only a fictitious one, and of a like kind
with that which we ascribe to vegetables and animal bodies. It cannot,
therefore, have a different origin, but must proceed from a like opera-
tion of the imagination upon like objects" (p. 259).

Under Hume's anatomizing scrutiny the self ceases to be an entity,
unified and unchanging; it becomes a necessary fiction, constructed by
an act of the imagination. It is this conception of the self with which
Jean-Jacques Rousseau undertakes the writing of *The Confessions*. The
flamboyant proclamation of his design should not obscure the perils and

the satisfactions of the enterprise: "I have resolved on an enterprise
which has no precedent, and which, once complete, will have no imitator. My purpose is to display to my kind a portrait in every way true to
nature, and the man I shall portray will be myself."[10] Behind the complex egoism, which denies the possibility of imitation even as it sanctions and invites it, lies another impulse to which Rousseau, and others,
respond: "Let the last trump sound when it will, I shall come forward
with this work in my hand, to present myself before my Sovereign Judge,
and proclaim aloud: 'Here is what I have done, and if by chance I have
used some immaterial embellishment it has been only to fill a void due to
a defect of memory. I may have taken for fact what was no more than
probability, but I have never put down as true what I knew to be false'"
(p. 17). For Rousseau there is no Sovereign Judge to whom he may appeal beyond his own consciousness. There is only the memory of past
experiences suggesting the existence of a self enduring in and through
time. But memory proves not altogether reliable. It is marked by gaps,
blanks, lacunae, which Rousseau covers with probabilities, with fictions
forming a connection, lending an illusion of continuity and identity.

In *The Confessions,* Rousseau sets out to create a narrative affirming
"the unbroken consciousness of [his] own existence." Defects of memory, and perhaps failures of nerve, require those immaterial embellishments to close the potential gaps in Rousseau's account: "There are
some events in my life that are as vivid as if they had just occurred. But
there are gaps and blanks I cannot fill except by means of a narrative as
muddled as the memory I preserve of the events" (p. 128). What is at
stake is not simply a well-wrought, convincing narrative. Unbridged
gaps threaten inconsistencies and voids in Rousseau's story, in his unbroken consciousness, in his self. Such voids, covered with the probable
rather than the necessarily true, raise the issue of the credibility of the
narrative and the authenticity of the self emerging in it. Within the narrative there is no sure way to determine where fact ends and fiction begins. But voids uncovered become pockets of unintelligibility or meaninglessness with which no one can live: finally, the probable is preferable
to the patently false or to the intolerable lacuna. When he stands before
his Sovereign Judge, Rousseau will hold in his hands that text he wittily
presents *as* his self.

The autobiographical process, the one in which Dickens's David
Copperfield will participate, becomes an act of self-creation. It repeat-

edly draws attention to the fictive status of the self, especially through its appropriation of other narrative conventions. *The Confessions* often reads like a picaresque novel with Rousseau as the morally ambiguous picaro, on the road. Rousseau's account of his childhood reading, a haunting anticipation of the fictional David Copperfield's words, reveals how other narratives influence his autobiographical act: "My restless imagination took a hand which saved me from myself and calmed my growing sensuality. What it did was to nourish itself on situations that had interested me in my reading . . . [so that] I became one of the characters I imagined" (p. 48). The fictions of youth and those of maturity are designed to sustain Rousseau and his idea of himself. The autobiographical I of *The Confessions* emerges as a creation of the artist's imagination—in fact, as his most important creation, his hypothetically authentic self: "I have displayed myself as I was, as vile and despicable when my behaviour was such, as good, generous, and noble when I was so. I have bared my secret soul as Thou thyself hast seen it, Eternal Being!" (p. 17).

But throughout *The Confessions* Rousseau requires of his reader constant attention: the reader "must never lose sight of me for a single instant, for if he finds the slightest gap in my story, the smallest hiatus, he may wonder what I was doing at that moment and accuse me of refusing to tell the whole truth" (p. 65). The test of sincerity and authenticity becomes the coherence, thoroughness, and plausibility of the narrative.[11] The reader becomes the ultimate judge of Rousseau's secret soul: "His task is to assemble these elements [of the narrative] and to assess the being who is made up of them. The summing-up must be his. . . . it is not enough for my story to be truthful, it must be detailed as well" (p. 169). Rousseau never doubts his capacity for deception, of himself and of others. He strives for a truth that may elude his own consciousness, his own unreliable memory. Rousseau's self-consciousness seeks out a responsive awareness in the reader of his imagination. The Cartesian assurance of the cogito has waned. Autobiography, almost at the moment of its inception in the modern period, is an intersubjective venture, an encounter between two imagined consciousnesses. The hypothetical reader displaces that desiccated abstraction, the Eternal Being, to become the Other with whom Rousseau engages.[12]

Rousseau asks of his reader precisely the same attentiveness that Freud exercised in the last decades of the nineteenth century as he listened to those men and women who came to him with their stories, their autobiographical accounts that no longer sustained them. For Freud, as for Rousseau, man remains a narrative being, creating himself through the story of his life that he unfolds: "There seems to be a necessity for bringing psychical phenomena of which one becomes conscious into causal connection with other conscious material. In cases in which the true causation evades conscious perception one does not hesitate to attempt to make another connection, which one believes, although it is false" (*SE*, 2:67, n. 1). Freud has returned to those embellishments of *The Confessions*, no longer ironically alluded to as immaterial. We are in the world that Hume and Rousseau have created for modern consciousness, a world Freud elaborates upon as he charts the psychopathology of everyday life and devises a grammar of dreams and symptoms.

As a physician, Freud listens to the stories, the spoken autobiographies, of patient after patient. The stories may be garbled, incoherent, or suspect in their coherence. And in them Freud pursues the story within the story that may be true. In his part of the theoretical conclusion to *Studies on Hysteria*, he writes: "But if we examine with a critical eye the account that the patient has given us . . . , we shall quite infallibly discover gaps and imperfections in it. At one point the train of thought will be visibly interrupted and patched up by the patient as best he may, with a turn of speech or an inadequate explanation. . . . The patient will not recognize these deficiencies when his attention is drawn to them" (*SE*, 2:293). Freud's words echo Rousseau's: he remains alert to the slightest gap or the smallest hiatus in what the patient tells him. He responds to the apparently meaningless and, through the technique of free association, encounters a new method of answering, in which isolated and unintelligible words may finally be transformed into a coherent narrative. In *The Confessions* Rousseau speaks of "the dark and miry maze of [his] confessions" through which he makes his way, sustained by the thread of his narrative line. Freud becomes a latter-day Theseus, "standing before a wall [of words] which shuts out every prospect and prevents us from having any idea whether there is anything behind it, and if so, what" (*SE*, 2:293). Freud reverses Theseus, as Rousseau has done, and pursues the "logical thread" running through "lacunas which are often covered by 'false connections'" in order to penetrate the labyrinth of words and push to the center of the true story, the lair of the repressed fact.[13]

Freud, like Rousseau, is engaged in an intersubjective project. He cooperates with his patient to create a coherent account of the patient's life, an account unmarred by lacunae or symptomatic modes of expression, for only a properly coherent account explains and dispels the patient's condition. For Freud, the final test of the truth of a newly rendered story is its power to effect change. In the case of Frau Emmy von N., he observes, "I accustomed myself to regarding as incomplete any story that brought about no improvement, and I gradually came to be able to read from patients' faces whether they might not be concealing an essential part of their confessions" (*SE*, 2:79). But truth for Freud, as for Rousseau, to whom he indirectly alludes here, remains complicated and elusive. Freud seeks to reconstruct the forgotten, or the repressed, past to liberate the patient from a compulsive and futile repetition of it in that disguised form the patient cannot recognize. The concept of the unconscious guarantees the existence of that latent memory, neither incomplete, vague, nor "mutilated"—a memory "which is not at the ego's disposal and which plays no part in association and memory, [but] nevertheless in some fashion lies ready to hand and in correct and proper order" (*SE*, 2:287). Freud demands the existence of the unconscious, reaffirming a quintessential romantic credo. In his *Confessions of an English Opium-Eater,* Thomas De Quincey proclaims, perhaps a little stridently, that

there is no such thing as *forgetting* possible to the mind; a thousand accidents may, and will interpose a veil between our present consciousness and the secret inscriptions on the mind; accidents of the same sort will also rend away this veil; but alike, whether veiled or unveiled, the inscription remains for ever; just as the stars seem to withdraw before the common light of day, whereas, in fact, we all know that it is the light which is drawn over them as a veil—and that they are waiting to be revealed, when the obscuring daylight shall have withdrawn.[14]

De Quincey's use of the phrase "secret inscriptions," recorded within the "dread book of account" which is the mind, is a witty play upon the tabula rasa of British empiricism; an allusion to the work Rousseau will offer to his Sovereign Judge; and a reference to those secret inscriptions, the Egyptian hieroglyphs, obsessing the English public in 1821 and 1822.

De Quincey's words nicely foreshadow Freud's "Constructions in Analysis." The biologist of the mind has become, not surprisingly, the archaeologist of the mind: "[The analyst's] work of construction, or, if it is preferred, of reconstruction, resembles to a great extent an archaeologist's excavation of some dwelling-place that has been destroyed and

buried or of some ancient edifice. . . . The analyst . . . works under
more favourable conditions than the archaeologist. . . . All of the essentials [in the mind] are preserved; even things that seem completely forgotten are present somehow and somewhere, and have merely been
buried and made inaccessible to the subject" (SE, 23:259–60). In his
effort to make the invisible visible, Freud has recourse, yet again, to a
figurative language peculiar to psychology. The language makes it possible to become aware of certain mental processes and may, in fact, create
them. The idea of the unconscious may be no more than another romantic fiction essential to the psychoanalytic project, an attempt to confer
upon the self that unity and identity denied it by the scrutiny of David
Hume and the curious integrity of Jean-Jacques Rousseau.

Armed with his archaeological trope, Freud examines the hieroglyphic
events of the patient's past. He reconstructs the "ancient edifice" that is
the patient's memory, the patient's self. In his treatment of "Dora,"
Freud restores "what is missing" in Dora's story and in her memory:
"Like a conscientious archaeologist, I have not omitted to mention in
each case where the authentic parts and my constructions begin" (SE,
7:12). Even unconscious memory may fail to provide the complete story.
The correct and proper order of events explaining the patient's dilemma
may not exist intact somewhere within the figurative strata of the mind.
In the therapeutic process Freud, with the patient's cooperation, may
find himself *creating* memory, forging a coherent past in narrative form
to replace the lacuna or the symptom making life intolerable. Paul
Ricoeur calls the therapeutic act a praxis, a work, the "great work of 'becoming conscious,'. . . the process of understanding, of remembering,
of recognizing the past and of recognizing oneself in [the] past." [15] But if
the physician and the patient create a past with which the patient may
live, they are, in fact, creating a self at the same time, the patient's fictive
self that finds its meaning in a reconstructed past possessing the ring of
narrative truth. The self emerging from the therapy is no less an imaginative construct than the self Rousseau offers in *The Confessions*.

Autobiography as practiced by Rousseau and Freudian case history
become versions of each other. In that romantic tradition within which
Freud writes, the self as construct, as fiction, incorporates and deals with
the potentially discontinuous events of the patient's life so that the patient can remain in touch with time, with a hypothetical past, present,
and future. It is within this context, I imagine, that Steven Marcus

offers his revision of Freud in "Freud and Dora: Story, History, Case History":

Freud is implying that a coherent story is in some manner connected with mental health . . . and this in turn implies assumptions of the broadest and deepest kind about both the nature of coherence and the form and structure of human life. On this reading, human life is, ideally, a connected and coherent story, with all the details in explanatory place, and with everything (or as close to everything as is practically possible) accounted for, in its proper causal or other sequence. And inversely, illness amounts at least in part to suffering from an incoherent story or an inadequate narrative account of oneself.[16]

Marcus's reading of Freud points to the affinity between conceptions of self in romantic autobiography and psychoanalysis. It suggests that a continuum of assumptions informs autobiography, case history, and the great nineteenth-century novels. The autobiographer, the physician, and the novelist seek out a connected and coherent story for the characters they depict. Details are "accounted for in [their] proper causal or other sequence." Chronology alone is not the aim. The perception of thematic patterns, of coincidences that become co-incidences, may make the fictional character's adventures intelligible or the patient's life endurable. In the course of autobiography, the novel, or the therapeutic process, "nothing less than 'reality' itself" is made. An adequate narrative account of the self emerges: the authentic self proclaims its existence through, in Marcus's words, "a story, or a fiction, . . . [with] a narrative structure . . . rendered in language, in conscious speech, and no longer . . . in the deformed language of symptoms, the untranslated speech of the body. At the end—at the successful end—one has come into possession of one's own story." [17] The success or failure of the novel as aesthetic venture and of psychoanalysis as therapeutic adventure may be judged by curiously analogous criteria: in the case of analysis the aesthetically satisfying may well effect a cure; in the novel, an adequate account of a character's past may make change possible. The words of Jane Austen's Elizabeth Bennet mark a turning point in English fiction: "Till this moment, I never knew myself."

The tendency of fiction and case history to merge strikes Freud early on. His comments upon his analytic constructions or reconstructions, those fictions he employs to cover the gaps in the patient's story, reveal his uneasiness. In *Studies on Hysteria* Freud, with his characteristic integ-

rity, acknowledges the problem: "I have not always been a psychotherapist. . . . and it still strikes me myself as strange that the case histories I
write should read like short stories and that, as one might say, they lack
the serious stamp of science. I must console myself with the reflection
that the nature of the subject is evidently responsible for this, rather than
any preference of my own" (*SE*, 2:160). It is precisely the way in which
Freud imagines the subject, the subjectivity of the patient, that compels
him to write as he does. Freud relies on the form of the short story because he shares the ontological assumptions of nineteenth-century writers about the narrative structure of the self. The physician explores the
unconscious and "must behave as 'timelessly' as the unconscious itself, if
he wishes to learn anything or to achieve anything" (*SE*, 17:10). But in
conducting a therapy or in writing a case history, the physician is no
longer free to behave timelessly: he must render in a linear fashion the
nonlinear, atemporal unconscious to deliver the patient from the domi-
nation of the past and the reader from bewilderment. He must have recourse to those "detailed description[s] of mental processes such as we
are accustomed to find in the works of imaginative writers" (*SE*, 2:160).
Freud turns to fiction, to the nineteenth-century novel, as a model for
his own studies in hysteria.

In *Studies on Hysteria*, Freud seems genuinely perplexed that his case
histories read like short stories. He is not yet comfortable with his own
artistic genius, with the fact that he is, after all, a gifted raconteur, a
man of letters as well as a man of science. By the time of the writing of
the case histories of "Dora" and the "Wolf Man," this has changed: he
revels in his own artistry. However, even in the *Studies* he does refer to
"the works of imaginative writers" who precede him and whom he emulates. *David Copperfield*, his favorite Dickens novel, is rich in the "detailed description of mental processes" Freud so prizes. In a letter to his
fiancée, Martha Bernays, he writes: "You must have noticed that all our
writers and artists have a 'mannerism,' a stereotyped series of motives
and arrangements which indicate the limits of their art: . . . To these
mannerisms belong, in the case of Dickens, those flawless girls, . . . so
good they are quite colorless; then the fact that all the good people immediately become friends . . . ; then the sharp distinction between virtue and vice which doesn't exist in life (where should I be, for example?); . . . *Copperfield* has the least of all this. The characters are
individualized; they are sinful without being abominable."[18] The letter

was written in 1883, thirteen years after Dickens's death, seventeen years before *The Interpretation of Dreams*. And the parenthetical observation, "where should I be, for example," resonates. Dickens's art in *David Copperfield* reminds Freud of his own subject, and subjects. The psychoanalyst inhabits daily a world in which there can be no sharp distinctions between virtue and vice. He confronts with imagination and sympathy human beings who are, in a conventional sense, sinful without being abominable. And he does not recoil from them. In the case histories, Freud strives to do justice to their humanity and to the complexity of his own enterprise.

Freud writes with an awareness of both Jean-Jacques Rousseau and Charles Dickens. Dickens writes, poised between the two: he responds to *The Confessions* and intuitively anticipates, and influences, Freud's psychoanalytic investigations. This is nowhere clearer than in *David Copperfield*, written almost in midcareer as the eighth of Dickens's fifteen novels. At one point Dickens entertained the idea of entitling his novel *The Copperfield Confessions,* pointing clearly to the parallels between the fictive David Copperfield and the historical Rousseau.[19] David writes as a poet of the memory, the heir of Rousseau and De Quincey before him, and the precursor of the Freud of *The Interpretation of Dreams:* "I think the memory of most of us can go farther back into such times [in infancy] than many of us suppose."[20] But it is David's awareness of the nature of the autobiographical enterprise that echoes Rousseau and foreshadows Freud: "It is not my purpose, in this record, though in all other essentials it is my *written memory,* to pursue the *history* of my own *fictions*. They express themselves, and I leave them to themselves. When I refer to them, incidentally, it is only as a part of my *progress*" (chapter 48, emphasis mine). In this passage David apparently isolates his personal narrative, his "written memory," from his novels, those fictions that have made him a public figure. But the attempt to distinguish his autobiography from his novels falters: the words in the passage gravitate towards each other, dislodging themselves from their positions on the page. David's personal history and his fictions fuse, revealed as curiously akin to each other by the word *progress*. The trope suggests the fictive elements inherent in David's story of his life; it reminds us that his narrative, like Rousseau's, is informed by fictional structures, by the progress and its secular analogue, the picaresque novel. As a child David read *Don Quixote, Roderick Random,* and *Tom Jones*. He has imagined himself as "Tom

Jones (a child's Tom Jones, a harmless creature) for a week together."
His mind has been expanded: "I have sustained my own idea of Roderick Random for a month at a stretch, I verily believe" (chapter 4). David's autobiography inevitably merges with his novels. The status of the
autobiographical I has become problematic, another character in that
galaxy of characters generated by the artist's imagination. The ontological assumptions underlying his creation of his characters inform David's
creation of his self in his personal history.

For Dickens, for David Copperfield, the hero of autobiography and
the hero of fiction merge. They are both imagined characters, created to
provide a chronological and causal account of the self. In a novel, David
creates character and a narrative line. In his personal history, he must
perceive that narrative thread in lived experiences and depict a character
to whom he refers as himself. In the pages of *David Copperfield*, Dickens
completes a movement implicit in his earlier works: the self has become
a construct, a compelling fiction. Dickens's characters, David Copperfield among them, are revealed as narrative beings. They are no longer
brilliant, if potentially solipsistic, monologuists. They are, like Freud's
patients, inveterate tellers of those stories by which they endeavor to define themselves and their perplexing relationships to others.

Jean-Jacques Rousseau, Charles Dickens, and Sigmund Freud share a
similar vision of the human situation, reaffirmed in the twentieth century by José Ortega y Gasset: "It is too often forgotten that man is impossible without imagination, without the capacity to invent for himself
a conception of life, to 'ideate' the character he is going to be. Whether
he be original or a plagiarist, man is the novelist of himself."[21]

Men and women, and fictional characters in romantic narratives, become
the novelists of themselves by imaginatively creating the self upon which
each acts. Such self-creation never occurs in a vacuum: it involves a response to those other selves impinging upon the single self within a historical situation. And the self-creating act is never completed, never
final. For the romantics, as for those existentialists like Ortega who are
indebted to their "[romanticist] predecessors,"[22] men and women are
beings with histories, existing within the medium of time. In forging the
account of oneself, in establishing those connections between discrete
events in one's life, the individual engages in an act of interpretation that
never ends. Circumstances may be established as real, as given, but their

meanings may be, at best, only imminent or subject to continuous revision. In discussing Freud and psychoanalysis in "Cézanne's Doubt," Maurice Merleau-Ponty observes: "The very decisions which transform us are always made in reference to a factual situation; such a situation can of course be accepted or refused, but it cannot fail to give us our impetus nor to be for us, as a situation 'to be accepted' or 'to be refused,' the incarnation for us of the value we give to it."[23] The circumstances of an individual's life, embedded in a fragile narrative structure, become romantic images whose ultimate meanings remain elusive. The narrative construct designed to accommodate the interpretations changes, however subtly, as meanings change.[24]

This dynamic, temporal dimension of the romantic self is another legacy of that triumph of the science of biology in the late eighteenth century of which Foucault writes in *The Order of Things*. Foucault's "science of life" celebrates the animal as "the privileged form" and provides a controlling trope for a self embued with the qualities of a living organism: "There is being only because there is life, and in that fundamental movement that dooms them to death, the scattered beings, stable for an instant, are formed, halt, hold life immobile—and in a sense kill it—but are then in turn destroyed by that inexhaustible force" (p. 278). The fate of an animal organism, of a species, is to be born, to achieve a fragile form, and to move toward nonbeing, spent life. Analogously, the particular self appears for "which individuality, with its forms, limits, and needs, is no more than a precarious moment, doomed to destruction, forming first and last a simple obstacle that must be removed from the path of that annihilation" (p. 279).

For the nineteenth and the twentieth centuries, the lowly caterpillar becomes an apt emblem for a conception of the self suggested by Foucault's observations. With its impending metamorphoses, the caterpillar proclaims the radical discontinuity of the post-Humean self. For writers as apparently diverse as Thomas Carlyle, Lewis Carroll, and Vladimir Nabokov, in *Speak, Memory* and elsewhere, the caterpillar and the butterfly proclaim the romantic self as at once a construct and a process, subject to curious permutations. The identity of the creature fated to become first a chrysalis and then the ephemeral Psyche can be established through an imagined, if not imaginary, unity pervading three discrete stages of existence. Any interruption in the process of change marks a figurative (sometimes a literal) death, as it does for Carroll's somnolent blue Caterpillar, which seeks stasis in its desire to retain its precious form as a caterpillar, and to resist the forces driving it on into different forms, ultimately into that of the butterfly, fated to die. Dickens exploits the romantic emblem of the caterpillar in *Dombey and Son* through Mrs. Chick as she rushes in upon Lucretia Tox to announce Mr. Dombey's engagement to Edith Granger:

> "It's a world of change. Any one would surprise me very much, Lucretia, and would greatly alter my opinion of their understanding, if they attempted to contradict or evade what is so perfectly evident. Change!" exclaimed Mrs. Chick, with severe philosophy. "Why, my gracious me, what is there that does *not* change! Even the silkworm, who I am sure might be supposed not to trouble itself about such subjects, changes into all sorts of unexpected things continually."[25]

It is the unexpected and often convulsive nature of change, both personal and social, that causes Mrs. Chick to wax philosophical. Mrs. Chick's silkworm, like Carroll's Caterpillar, suggests, in the realm of the personal, the discontinuities in the life of the self and the ephemerality of that identity to which each character in Dickens's novels so tenaciously clings as he, or she, embraces what Steven Marcus has called the "furious activity of stasis."[26]

Mrs. Chick's observations about the silkworm are echoed, in more explicit terms, by Mr. Morfin, Dombey's musical clerk, as he ponders the realities of time and change and the way in which he and others inadequately cope with them: "We go on in our clock-work routine, from day to day, and can't make out, or follow, these changes [in others]. They—they're a metaphysical sort of thing. We—we haven't leisure for it. We—we haven't courage" (chapter 33). In an age of existentialism and phenomenology, and more recently of deconstructionism, we would say that Mr. Morfin is musing upon ontological sorts of things: "One don't see anything, one don't hear anything, one don't know anything; that's the fact. We go on taking everything for granted, and so we go on, until whatever we do, good, bad, or indifferent, we do from habit. Habit is all I shall have to report, when I am called upon to plead to my conscience, on my death-bed" (chapter 33). Many of Dickens's most memorable characters, with their set patterns of speech, with their theatrical routines, passing so feebly for authentic selfhood, are no more than frightened refugees from time and change, "deaf, dumb, blind, and paralytic, to a million things, from habit." That habit which a character adopts, that role each unrelentingly portrays, "hardens [him], from day to day, according to the temper of [his] clay, like [an image], and leaves [him] as susceptible as images to new impressions and convictions" (chapter 53). Mr. Morfin is probing the nature of the self, its need for change and growth; its remarkable fragility; and its susceptibility to a paralytic state impeding change and inducing a self-absorption so deaf, dumb, and blind to others that it borders upon solipsism and figurative death.

Mrs. Chick and Mr. Morfin become unwitting fictional participants in the historical dialogue, explored by Michel Foucault, that generates romantic conceptions of the self and the attendant anxiety about the nature of personal identity. Mrs. Chick, with her observation that it's "a world of change" and with her significant, if self-serving, reference to the continually changing silkworm, has touched upon the issue of identity and the hypothetical unity of the self. Mr. Morfin, obsessed with change and habit, has engaged with a crucial issue in a romantic ontology positing a self whose unity, if it exists, evolves through a complex, temporal progression.

Mr. Morfin is speaking, as Dickens is writing, after the historical shift in which Foucault's "great dichotomy" between the living and the nonliving is established: "The organic becomes the living and the living is that which produces, grows, and reproduces; the inorganic is the nonliving, that which neither develops nor reproduces; it lies at the frontiers of life, the inert, the unfruitful—death. And although it is intermingled with life, it is so as that element within it that destroys and kills it" (p. 232). Mr. Morfin's preoccupation with habit and paralysis makes sense within this historical situation.[27] He speaks of the habit that hardens, figuratively, our mortal clay, referring to the statue or monument, the image, impervious to change. His words anticipate characters like Lady Dedlock, Mrs. Clennam, and Bradley Headstone, each of whom becomes an effigy of ice or stone, possessed by a fixed identity frustrating the human impulse to change. Implicit from the start in Mr. Morfin's observations is that Goethean conception of the self described by Ortega y Gasset: "[Goethe] is the man in whom for the first time there dawned the consciousness that human life is man's struggle with his intimate and individual destiny—that is, that human life is made up of the problem of itself, that its substance consists not in something that already *is* . . . but in something which has to make itself, which, therefore, is not a *thing* but an absolute and problematical *task*."[28] This conception of the self rejects being as a static and given nature: it argues "not that man *is,* but that he *lives.*"[29] The self is living, dynamic, and growing. Within this context Mr. Morfin's habit denies the imperatives of the dynamic self; it produces a figurative, if not a literal, death. The self is no longer an entity, the substance of medieval philosophy; it is an evolving process whose present structure can, at best, only be approximated in language and in thought.

Image as a figure of speech for statue or effigy alludes to the dangers of paralysis, of a psychological ossification. Yet, connected as it is to the word *imagination,* and to the imaginative activities of a self, the trope returns us to Rousseau and to those images of himself and of others by which he tries to live. Mr. Morfin's image alludes also to the status of the romantic self as fiction or construct. In a Dickens novel, characters often possess images of themselves upon which personal identity rests precariously. Dick Swiveller, in *The Old Curiosity Shop,* has a conception of himself as a genteel youth that he encourages his friends to accept and to perpetuate. In *Dombey and Son,* the poor, buffeted Miss Tox, dreaming that Mr. Dombey must soon remarry, perhaps someone like herself, turns "her head, and [is] surprised by the reflection of her thoughtful image in the chimney-glass" (chapter 29). In the image of her flushed face Miss Tox sees the version of herself as the future Mrs. Dombey that has, until now, harmlessly constituted her fragile identity. It is an image to be shattered momentarily by a Mrs. Chick determined that *she* will not be accused of conspiring to foist Miss Tox upon her widowed brother. Mrs. Chick has her own precious image of herself to protect. She acts to get in the first word, following Mr. Dombey's engagement to Edith Granger. She will dispel any hint of complicity in an ineffectual plot: to foster her own conception of herself Mrs. Chick will, if necessary, dash to the ground Lucretia Tox's modest hopes, and her self: "If my brother Paul had consulted with me . . . I should have said, 'Paul! You to marry a second time without family! You to marry without beauty! You to marry without dignity! You to marry without connexion! There is nobody in the world, not mad, who could dream of daring to entertain such a preposterous idea!'" (chapter 29). Mrs. Chick relies upon the power of the word to create a reality with which she can live and so face her brother without embarrassment. Miss Tox, whose own fragile reality has been swept aside, can only—faint into the arms of Major Bagstock's native servant. The design to which Mrs. Chick has, in part, committed herself has collapsed; she acts to extricate her *self* from it. Miss Tox, ex-communicated from the Dombey world, must contrive to exist in limbo as best she can.

But it is not only minor characters who confront the riddles posed by Mrs. Chick's unsuspecting silkworm. Florence Dombey, trying to pre-serve her own threatened identity, loves an idealized version of her fa-ther. "But the father whom she loved began to be a vague and dreamy idea to her: hardly more substantially connected with her real life, than the image she would sometimes conjure up, of her dear brother yet alive" (chapter 47). Such an image, of oneself or of another, is neces-sarily obsolete in the moment of its inception. Florence's idea of her fa-ther, divorced from the real man and the changing world in which he must live, is like her idea of Paul: it is a dead, and a potentially deaden-ing, thing. It has nothing to do with real life and, in the ordinary course of events in the Dickens world, removes the character entertaining the image from the medium of time inhabited, always anxiously, by Dick-ens's characters. However impervious to change such an image—as effigy or idea—may seem, it remains forever vulnerable to disruption. In his rage and humiliation over Edith's elopement with James Carker, Mr. Dombey strikes Florence, the only person who truly loves him, upon her breast. He inevitably strikes at the image of him that his daughter has nurtured in her mind and in her heart: "For as she looked, she saw him murdering that fond idea to which she had held in spite of him. . . . She saw she had no father upon earth, and ran out, orphaned, from his house" (chapter 47). Florence can no longer inhabit her father's house or that edifice of her imagination in which she has succored an illusory version of her father, and of herself. She is cruelly orphaned. But she is freed from a constellation of images to which she has become habitu-ated. And she is thrust back into time.

The multifaceted image of which Mr. Morfin speaks may be a statue or an effigy, in stone, wood, or ice; it may be an idea within the mind of a character, an idea of oneself, or of another; it may be a reflection float-ing upon the surface of a potentially magic glass, or a striking likeness in a portrait, like the one of Lady Dedlock in the drawing room of Chesney Wold. The "freezing mood" into which Lady Dedlock has fallen is caught in the portrait, "a perfect likeness, and the best work of the mas-ter" in Rosa's rote description.[30] The portrait captures the ennui and grace of Lady Dedlock's acquired expression, the mask she habitually wears in her dealings with the fashionable world. But the mask, however voluntarily donned, acquires a primacy of its own, shutting Lady Dedlock off temporarily, and perhaps fatally, from time and change. Behind the mask the self slowly combusts, disintegrates, producing at best an ashy residue, at worst, a void. For to surrender or to lose one's capacity for change is to negate one's being.

For Mr. Morfin, the whimsical metaphysician, and for Dickens the novelist, man becomes, as he does for Ortega, "a substantial emigrant on a pilgrimage of being."[31] But it is a Faustian pilgrimage without an end other than that deathbed to which each of us, like Mr. Morfin, moves. Mrs. Skewton in her fear of change and the pilgrimage of being takes refuge in her static role of Cleopatra. She is a grotesque because the role induces a form of premature paralysis, a version of that ultimate paralysis, Death, which strikes her, appropriately, at her glass and reduces her to "a horrible doll that had tumbled down." Human life, like the silk-worm's, remains a series of metamorphoses, literal and figurative, in time. The metamorphoses cannot be as radical as those the unsuspecting silk-worm must endure. In human life authors and their characters demand a pattern, a thread of continuity, for "if there were no repetition, what then would life be? Who would wish to be a tablet upon which time writes every instant a new inscription? or to be a mere memorial of the past?"[32] In his *Repetition: An Essay in Experimental Psychology,* Kierke-gaard is writing about a self persisting in and through time for which the flux of words flowing endlessly, and meaninglessly, upon the tablet or the awful fixity of words engraved in stone suggests modes of nonbeing. Each condition, explored by Kierkegaard in his complex linguistic trope, represents the literal or figurative death of the self through fragmenta-tion or paralysis. The viable self postulated by Kierkegaard unites past, present, and future in the fluid dance of an unfolding poem. The self is engaged in life-sustaining gestures, rhythmic modulations of its past that attest to the vitality of its evolving center.

In Kierkegaard's epigrammatic observation, two traditions central to romantic conceptions of the self converge. The literary trope comparing the self to an inscription points to the self as a construct in Rousseauistic terms. The verbal play upon the monument of stone dwells upon the self as process, as evolutionary activity. The movement toward a constructed unity is unending. If it is interrupted, if it is temporarily or permanently halted, the individual abandons the pilgrimage of being to become a monument to a dead self. In Dickens's novels the two most powerfully rendered monuments to their dead, or dying, selves become Bradley Headstone and John Jasper, whose stony names proclaim their paralysis. Their inability to change transforms them into living headstones, bizarre memorials to the romantic quest abandoned. In his sustained first-person narratives—those of David Copperfield, Esther Summerson, and Pip—Dickens reveals his part in that indigenous romantic tradition marked out by *The Prelude*. Dickens shares Wordsworth's fascination with childhood sensations and with the capacity of the memory to rescue those sensations from a phenomenological limbo. He allies himself with Wordsworth and with those romantics who place their faith in the power of the imagination to create a self by perceiving an exchange between the future and the past and by musing upon riddles whose "final meaning," as Merleau-Ponty observes, is "nowhere written down."

The recurrence within his novels of characters fatally estranged from the medium of time, in betrayal of their ontological status as historical beings, suggests that Dickens writes with a Carlylean, a Goethean, celebration of Becoming. In Teufelsdröckh's "Close thy *Byron;* open thy *Goethe*," [33] Carlyle embraces the Faustian credo, later to be quoted by Freud, "In the beginning was the Deed." Only in the field of action does the individual understand himself, realize himself: "A certain inarticulate Self-consciousness dwells dimly in us; which only our Works can render articulate and decisively discernible. Our Works are the mirror wherein the spirit first sees its natural lineaments. Hence, too, the folly of that impossible Precept, *Know thyself;* till it be translated into this partially possible one, *Know what thou canst work at*" (pp. 162–63). A Faust *translates*, and interprets, the Gospel according to John; Carlyle translates Socrates, Aristotle, in a Goethean manner to argue that "*The end of Man is an Action, and not a Thought*" (p. 155). And the supreme action of Carlylean man is the ongoing creation of the self. Like the obsolete Christian Mythus, which must be swept away to prepare for a new, a living Mythus, the obsolete self must be relinquished to prepare for a new, living self, which in time will undergo yet another metamorphosis, another "Spiritual New-birth, or Baphometic Fire-baptism." As Teufelsdröckh writes, "What the Father has made, the Son can make and enjoy; but has also work of his own appointed him. Thus all things wax, and roll onwards; Arts, Establishments, Opinions, nothing is completed, but ever completing" (p. 247).

Throughout *Sartor Resartus* there runs an undercurrent of perplexity as Carlyle embraces the evolutionary process of Becoming. The incantatory rhythms of "Produce! Produce!" reveal his anxiety that the imprisoned chrysalis may fail to become the winged Psyche. If it is "man's nature to change his Dialect from century to century he cannot help it though he would" (p. 189); there is nonetheless a "law of Perseverance . . . in man: by nature he hates change; seldom will he quit his old house till it has actually fallen about his ears" (p. 237). The tendency to preservation of an existing condition haunts Carlyle's imagination in *Sartor Resartus* as it engages the imagination of Goethe in *Faust* and of Freud in *Beyond the Pleasure Principle*. Within the living self, perceived as organism, there exists an impulse to stasis. In *Faust* it is Mephistopheles who embodies this human tendency to abandon activity and to take refuge in the illusory ease of stasis:

> I am the spirit that negates.
> And rightly so, for all that comes to be
> Deserves to perish wretchedly;
> 'Twere better nothing would begin. . . .
> I am part of the part that once was everything,
> Part of the darkness which gave birth to light,
> That haughty light which envies mother night
> Her ancient rank and place and would be king.[34]

So Freud writes in *Beyond the Pleasure Principle*—his profound reading of *Faust*, the central literary text of his imaginative life—of "the *conservative* nature of living substance" and of the "organic compulsion to repeat," leading to the "hypothesis that all instincts tend towards the restoration of an earlier state of things" (*SE*, 18:36–37): "The elementary living entity would from its very beginning have had no wish to change; if conditions remained the same, it would do no more than constantly repeat the same course of life" (*SE*, 18:38). With his conception of the principle of Thanatos, Freud argues for the existence of something "more primitive, more elementary, more instinctual than the pleasure principle which it over-rides" (*SE*, 18:23) to explain the compulsion to repeat the painful past. Thanatos, as the principle of stasis, of paralysis, is the impulse for which Mephistopheles speaks when he cries, "'Twere better nothing would begin." The light against which Mephistopheles rails is both the light of Eros and of consciousness, sublimated Eros, latecomers to the biological and psychological organism without which there would be no change, no human life, but only stasis and insensate matter. Faust, in his pursuit of sexual love and of self-fulfillment in creative activity, serves Eros in its diverse forms. Eros, in Goethe's words, *"ungebändigt immer vorwärts dringt'* [presses ever forward unsubdued]. The backward path that leads to complete satisfaction is as a rule obstructed. . . . So there is no alternative but to advance in the direction in which growth is still free—though with no prospect of bringing the process to a conclusion or of being able to reach the goal" (*SE*, 18:42). Mephistopheles, for whom Naught is the only reality, serves literal and figurative death. Faust, and Eros, advance in the direction in which growth is still free in a process without end. In *Beyond the Pleasure Principle,* the encounter between Faust and Mephistopheles recurs in the struggle between Eros and Thanatos.

In his recourse to the figurative language of psychology, Freud transfers the "organic compulsion to repeat" to the human psyche, to render intelligible the patient's inertia, his tendency "to be content with an incomplete solution" of his conflict (*SE*, 23:231). Freud uses a biological perspective to capture the patient's tendency to cling to an obsolete version of the self that alienates him from time. The pessimism of "Analysis Terminable and Interminable" comes from Freud's recognition that the patient refuses to abandon, or abandons only with reluctance, those defenses against perplexing circumstances that once served him in the past: "The adult's ego . . . continues to defend itself against dangers which no longer exist in reality; indeed, it finds itself compelled to seek out those situations in reality which can serve as an approximate substitute for the original danger, so as to be able to justify . . . its maintaining its habitual modes of reaction" (*SE*, 23:238). But Freud discusses this ego, with its defense mechanisms, not only through biological tropes, but through the analogy of a censored text: "Repression has the same relation to the other methods of defence as omission [of words or passages, with the substitution of new sentences] has to distortion of the text, and we may discover in the different forms of this falsification parallels to the variety of ways in which the ego is altered" (*SE*, 23:236–37). The fixated ego is a censored text and the modification of the ego is the restoration to that fragmentary text of those passages from the past deleted in the act of repression. The self is returned to time by a figurative rewriting of its narrative structure, a structure now accommodated to changed circumstances in the patient's life, permitting him "to advance in the direction in which growth is still free—though with no prospect of bringing the process to a conclusion" (*SE*, 18:42).

In Freud's discussion of the ego in "Analysis Terminable and Interminable," we return to the romantic self in its fully articulated form, to that conception of the self generated by the tradition in which Rousseau, Goethe, Kierkegaard, and Freud participate. The romantic self, like the Freudian ego, embraces life by rejecting inertia. This self remains a fragile narrative construct forever part of a process of Becoming, connected through its various stages of revision by yet another romantic concept, the unconscious, which apparently guarantees the unity and identity of a self evolving in and through time. The Faustian self, moving toward an integration never to be fully achieved, vacillates between the two poles of fragmentation or paralysis. Mephistopheles tempts Faust in two seemingly antithetical directions, each a version of nonbeing: he lures Faust toward Walpurgisnacht, the disintegration of the self in pure debauchery, or toward the paralysis of the self in a form of sodden, self-satisfied inertia.

For Dickens, as for those other romantic writers who anticipate him and for those whom he intuitively anticipates, the two poles of the living self remain fragmentation or paralysis. In *Our Mutual Friend*, Silas Wegg, in quest of his amputated leg bone, visits Mr. Venus—Preserver of Animals and Birds, Articulator of human bones—to ask, "Where am I?" [35] Wegg's leg bone—part of Mr. Venus's collection of bones "warious" and "miscellaneous"—and his wooden stump serve as the germ of an elaborate Dickensian conceit. The bone and stump allude to various fates confronting the romantic self. Wegg, in identifying his self with the amputated leg bone in Mr. Venus's possession, comically discourses upon the dangers of the fragmented self in the urban wasteland: "I have a prospect of getting on in life and elevating myself. . . ," says Wegg, feelingly, "and I shouldn't like—I tell you openly I should *not* like—under such circumstances, to be what I may call dispersed, a part of me here, and a part of me there, but should wish to collect myself like a genteel person" (book 1, chapter 7). The process of dispersal may lead to psychic disintegration, to the collapse of the fragile self. It is the fate John Harmon circles in his attempts to free himself from the terms of the Harmon Will as he takes on the name first of Julius Handford, then of John Rokesmith, and of George Radfoot. Each name is a harbinger of a potential self, a way of responding to the complex circumstances in which Harmon finds himself. Yet each name represents only a partial expression of that fully integrated self Harmon must forge as the smithy of his own identity.

Silas Wegg's comic embodiment of the danger of dispersal, of fragmentation, is matched by his equally comic inclination to paralysis, to petrification. As he seeks out himself in the leg bone Mr. Venus charmingly calls a "Monstrosity," Wegg stumps along on the wooden leg that is the true signifier for his dislocated self. Psychically, Wegg is as dead as the piece of wood serving him as a limb. Greed so thoroughly pervades his life that his actions become a virtual compulsion toward repetition. He is as "paralytically animated" as the animals and the skeletons in Mr. Venus's shop. Wegg, possessed of an unmanageable member with a curious will of its own, becomes Dickens's Osiris of the Thames. As he reads to Mr. Boffin about misers and their hoarded wealth, Wegg's wooden leg elevates itself in a parody of an erection. Wegg's life has centered itself in that wooden effigy of a phallus that rises only in response to the lure of gold. The spurious sexuality of the wooden leg reveals the spurious vitality of Wegg's self. He is an automaton, a comic version of the literal and figurative automatons in Freud's reading, in "The 'Uncanny,'" of E. T. A. Hoffmann's "The Sandman." Wegg's bizarre sexuality is the logical extension of a self "deaf, dumb, blind, and paralytic" through its habitual pursuit of filthy lucre.

Inevitably, in the art of analogy Dickens so skillfully employs, Wegg's comic predicament comments upon the serious plights of other characters. Wegg's compulsive actions refer to the conditions of both Eugene Wrayburn and Bradley Headstone and to the chase in which they routinely participate. But the situation of John Harmon, tentatively embarked upon his pilgrimage of being, is also alluded to through Wegg's mischievous wooden limb. The terms of the Harmon Will, the substitute for old John Harmon's tyrannical will, tempts John Harmon, the son, to violate his own values and integrity. If he succumbs to the lure of the Harmon fortune and marries Bella Wilfer for its sake, Harmon will truly become his father's namesake, a mere memorial to twisted values and a dead past. Harmon runs the risk of becoming an appendage to the past, a lifeless limb of a dead family tree paralytically animated by the father's greed and the conservative tendency to restore an earlier state of things.

John Harmon's is the story of the quintessential romantic self. He
journeys between the poles of psychic fragmentation and of psychic paralysis. For Dickens, however, paralysis is often the prelude to fragmentation, to the spontaneous combustion of a self silently disintegrating
behind the gargoyle façade of the habitual self. The gorgon's head, in
one guise or another, presides over the later novels. It is the head that
turns men and women to stone, the visage of a social or a personal past
whose gaze fixes its victims in forms of life, social and personal, now
obsolete and ossified. But, like Silas Wegg's wooden leg, such structures
will elevate themselves to proclaim a semblance of life, however distorted
or perverted. Charles Darnay meets the gorgon's head of the French aristocracy. John Harmon encounters it in the granite terms of his father's
will. But Harmon defies the past by exploiting his near-fatal immersion
in the Thames. He risks the dangers of self-dispersal in the various dis-
guises he adopts. But he prevails, piecing himself together, reinventing
himself upon terms different from those embedded in the Harmon Will:

Man invents for himself a program of life, a static form of being, that gives a
satisfactory answer to the difficulties posed for him by circumstance. He essays
this form of life, attempts to realize this imaginary character he has resolved to
be. He embarks on the essay full of illusions and prosecutes the experiment with
thoroughness. This means that he comes to *believe* deeply that this character is his
real being. But meanwhile the experience has made apparent the shortcomings
and limitations of the said program of life. It does not solve all the difficulties,
and it creates new ones of its own. . . . Man thinks out another program of life.
But this second program is drawn up in the light, not only of circumstance, but
also of the first.[36]

The kinship of Ortega y Gasset's ideas to Rousseau's and Goethe's, to
Dickens's and Freud's, is significant. For if someone falls prey to the belief that his imaginary character is his real being, he becomes a creature
of Mr. Morfin's dreaded habit: he becomes fixated upon a form of life
that once may have served a legitimate function within a set of circumstances now irreversibly altered by time. The figure refusing to reinvent
himself imaginatively succumbs to the conservative tendency to repeat
the past, to deny the need for change because such change is always
threatening. In Ortega's credo we see how, in the compulsion to repeat
the past, either a past lived by another or by oneself, the romantic pil-

grim, perforce the "novelist of himself," must fail to be original and end only as a plagiarist.

In this book I shall be exploring the pilgrimage of being upon which various Dickens heroes and heroines embark and the vicissitudes they encounter in their successful, or failed, acts of self-creation. In imagining the life of the self, Dickens, like Freud, has recourse to those romantic paradigms available to him, paradigms that help to constitute the recent invention, man. Dickens's sense of psychic dislocation is hauntingly proto-Freudian and utterly romantic. Dickens in his novels and Freud in his case histories record the experiences of fictional characters and living men and women "'fixated' to a particular portion of their past, as though they could not manage to free themselves from it and . . . for that reason alienated from the present and the future" (*SE*, 16:273). The dynamic, the living self of Goethe and of Kierkegaard falls prey to stasis, to paralysis, to habit.

The book begins in medias res with *Dombey and Son* and *David Copperfield*. In *David Copperfield* Dickens for the first time, after his own abortive effort to write an autobiography, directs his attention to the problem of memory and to the minutiae of personal history. He moves away from the melodramatic presentation of the theatrical self to a study of the narrative self in action. In this fictional autobiography, Dickens explores David's attempts to integrate his troubling past into a narrative account of his self in his effort to move forward in time toward an elusive, integrated self—toward the "winged Psyche" of *Sartor Resartus,* a fragile form achieved for the moment, but tending always to dissolution.[37]

The vision of the narrative self emerging in *David Copperfield* then informs Dickens's exploration of other fictional characters flirting always with paralysis. Such a conception of the self, and the dangers it confronts, is not confined to the first-person narratives of an Esther Summerson or of a Pip. The vision of the self emerging in *David Copperfield* illuminates the plight of a Charles Darnay and the apparent impasses of John Harmon and Eugene Wrayburn in *Our Mutual Friend*—even, I shall argue, the condition of the opium-addicted John Jasper in *The Mystery of Edwin Drood*. But *David Copperfield* does not materialize ex nihilo. Dickens has been moving toward this seminal novel from the beginning of his career. In *Dombey and Son* the characteristic language and motifs pervading the later novels, informed by the ontology of the romantic self, appear in crystallized form. *Dombey and Son* has always been celebrated as the novel in which Dickens finally comprehends the great issue of social change in nineteenth-century England. For me it reveals, just as clearly, Dickens's comprehension of the issue of personal change to which he insistently returns in the novels written in the last two decades of his life.[38]

Part One

The Living Self

Dombey and Son and David Copperfield

Chapter 1

> "Do you know," simpered Cleopatra, revers-
> ing the knave of clubs, who had come into her
> game with his heels uppermost, "that if any-
> thing could tempt me to put a period to my
> life, it would be a feeling of curiosity to find
> out what it's all about, and what it means; there
> are so many provoking mysteries, really, that
> are hidden from us. Major, you to play!"
> —Mrs. Skewton, *Dombey and Son*

The Mysteries of the Self

In passing, before she returns to the more engrossing subject of cards, Mrs. Skewton speaks, somewhat frivolously, of life's "provoking mysteries." The phrase reverberates through *Dombey and Son* and is a useful reminder that, although his characters often flee from such mysteries, Dickens the novelist does not. Death is the mystery that causes Mrs. Skewton to neglect, however briefly, her game of cards. She resumes her role as Cleopatra as she evades those other mysteries revealed in Mrs.

Chick's observation that "It's a world of change." Mrs. Skewton becomes imprisoned in her habitual pose as Cleopatra, evading the romantic imperative to change and self-creation, while Major Bagstock denies the realities of time, change, and death through those verbal repetitions by which he seeks to perpetuate himself: "Would you give Joey B. the go-by, Ma'am? Not yet, Ma'am, not yet! Damme, not yet, Sir. Joe is awake, Ma'am. Bagstock is alive, Sir. J. B. knows a move or two, Ma'am. Josh has his weather-eye open, Sir. You'll find him tough, Ma'am. Tough, Sir, tough is Joseph. Tough, and de-vil-ish sly!"[1] Major Bagstock thinks and talks of himself in the third person: he has no "I" to speak of as he pirouettes around the void of an absent self. His unchanging verbal mannerisms indicate that, although he is speaking English, he is, no less than Miss Blimber, "working in the graves of deceased languages." As Dickens makes clear, "None of your live languages for Miss Blimber," or for Major Bagstock (chapter 11). His "stone dead" personal language, addressed primarily to an absent self, reveals the extent to which "Bagstock is [not] alive, Sir," in any genuine sense. Like Mrs. Skewton in her role as Cleopatra, he has chosen paralysis—until Paralysis chooses him—to avoid the romantic pilgrimage of being. Each becomes a self-plagiarist, with a version of the self constructed upon an originally specious and now outmoded pose.

Dickens's characters flee the mystery of death and betray the dynamics of the living self only to become imprisoned in the "cold hard armour" of their roles and to encounter yet another mystery, a terrible isolation from themselves and others. Dickens recurrently explores such isolation in the language of metal, stone, and ice. This language of figurative petrification establishes a poetic continuum between the self in stasis and the self in isolation, for isolation engenders stasis in the intersubjective realm of Dickens's novels. The opening pages of *Bleak House* serve as the almost inevitable introduction to this dimension of the Dickens world: critics, like Dickens's characters, succumb to habit. But an even starker vision appears in *Little Dorrit*. The second book of that novel opens upon a group of travelers as they ascend the Alps by mule, making their way toward the convent of the Great Saint Bernard. This scene grew out of Dickens's own visit to the convent in the first week of September 1846, when he was at work on the opening numbers of *Dombey and Son*. His visit was recorded in a letter to John Forster:

I wish to God you could see that place. A great hollow on the top of a range of dreadful mountains, fenced in by riven rocks of every shape and colour: and in the midst, a black lake, with phantom clouds perpetually stalking over it. Peaks, and points, and plains of eternal ice and snow, bounding the view, and shutting out the world on every side: the lake reflecting nothing: and no human figure in the scene. . . . Nothing of life or living interest in the picture, but the grey dull walls of the convent. No vegetation of any sort or kind. Nothing growing, nothing stirring. Everything iron-bound, and frozen up.[2]

The language of this and other letters, more clearly even than the later language of *Little Dorrit,* conjures up the desolation, the pure otherness of nature and the universe. In the 1846 letter to Forster, Dickens wrote in a manner reminiscent of Shelley's "Mont Blanc" and Mary Shelley's *Frankenstein.* He captured an internal and an external landscape, touching upon the estrangement of men and women from a hostile universe no longer succoring the human spirit and intensifying the pain of their estrangement from each other.[3]

The fictive pilgrims of *Little Dorrit* move through the darkness of encroaching night, separated no longer by London fog, but by the Alpine mist and clouds enveloping them: "The breath of the men was cloud, the breath of the mules was cloud, the lights were encircled by cloud, speakers close at hand were not seen for cloud, though their voices and all other sounds were surprisingly clear."[4] They suddenly speak in a babel of foreign tongues after the silence resulting from fatigue and sharp cold. Experiencing the isolation imposed by separate and finite selves, they are foreigners to each other, each single and solitary as a consequence of the fact of embodied consciousness. The romantic vision dictates that each traveler speak in a foreign, or a dead, language to every human Other who is encountered.

The living travelers of *Little Dorrit* are curiously akin to those "dead travellers found upon the mountain" whose frozen corpses are "silently assembled in a grated house" adjacent to the convent: "The mother, storm-belated many winters ago, still standing in the corner with her baby at her breast; the man who had frozen with his arm raised to his mouth in fear or hunger, still pressing it with his dry lips after years and years. An awful company, mysteriously come together!" (book 2, chapter 1). But the dead travelers are no more mysteriously come together than the living ones, who think "little or nothing of the dead" in the grated house enfolded by the same cloud and snow flakes. The frozen bodies, standing upright in their jail-like house, comment on the condition of the uncomprehending living. They announce the death-in-life of absolute isolation, with the psychic and the spiritual hunger it engenders: "I and my child will dwell together inseparable, on the Great Saint Bernard, outlasting generations who will come to see us, and will never know our name, or one word of our story but the end" (book 2, chapter 1). Isolation ensures that one's name and story are never to be fully understood by others. But the story itself may be interrupted permanently, not only through physical death, but also through the death-in-life of pure stasis. The dynamic self for whom the pilgrimage of being is a necessary activity becomes cut off from time and the possibility of change. Within *Little Dorrit* those three frozen figures—the mother, the child, and the man—serve as eternal hieroglyphs for the riddle of the human condition.

The provoking mysteries of the human condition may prove so compelling for Dickens that he will interrupt the narrative line of a novel, as in *A Tale of Two Cities,* to engage in an elegiac speculation:

A wonderful fact to reflect upon, that every human creature is constituted to be that profound secret and mystery to every other. A solemn consideration, when I enter a great city by night, that every one of those darkly clustered houses encloses its own secret; that every room in every one of them encloses its own secret; that every beating heart in the hundreds of thousands of breasts there, is, in some of its imaginings, a secret to the heart nearest it! Something of the awfulness, even of Death itself, is referable to this.[5]

For Dickens, these two ineluctable facts exist at the core of the human predicament. Death is the "consolidation and perpetuation of the secret" that constitutes the individuality, the identity, of every man and woman. Unknown by those most dear to them, each of Dickens's characters endures the imprisonment that the romantic emphasis upon individuality imposes upon those who feel like Rousseau and who claim with him, "I am like no one in the whole world. I may be no better, but at least I am different."[6]

But behind the musing upon the fact that each person—my friend, my neighbor, my love, the darling of my soul—remains a mystery, there lies yet another recognition: each person remains a mystery to himself. The passage, dwelling upon the ineradicable foreignness of the Other, suggests the foreignness of one's own self: "No more can I look into the depths of this unfathomable water, wherein, as momentary lights glanced into it, I have had glimpses of buried treasure and other things submerged. . . . It was appointed that the water should be locked in an eternal frost, when the light was playing on its surface, and I stood in ignorance on the shore" (book 1, chapter 3). Dickens returns to the "black lake" near the Saint Bernard convent where "everything [is] iron-bound, and frozen up." He returns to the grated house of *Little Dorrit,* to the riddle posed by the frozen mother and by the man with his arm raised to his mouth in either fear or hunger. The watery depths of the Other, "locked in an eternal frost," refuse to relinquish their secrets. But the water also serves as a trope for the unfathomable depths of the musing "I." Beneath the surface lie things submerged and inaccessible. The surface catches the light prior to the moment of freezing. It is always potentially a mirror reflecting tentative speculations upon others and revealing the otherness of one's own innermost personality.

Dickens's characters often stand in ignorance upon the shore, gazing into the waters of the self, encountering only reflections, only images, of themselves. Dickens follows Teufelsdröckh in *Sartor Resartus* in remaining skeptical about the possibilities of self-knowledge: "A certain inarticulate Self-consciousness dwells dimly in us; which only our Works can render articulate and decisively discernible. Our Works are the mirror wherein the spirit first sees its natural lineaments. Hence, too, the folly of that impossible Precept, *Know thyself*."[7] I have suggested how such a passage echoes the words of Goethe's Faust, "In the beginning was the Deed." But it also underlies the significance of those literal and figurative mirrors into which characters in Dickens's novels so often look. Charles Darnay, on trial in the Old Bailey, glances upward to see the mirror over his head in which his reflection seems to mingle with the reflections of those who have stood in the prisoner's dock before him: their images rise from the watery depths of the mirror. What Darnay glimpses, fleetingly, is a version of himself, perhaps as others in the crowded courtroom view him. Esther Summerson, after her disfiguring illness, must look into the glass to see her altered face so that she can learn to live with her altered self. Even Mr. Dombey, in a rare act of introspection, can be caught looking down "into the cold depths of the dead sea of mahogany on which the fruit dishes and decanters lay at anchor; as if the subjects of his thoughts were rising towards the surface

one by one, and plunging down again" (chapter 30). Dickens characteristically unites the mirror and the sea to suggest the deceptive veneer
that seals off the submerged self. The glassy surface yields reflections of
light and obscure images drifting to the surface, only to be immediately
dissolved.

Self-knowledge is always elusive for Dickens's characters. The mirror
recurrently captures the image of a character: it casts back not the self,
but a complex approximation of it. As Edith Granger, soon to be Mrs.
Dombey, passes through the Dombey house, the "broad high mirrors
[show] her, at full length, a woman with a noble quality yet dwelling in
her nature, who was too false to her better self, and too debased and
lost, to save herself. She believed that all this was so plain more or less, to
all eyes, that she had no resource or power of self-assertion, but in pride"
(chapter 30). What Edith sees is not necessarily herself at all; in part, she
sees what she assumes others see *in* her. She cannot define herself in isolation, but only in an imaginary intersubjective exchange with the others
who gaze upon her. Dickens's understanding of the complex relationship of the self to itself stunningly anticipates the anti-Cartesian, post-
Christian thrust of current French thought that leads Roland Barthes to
a Lacanian reverie in his paradoxical autobiographical enterprise, *Roland
Barthes par Roland Barthes*:

*"But I never looked like that!"—How do you know? What is the "you" you might or
might not look like? Where do you find it—by which morphological or expressive calibra-
tion? Where is your authentic body? You are the only one who can never see yourself
except as an image; you never see your eyes unless they are dulled by the gaze they rest
upon the mirror or the lens . . . : even and especially for your own body, you are condemned to the repertoire of its images.*[8]

Barthes is speaking not only of the knowledge of the body, but of the
knowledge of the elusive "you," the Cartesian "I" whose existence was
once so confidently proclaimed in the formula of the cogito. But in a
universe no longer sustained by God's informing presence, the individual must sustain himself, or herself, through an act of the imagination.
The words of St. Paul acquire a new and secular meaning. In Dickens's
novels, characters continue to see through a glass darkly. But there is no
longer confidence in the hope that a self which cannot be known now
shall be known in a life after death, that one shall see face to face and

know "even as also [he is] known" in the present. For God no longer
countenances the knowledge of the self.

In Dickens's novels, no character ever sees face to face in the Pauline
sense. Never glimpsing their own faces, Dickens's characters scrutinize
the faces of others in the hope of seeing themselves reflected and defined
there. On his first visit to the Carker household, Mr. Morfin tells Harriet
Carker that the face is the mirror of truth. Her face *may* mirror the
depths of Harriet's inaccessible self. It may, however, mirror back to Mr.
Morfin only his conception of Harriet, as well as Harriet's idea of him,
itself a complicated response to his professed faith in her goodness. The
complex intersubjective exchange reassures Mr. Morfin about himself
and his motives. Florence Dombey encounters the far different gaze of
her father. Like Sleeping Beauty, she finds herself incarcerated in an enchanted castle, cut off from time itself: "Florence lived alone in the great
dreary house, and day succeeded day, and still she lived alone; and the
blank walls looked down upon her with a vacant stare, as if they had a
Gorgon-like mind to stare her youth and beauty into stone" (chapter 23).
The stare of the blank walls is like her father's stare; like his, it seeks to
deny and destroy the gift of love and of life that she possesses. But Florence does not succumb to the gorgon gaze of the father. She does not,
finally, see herself reflected there in a way that would turn her to stone,
paralyzed by her father's hatred. The face of the dying Mrs. Dombey
responds to Florence's imploring words: "For a moment, the closed eye-
lids trembled, and the nostril quivered, and the faintest shadow of a
smile was seen" (chapter 1). In the mirror of her mother's face, Florence
sees herself as someone with the capacity to love and to evoke love in
others. She exists in a state of grace throughout *Dombey and Son:* the
mother's last, and most significant, smile envelops Florence in the wings
of the dove.[9]

For Mr. Dombey there is no state of grace. Little Paul thinks and
speaks of his father as being two in one, Dombey and Son. Paul's father
may well be little more than an idée fixe grotesquely embodied. He is
what John Harmon in *Our Mutual Friend* struggles not to be—the dead
appendage of a dead father. His wooden stiffness and frozen inflexibility
reveal the extent to which he is merely a memorial to an abstract idea.
When he fiercely rebukes Walter Gay with the words "You are a boy . . .
and what you think of, or affect to think of, is of little consequence,"

Dombey is like a ventriloquist's dummy—an effigy like the Wooden Midshipman—mouthing the words of his own father (chapter 6). It is altogether appropriate that in his private office Dombey is "stared at, through a dome-shaped window in the leads, by ugly chimney pots and backs of houses, and especially by the bold window of a hair-cutting saloon on a first floor, where a waxen effigy . . . showed him the wrong side of its head for ever" (chapter 13). Dombey is the dead past—"paralytically animated"—turning his gorgon visage upon Paul to impose the fatal legacy he has inherited. But Dombey remains a beleaguered plagiarist, susceptible to self-doubt, however muted: "Towards his first wife, Mr. Dombey, in his cold and lofty arrogance, had borne himself like the removed *Being he almost conceived* himself to be" (chapter 40, emphasis mine). Dombey almost believes in this imaginary character he has resolved to be, not of his own choosing, but of his father's. Cut off from time, a mere creature of another's will, Dombey cultivates the precious image of himself as Dombey and Son that serves only to destroy any original, living identity he might create. He has become habituated to the role he plays, has become one of Mr. Morfin's images, and is as "susceptible as images to new impressions and convictions."

The role implicitly forged by the dead father—as Dombey tries to forge a similar role for little Paul, who will prefer not to follow in his father's footsteps—has a dual function. Through the male heirs the firm of Dombey and Son tries to deny the reality of death, much as Major Bagstock and Mrs. Skewton try to deny it. There is also an attempt to deny the reality of time in general, to deny that the idea of Dombey and Son as a firm might ever become, in Ortega's sense, obsolete. Dombey and Son, as a "program of life, a static form of being, . . . does not solve all the difficulties, and it creates new ones of its own." Mr. Dombey's stiffness is not mere pride; it is a flawed response to economic reality and to the ontological realities of the self. The waxen effigy in the hair-cutting saloon ironically mocks Mr. Dombey. But his essence—since Dombey seeks to affirm an indestructible essence—is captured in the most demonic effigy of all. Dickens moves from Florence's scrutiny of her father's face to the Wooden Midshipman before Sol Gills's instrument shop: "If anything had frightened [Florence], it was the face [her father] turned upon her. The glowing love within the breast of his young daughter froze before it, and she stood and looked at him as if stricken into stone" (chapter 18). The scene shifts to Solomon Gills sadly anticipating Walter Gay's departure. Old Sol rests "his weary wig so near the shoe-buckles of the guardian genius of his trade and shop as he could. But no fierce idol with a mouth from ear to ear, and a murderous visage made of parrot's feathers, was ever more indifferent to the appeals of its savage votaries, than was the wooden Midshipman to these marks of attachment" (chapter 19).

The Wooden Midshipman with its murderous visage suggests the gorgon's spell under which Dombey seeks to cultivate an apparently indestructible image. It is also a talisman for the figurative death of Dombey and others in the novel. Dombey's habitual coldness and stiffness make him like the frozen man in the grated house near the convent of Saint Bernard. At the cold collation following young Paul's baptism, Dombey remains unmoved: "He might have been hung up for sale at a Russian fair as a specimen of a frozen gentleman" (chapter 5). In a state of psychic arrest, he is isolated from others and from any vestige of a living, dynamic self that might have survived the murderous glance of his father and of his own stern visage. Yet Dombey's social and personal rigidity, negating the romantic ontology informing Dickens's novels, marks the unreality of the inflexible fiction by which he tries to live. Dombey is understandably not given to introspection, to standing upon the figurative shore and gazing into the depths of himself. Such activity threatens to dissolve his precious and fragile image of himself. Meditating upon his approaching marriage, upon his daughter, and himself, Dombey stares into the mirrorlike surface of a mahogany table, but understands himself "indifferently well, perhaps, at best; for marriage company and marriage altars, and ambitious scenes—still blotted here and there with Florence—always Florence—turned up so fast, and so confusedly, that he rose, and went up-stairs to escape them" (chapter 30). Dombey flees from the image of Florence and from perplexing thoughts rising to the surface of his mind. He seeks that image of himself in the reflecting surface of the table that he ordinarily finds reflected in the faces of those who flatter and toady to him. His thoughts subvert his conception of himself. Florence's image reminds him always of little Paul's preference for his sister and of his namesake's death. Through his daughter, Dombey is confronted with his own mortality and encounters the nearly unthinkable, that his extended identity as Dombey and Son is a mere construct vulnerable to the vicissitudes of time. Lacking a "Son and Heir"—the name of the ship carrying Walter Gay to his apparent death—Dombey is radically incomplete. He is as crippled as the man with the wooden leg, the curious precursor of Silas Wegg who witnesses the marriage of Florence and Walter.[10]

Dombey, who cannot see himself, is "*condemned to the repertoire of the images*" he mistakes for himself. The marriage to Edith Granger is designed, in part, to produce that son and heir who will make Dombey truly Dombey and Son. But Edith lures Dombey for other reasons. She seems both an extension of Dombey's self and a confirmation of it. Edith sits "like a handsome statue; as cold, as silent, and as still" (chapter 30). She is always at Dombey's disposal: it flattered him to think how haughtiness and coldness "deferred to him, in Edith's case, and seemed to have no will apart from his. It flattered him to picture to himself, this proud and stately woman doing the honours of his house, and chilling his guests after his own manner" (chapter 30). Dombey wants Edith to exercise her gorgon spell upon others, as he seeks to do. He cannot know that Edith, like himself, is the victim of the same spell, that her face will strive "for composure until its proud beauty [is] as fixed as death" (chapter 35).

It is Edith Granger, perhaps more than any other character in *Dombey and Son* and in the novels to follow, who dramatizes the power of the imaginative construct we call the self to achieve a frightening and constricting autonomy. Edith, molded by "the daily working of [her mother's] hands," sees herself as a thing to be placed upon the auction block and to be sold to the highest bidder. The process begins most clearly when Edith is Florence's age, but it is based upon an earlier experience, depicted by Dickens in *Bleak House,* when a child acquires a specular image of itself. Esther Summerson's identity is founded upon the vision of herself that she sees as a child in her little glass and upon that version of herself she sees reflected in her aunt's stern face. The image in the mirror establishes a sense of physical boundaries and anticipates the boundaries of an emerging, if fragile, self. The outlines of a body, and a self, seem to take form within the mirror's frame. This outline, tentatively established during what Jacques Lacan and Maurice Merleau-Ponty discuss as the mirror stage, replaces both the self once seen and known by God and the Cartesian cogito.[11]

But the outline, the boundary between self and Other, never remains fixed or absolute. Rather, it is a fragile membrane, easily penetrated by the thoughts and feelings of others, which are inferred from those adult faces the child inevitably scrutinizes for confirmation of its existence and its nature. The image in the mirror subtly fuses with the image perceived in the mirroring face of the adult: "I happened to look timidly up from my stitching, across the table, at my godmother, and I saw in her face, looking gloomily at me, 'It would have been far better, little Esther, that you had had no birthday; that you had never been born!'" [12] No words are spoken. In this intersubjective exchange with the unyielding face of her aunt, Esther comprehends what Miss Barbary sees within her. Esther submits to that "darkened face [that has] such power" over her; she is frozen by the face and by the ensuing words with which Miss Barbary seeks to establish, permanently, that version of her self with which Esther is to live (chapter 3). This conception of herself is frozen in her consciousness so that, rebel as she might, Esther will remain haunted and impelled by the aunt's version of her. Esther Summerson, like Edith Granger, is molded by another; she loses her self to an Other and lives with an idea of herself alien to her own feelings and desires. [13]

An Esther Summerson or an Edith Granger identifies herself with the face in the mirror. Each is then prepared to identify with that version of her face, her self, reflected in an aunt's or a mother's face. Edith Granger, like the frozen Esther, becomes transfixed by the image perceived in the mother's countenance. She clings as best she can to her belief in the existence of a better self, her "own inward self." But as she hardens, like a statue or an image, into the role she plays, as if to deny her voluntary participation in the role, she loses touch with the hypothetical better self. The mask she dons, in repugnance for what she does, hardens; it consolidates itself, becoming impervious to change. Edith runs the risk of *becoming* the face, as "fixed as any statue's," that she and others see in those literal and figurative mirrors into which she looks.

This is the woman Mr. Dombey marries and upon whom he seeks to impose his own inflexible will. In her attempt to deny any complicity in her mother's dealings with Dombey, Edith becomes frozen into a refusal to please. She becomes the bartered thing she abhors. In playing the haughty role fully, she wants to deny it, as if through a form of caricature; but she is so habituated to the role that it will lead to her elopement with James Carker, Dombey's manager:

"Never seek to find in me," said Edith, laying her hand upon her breast, "what is not here. . . . Little by little you will know me better, and the time will come when you will know me, as I know myself. . . ."

The tears that were visible in her eyes as she kept them fixed on Florence, showed that the composed face was but as a handsome mask; but she preserved it, and continued. (Chapter 35)

The mask displaces Edith's own inward self; the imaginative construct imposed on her—fixed, rigid, and unchanging—is finally accepted by Edith. It develops its own autonomy: Edith becomes her specular image seen in the glass of the world.

The interplay between Edith and Dombey, who demands confirmation of his way of thinking from his wife as from all others, leads to one of the more brilliant confrontations in all of Dickens's novels. Dombey seeks Edith out in her own apartment, "determined to bend her to his magnificent and stately will." He finds her before her glass: "Her face was melancholy and pensive, when he came upon her; but it marked him at the door; for, glancing at the mirror before it, he saw immediately, as in a picture-frame, the knitted brow, and darkened beauty that he knew so well" (chapter 40). Neither Dombey nor Edith sees the other directly from the start. Each sees the face, the image, of the other reflected in the mirror. Dombey remains ignorant of his wife's inner state, of her attitude toward herself and her marriage. He sees Mrs. Dombey as his possession caught in the frame of the mirror. But Edith is no less alienated from her self. In the glass she sees Dombey's reflected face beside her own. She sees her face as she assumes others, like the phantasmal Dombey reflected in the mirror, must see it. Her conception of the way in which her husband perceives her ultimately informs her own relationship to herself. Edith Dombey gazes upon the face in the mirror that others see, or so she thinks. She is no longer sure whether the face hovering in the glass is her own inward self or some foreign presence with the power to consume or to paralyze the fragile self of one's dreams.[14]

In turning to Dombey, Edith offers him the face he has seen in the mirror, the cold and handsome mask of her acquired self. The mask might dissolve if Dombey were other than he is. As a construct, in time, it is subject to change. But such a change requires the help of others, an intersubjective exchange through which the constitution of the image, the self, is altered. The image in the mirror may change with others' changing perceptions of it, as they are perceived or intuited. Edith Dombey's face may yield its hard composure if Dombey ceases to treat her as his purchased thing, a framed likeness. But this requires Dombey to abandon his idée fixe, his rigid belief in Dombey and Son as some kind of enduring entity in a world of flux. He must relinquish his own habitual self, Ortega's "imaginary character," in which he has come deeply to believe, and penetrate the habitual self that is imprisoning Edith.

But the habitual self upon which Mr. Morfin has mused seeks to conserve itself and to repeat a dead past. "Deaf, dumb, blind, and paralytic, to a million things, from habit," such a self operates upon the principle of the repetition compulsion. Dombey's self, an institution, like the firm of Dombey and Son, struggles "to keep . . . in existence after the time of its usefulness has passed" (*SE*, 23:237–38). Toward his first wife, Mr. Dombey, "in his cold and lofty arrogance, had borne himself like the removed Being he almost conceived himself to be. . . . He had asserted his greatness during their whole married life, and she had meekly recognised it" (chapter 40). In his encounter with Edith, Dombey wants to reestablish the past relationship with the dead first Mrs. Dombey in order to restore his illusory conception of himself. He wishes to reaffirm "the cold hard armour of pride in which he [lives] encased," seemingly protected from a hostile world: "'Madam,' said Mr. Dombey, with his most offensive air of state, 'I have made you my wife. You bear my name. You are associated with my position and my reputation. I will not say that the world in general may be disposed to think you honoured by that association; but I will say that I am accustomed to "insist," to my connexions and dependants'" (chapter 40). Dombey has denied Edith's existence, her autonomy, her self. With these words, spoken out of habit, Dombey seals his fate, and Edith's.

Dombey responds to Edith's pleas, if she can be said to plead before any man, with repeated references to his ultimatum. He demands submission "—To Me—To Me!" Edith responds, after revealing a "pale blank earnestness," with a face that changes "to its old expression, deepened in intensity!" The face first seen in the glass, by Dombey and by Edith upon Dombey's entrance into the room, returns as a presence more real than the chaotic feelings to which Edith has briefly yielded. The return of her "old expression" marks Edith's permanent alienation from her "inward self," a self capable of responding to thoughts of Florence; it marks the degree to which she has become a captive to Dombey's conception of her.[15] Edith turns "her back upon [Dombey], and, without reply, [sits] down before her glass," but "he saw no more expression of any heed of him, in the mirror, than if he had been an unseen

spider on the wall, or beetle on the floor, or rather, than if he had been
the one or other, seen and crushed when she last turned from him, and
forgotten among the ignominious and dead vermin of the ground"
(chapter 40). The scene ends as it begins, with Edith before her glass "as
if she were a beautiful Medusa" with the capacity not simply to turn men
to stone, but to annihilate them completely. Yet she, too, has been turned
to stone, not only by her own stern gaze, but by Dombey's cold countenance. They have not met face to face; they have encountered each other
through the mediating surface of the glass: "He looked back, as he went
out at the door, upon the well-lighted and luxurious room, the beautiful
and glittering objects everywhere displayed, the shape of Edith in its
rich dress seated before her glass, and the face of Edith as the glass pre-
sented it to him" (chapter 40). And to her. She is a shape in a fixed position, once again the marble image—immovable, cold, and indifferent.
Dombey has done this to her, consolidating her alienation from a self
perhaps still capable of love and change. She retaliates by denying his
existence. She refuses to acknowledge his retreating image in the mirror,
the image he seeks to project to himself and to others. In doing so, Edith
becomes the captive of the image in the glass, that alienating construct
sustained by the almost perverse cooperation of Mrs. Skewton, Dombey, and Edith herself. Edith abandons a sense of her own capacity to
will and to choose. Whatever authentic self she had tentatively cultivated
has receded into the depths of the mirror, lost to her searching gaze.[16]

Mr. Dombey and Edith fail to respond to the imperatives of the romantic self, to that dynamic process evolving, in time, toward some hypothetical unity. They remain on the shore, at best only glimpsing in
"the depths of this unfathomable water" the "buried treasure and other
things submerged" there. Their alienation from themselves and their
isolation from others is complete. Each has become, in every sense of the
word, one of Mr. Morfin's images: an effigy; a reflection in a mirror; a
figure in a portrait; an idea in the consciousness of each. They are "deaf,
dumb, blind, and paralytic, to a million things, from habit." But such
rigidity only obscures the fragile nature of the constructed self. Edith's
image in the glass seems stable, permanent, impervious. Her true condition is revealed in the "wealth of colour and voluptuous glitter" of her
apartment, a glitter that repeats her "repellant beauty," as Dombey sees
it, as "in so many fragments of a mirror." The acquisition of the specular
image, at once necessary and potentially dangerous to a person possess-

ing or possessed by it, remains at best a temporary achievement, a form of the self always subject to disruption. For the image is never self-sustaining, however hardened and impervious to change it becomes. It may, like the "Wooden Midshipman, [go] to Pieces." Edith Dombey has been turned to stone, and only in the concluding pages of the novel does she relent and melt in tears for a brief moment. Dombey's case proves to be different. However, Dombey does not go to pieces as long as his conception of himself—as Dombey and Son—is sustained by others. As James Carker observes to Edith, "We who are about him, have, in our various positions, done our part, I dare say, to confirm him in his way of thinking; but if we had not done so, others would—or they would not have been about him; and it has always been, from the beginning, the very staple of his life" (chapter 45).[17]

Carker the manager knows Dombey well. But though others are necessary to him to confirm his idea of himself, Dombey lives, like Edith and Carker, in a universe peopled by his own images, of himself and of others. Dombey inhabits a hall of mirrors, experiencing the isolation at the center of the romantic experience. This isolation from oneself and others is central to Dombey's career. With the fall of the two houses, commercial and domestic, Dombey finds himself shut up in his rooms, contemplating suicide as he sees in the glass the picture of "a spectral, haggard, wasted likeness of himself, [brooding] . . . over the empty fireplace. Now *it* lifted up *its* head, examining the lines and hollows in *its* face; now hung *it* down again, and brooded afresh. Now *it* rose and walked about; now passed into the next room, and came back with something from the dressing-table in *its* breast. Now, *it* was looking at the bottom of the door, and thinking" (chapter 59, emphasis mine). Dombey has ceased to exist as a unified body reflected in a glass. With the loss of the unified specular image, the model for the creation of identity, there occurs a loss of a sense of a unified self. Dombey has ceased to possess a viable identity. He has been reduced to the spectral likeness that he perceives as it, as a foreign presence, an alien image from which he must be freed if he is to live, or to die. He is saved by Florence and by the face she raises to him, mirroring back a new self able to accept that "Dombey and Son [is] no more," that time exists, that change is necessary and obsolete fictions of the self must be abandoned. But this change occurs under the aegis of the paradoxically unchanged Florence, who happens now to be a mother, and it is effected by the power of Florence's face. Dombey leaves the room where he has seen the picture in the glass and accompanies Florence into the city, "with her eyes upon his face." A tentative contact of sorts has occurred. It is not contact between the authentic self of Dombey and the authentic self of Florence, but rather an encounter between the specular image of each, impinging upon and altering the image of the other, making change, and life, possible.

Change is not altogether impossible in the fictive world of Dickens. But it is rare, and often harrowing. Among those who do not change are Major Bagstock and Mrs. Skewton—"her attitude . . . was one in which she had been taken in a barouche, some fifty years before, by a then fashionable artist" (chapter 21). They cling to their imaginary selves with a tenacity at once comic and grotesque. They quell whatever inner life might lead them to thoughtful reflection. But there are other characters, more complex, for whom change also proves to be impossible. They become like Dombey alone in his room. Their isolation and their attachment to the specular image compel them to live amidst the images generated by their own fancies. For them, the figurative and literal death of the self becomes the inevitable culmination of an irresolvable impasse. Dombey finally leaves the house that has never been freed from the gorgon spell cast by the legacy of Dombey and Son. But James Carker, the manager, succumbs to the spell and is finally destroyed by it: psychic paralysis leads, at last, to the fragmentation of the self.

For James Carker is the true Son of the firm and the novel. He models himself upon Mr. Dombey, partly as an act of conscious mockery and defiance, partly as a form of unwitting emulation: "The stiffness and nicety of Mr. Carker's dress, and a certain arrogance of manner, either natural to him, or imitated from a pattern not far off, gave great additional effect to his humility. He seemed a man who would contend against the power that vanquished him, if he could, but who was utterly borne down by the greatness and superiority of Mr. Dombey" (chapter 13). The pose Carker assumes, that of a subordinate vanquished by his employer, becomes more than a form of simple hypocrisy. Carker has truly been vanquished by the head of the House, the patriarch of the firm: his identity has been extinguished by Dombey's presence, upon whom he does, in part, model himself. This deeper truth cannot be acknowledged by Carker. Dickens hints at it during the episode in Leamington when Carker is introduced to Edith Granger and is subtly, but never explicitly, informed that Dombey intends to remarry. "Dombey's right-hand man," as Major Bagstock refers to him, stops "short of the extent of Mr. Dombey's stiffness: at once perhaps because he [knows] it to be ludicrous, and because in doing so he [finds] another means of expressing his sense of the difference and distance between them" (chapter 27). This is not merely Carker's ironic acknowledgment of Dombey's social and economic superiority. Carker seeks to differentiate himself from Dombey, to assert his existence independent of the master. He offers, in effect, a subtle caricature of Dombey, a disguised attack upon him. These are the tactics of a son, not of an employee. Carker is impelled to distance himself from Dombey in his need to prove he is not merely a dead appendage of the figurative father.

Carker tries to assert an identity, a self, of his own. But that identity is suspect. Like Dombey, Carker is at best only indifferently in touch with the fragile construct of his self. This becomes clear when he returns to his hotel room in Leamington to commune with his image in the glass: "There was a faint blur on the surface of the mirror in Mr. Carker's chamber, and its reflection was, perhaps, a false one. But it showed, that night, the image of a man, who saw, in his fancy, a crowd of people slumbering on the ground at his feet, like the poor Native at his master's door: who picked his way among them: looking down, maliciously enough: but trod upon no upturned face—as yet" (chapter 26). Looking into the mirror, Carker encounters a blurred reflection, the image of himself floating in the depths of his own consciousness. This moment anticipates the one of Dombey at the mahogany table, looking into its reflecting surface for "ambitious scenes" of his marriage to Edith Granger and of the births of innumerable sons to perpetuate himself and the firm—scenes never finally to materialize in his life. The image Carker sees is a false one because the sense of power it conveys to him is illusory. He is no more able to confront *his* master than the Native is able to confront Major Bagstock. Carker may very well contrive the financial ruin of the House. He may play upon Edith Dombey's sense of insult and injury to lure her into flight from her husband. But he cannot confront Dombey and challenge him directly, face to face.

Carker, instead, resorts to subtle acts of rebellion in the skills and

tastes he has developed. Unlike Dombey, he is a player of games, pic-
quet, backgammon, chess, and billiards. The house in which he lives, a
mere cottage, represents a rejection of the purely material values on display in the Dombey house. It suggests the life led by the second or the
third generation of a successful commercial family whose wealth permits
the cultivation of suspicious, avant-garde tastes: "Within, it is a house of
refinement and luxury. . . . the prints and pictures do not commemorate
great thoughts or deeds, or render nature in the poetry of landscape,
hall, or hut, but are of one voluptuous cast—mere shows of form and
colour—and no more" (chapter 33). The aesthetic sense lacking in the
Dombey quest for money has been transformed by Carker into an aes-
theticism tending to decadence, even to the perverse. The paintings on
the walls anticipate French Impressionism, Whistler, and Beardsley. Carker's cottage, like Dombey's house, is a trope for the man: "There issues
forth some subtle portion of himself, which gives a vague expression of
himself to everything about him!" (chapter 33).

   One of the paintings in the cottage has attained a place of honor before the table at which Carker breakfasts:

   "A most extraordinary accidental likeness, certainly," says he.
   Perhaps it is a Juno; perhaps a Potiphar's Wife; perhaps some scornful
Nymph—according as the Picture Dealers found the market, when they chris-
tened it. It is the figure of a woman, supremely handsome, who, turning away,
but with her face addressed to the spectator, flashes her proud glance upon him.
   It is like Edith. (Chapter 33)

There is a chilling quality to the passage, an uncanny anticipation of
John Jasper's obsession with the uncompleted portrait of Rosa Bud in
The Mystery of Edwin Drood. Carker, alone, salutes the woman whose
face is turned to him, the face an Edith presents to the social world she
scorns. But it is not truly Edith's face that Carker sees in the painting,
the allusion to Potiphar's wife implies that. Carker is lost in a world of
images detached from the real persons for whom they stand. If the
woman in the painting represents Potiphar's wife, the woman who tried
to seduce Joseph into violating his master's trust, then Carker becomes
Joseph and Dombey, Potiphar. Carker is immersed in an Oedipal fantasy
in which Dombey, Edith, and he are the principals. His fictive self is organized through his participation in a family of the imagination. In this
situation Dickens's romanticism anticipates Freud's. Robert Langbaum,

quoting Erik Erikson, places Freud, much as I would like to place Dickens, in the romantic tradition: "Despite the mechanistic model, Freud is a romantic who sees man as 'psychologically alone,' 'forever projecting his infantile family constellation on the "outer world"."'[18] Certainly Carker is not an anomaly in Dickens's novels. He represents many of Dickens's male characters who sustain their precarious selves by recreating the family constellation and imposing it upon the men and women in their adult lives. This recurring situation is yet another version of the romantic obsession with isolation and a self-absorption tending always to narcissism. The Family Romance acts as a complex trope. It permits the romantic artist to explore not only sexual realities, but the threat, the lure, of an estrangement from others beyond the family of the imagination: desexualized, the unresolved Family Romance, like other incest tropes, poses the dangers of projection and the issue of solipsism.

In his imagination Carker longs to be Joseph; he wants Edith to be the aggressor, the one to seek out an adulterous liaison. In such a relationship he can relish the retaliation against Dombey that, on one level of his consciousness, he so carefully plans. When he decides to use Carker as his agent to humble Edith, Dombey unwittingly feeds the fantasy sustaining his manager. Neither man is in touch with the real Edith. Each pursues the image of her dwelling in his fancy. Each sees a face, an image, whose inner reality must elude him. Here is a description of Dombey's first visit to Carker's cottage, another opportunity for him to be condescending to his second-in-command: "Cursorily as his cold eye wandered over [the pictures on the walls], Carker's keen glance accompanied his, and kept pace with his. . . . As it rested on one picture in particular, Carker hardly seemed to breathe, his sidelong scrutiny was so catlike and vigilant, but the eye of his great chief passed from that, as from the others, and appeared no more impressed by it than by the rest" (chapter 42). Carker wants Dombey to mark what seems to be Edith's resemblance to the portrait on the wall. Part of him desires to be found out, just as part of him is eager to shock and to offend. However, Dombey's uncomprehending glance also confirms Carker in his contempt for his chief. He can exploit Dombey's obtuseness, and does, by inviting Mr. Dombey to a chair with its back towards the picture, while he takes the seat opposite to it.

While Dombey reveals his plan to use Carker, a social inferior, to vanquish Edith, Carker will look first at Dombey, then at the painting "that resemble[s] Edith—as if it were a living thing." It is a bizarre and twisted gesture, a testament not to Carker's power, but to his impotence. Throughout the conversation, as Dombey talks on, Carker is in private dialogue with the picture, "his eager eye [scanning] Mr. Dombey's downcast face," then "[shooting] a strange triumphant look at the picture, as appealing to it to bear witness how he led him on again" (chapter 42). The portrait is more alive for Carker than the real Edith. It is far safer to gesture to this image than to the living woman. Even in her presence, Carker will be seeing his version of Edith as a seductive maternal figure eager to share in his act of revenge. Edith exists for Dombey only as his property, as an extension of his conception of himself as Dombey and Son. She exists only to adorn the name of the firm and to provide the male heir required to make his identity complete and enduring. Edith exists for Carker primarily as an instrument of his vengeance. The painting hovers over the two men, as elusive as the living Edith. It is not altogether clear whose attachment to the image is more suspect, Dombey's or Carker's. But it is only Carker who looks "with the evil slyness of some monkish carving, half human and half brute; or like a leering face on an old water-spout" (chapter 42). Dombey is an effigy to a dead past. Carker, a startling adumbration of John Jasper, becomes a fiendish gargoyle whose distorted features attest to the price he pays as "the organ of [Dombey's] displeasure." Carker's pun, conscious or unconscious, is not to be ignored. Dombey intones to Carker, "My will is law, and . . . I cannot allow of one exception to the whole rule of my life" (chapter 42). Dombey's pride, as well as his idea of himself, is at stake in his struggle with Edith. But Carker senses that the battle of wills is deeply sexual, too, a curious substitute for the consummation Dombey seeks and Edith shuns. As Dombey's "go-between," Carker is an agent of Dombey's phallic will, an instrument—an organ—of the figurative father of Carker's imagination.[19]

In his effort to humble both Edith and Carker, Dombey, of course, miscalculates. During the scene in which Edith demands a separation, a demand Dombey refuses to honor, Carker is a spectator to this heated and intimate exchange between man and wife. Florence, the daughter, has been allowed to leave the room before the climactic exchange occurs. But Carker is permitted to remain, to intensify Edith's feeling of humiliation and to negate more fully Carker's sense of himself as a person. He is to remain Dombey's cipher, the appendage of the father's will; it is a fate that John Harmon, in obligation to his own integrity, must avoid. Carker acquiesces to Dombey, convinced that he has defeated Dombey by exposing his motives to Edith:

"You were employed—"
"Being an inferior person, for the humiliation of Mrs. Dombey. I forgot. Oh, yes, it was expressly understood!" said Carker. "I beg your pardon!" (Chapter 47)

Throughout the exchange Carker keeps his eyes upon Edith's haughty face, just as he has gazed at the portrait—so like Edith?—upon Dombey's visit to his cottage. He remains the prisoner of his imagination, exploiting, even seeking out, the Oedipal situation in which mother and son turn finally against the father's tyrannical will.

It is not, then, as a lover that Carker arranges the rendezvous with Edith in Dijon. The meeting itself is a reenactment of the earlier scene in Edith's chamber when she turned her face to the glass, ignoring Dombey's retreat as if he were some "dead vermin." The room in which the two meet is an inner-drawing room at the center of a labyrinthine French apartment: "The glitter of bright tapers, and their reflection in looking-glasses, scraps of gilding, and gay colours, were confined, on this night, to one room—that smaller room within the rest, just now enumerated. Seen from the hall . . . it looked as shining and precious as a gem. In the heart of its radiance sat a beautiful woman—Edith" (chapter 54). Edith sits within another hall of mirrors, acting out a part that serves only to consolidate her alienation from herself. To achieve her victory over Dombey, she is willing to live in the eyes of the world as an acknowledged adulteress. She will become the image the world chooses to see, while clinging to the pretense of an inviolate inward self through her knowledge that the relationship with Carker has not been consummated. But a consummation of sorts does occur. Edith is forever wedded to her image, to the face with which she confronts the world. She may take refuge in the fact that if Carker boasts of his conquest, he serves as her instrument in her plan to avenge herself upon the "master" and his "man," upon Dombey and Son. But the psychic toll is great. Edith is "as firm as a rock." She may become yet another gargoylelike figure, another victim of the gorgon's stare, of the Dombey legacy. She speaks more truly than perhaps she understands when she says, "I stand alone in the world, remembering well what a hollow world it has been to me, and what a hollow part of it I have been myself" (chapter 54). The facade may be of stone, but the process of spontaneous combustion goes on apace within Edith. Her self may well become a void. She has been captured by the image in the glass, truly molded by her mother and society into a graven image that she will self-destructively serve.

The inner-drawing room, with its gilded and painted walls and ceilings and its waxed and polished floors, reveals Edith's isolation, her nearly solipsistic confinement within her own consciousness. This self-absorption is no less true of Carker. When he and Edith are finally alone, Carker compliments her upon her beauty with a telling phrase: "Even the picture I have carried in my mind during this cruel probation, and which I have contemplated night and day, is exceeded by the reality" (chapter 54). But the inner room with its reflecting surfaces suggests that the picture Carker carries in his mind is inseparable from the reality that he assumes he confronts. He is still contemplating the portrait in his cottage, still lost in his hall of mirrors, as he gazes upon the woman of his imaginings.

In pursuing Edith, Carker has pursued unwittingly the very person he dare not touch, confirming the extent to which he remains a part of Dombey and Son and the flawed patriarchal order for which it stands. In his infantile orality, he seems all teeth, but remains the toothless Son who cannot become a man, a husband, and a father. He has sought out Edith to confirm his own nonexistence. In meeting Edith—"face to face for the last time"—Carker encounters his own Medusa, who has "no more fear of him, than of a worm." His helplessness in her presence reveals his weakness, not simply her strength. The ultimate moment occurs when Edith holds "her hand up like an enchantress, at whose invocation the sound has come." The spell is cast and Carker is unmanned, rendered incapable of confronting face to face "the man whose confidence he [has] outraged." Little Paul has died rather than grow up to become another Dombey and Son. Carker, the figurative son, has turned to Oedipal fantasies that cut him off from time and change. His pursuit of Edith has, from the start, been a pursuit of death, a gradual dissolution of the blurred image in the hotel mirror in Leamington. Edith conjures up the presence of the avenging head of the House, slips through a

doorway she locks behind her, and leaves Carker to creep down the staircase, extinguishing his lamp "on seeing the street . . . where the stars
[are] shining." His retreat acknowledges the vulnerability of the self he
has constructed upon the complex triadic relationship; yet, without the
presence of Dombey and Edith, within his imagination if not in reality,
Carker has no self at all.

In Carker's flight from Dijon and from Dombey, a number of motifs
converge that anticipate the novels to follow. The self, a fragile construct,
undergoes the fragmentation that is the consequence of paralysis. The
process of disintegration occurs within the context of time denied and
within the paradigm of the family constellation to which Dickens will
return in novel after novel. Goethean stasis and Dickensian paralysis
become Freudian fixation. Carker's fixated self, unable to acknowledge
change in others or to participate in the change that constitutes the pilgrimage of being, undergoes a process culminating in a willed death:
"But the springing of his mine upon himself, seemed to have rent and
shivered all his hardihood and self-reliance" (chapter 55). His journey to
England, to a "remote country-place . . . deep [in] the inland green," is a
figurative and a regressive one, echoing the death of Smike in *Nicholas
Nickleby*. In its nightmarish quality it is a fevered recapitulation of Carker's life, in which there is the semblance of change and the reality of
stasis. The description of the journey is punctuated by a Dickensian refrain: "A vision of change upon change, and still the same monotony of
bells and wheels, and horses' feet, and no rest" (chapter 55). The monotony of the journey points to its meaninglessness: it is a journey neither
in space, nor in time. Carker has once said to Edith, "Dombey and Son
know neither time, nor place, nor season, but bear them all down"
(chapter 37). As the figurative Son and Heir of Dombey and Son, Carker
himself knows neither time, nor place, nor season. He is caught in the
role of the helpless son before the masterful father, unable to invent himself anew, to separate himself from the father, and to participate in the
continuum of self-evolution to which the romantic ontology informing
the novel commits him.

What has been implicit from the start in the relationship involving
Dombey, Carker, and Edith becomes almost explicit as Carker's temporal disorientation produces a "fevered vision of things past and present all confounded together; of his life and journey blended into one."

Carker has never escaped the past. He has continually projected Erikson's "infantile family constellation" upon the world: "Then, the old days before the second marriage rose up in his remembrance. He thought how jealous he had been of the boy, how jealous he had been of the girl, how artfully he had kept intruders at a distance, and drawn a circle round his dupe that none but himself should cross" (chapter 55). These are the jealousies of a child toward the rivals who appear to challenge an imagined, if precarious, primacy. The failure of his schemes against Dombey is part of some grotesquely Oedipal script: "To have his confidence in his own knavery so shattered at a blow—to be within his own knowledge such a miserable tool—was like being paralysed. With an impotent ferocity he raged at Edith, and hated Mr. Dombey and hated himself" (chapter 55). At one point in his journey, Carker's hired carriage stops, appropriately, near "an immense, old, shadeless, glaring, stone chateau, with half its windows blinded, and green damp crawling lazily over it, from the balustraded terrace to the taper tips of the extinguishers upon the turrets" (chapter 55). The glaring stone château suggests Carker's own psychic condition, his impotence and his paralysis. It is a metonymy for his gargoylelike state. It also foreshadows the St. Evrémonde château in *A Tale of Two Cities,* with its "heavy stone balustrades," stone urns and flowers, and "stone faces of men, and stone heads of lions"—a château that appeared "as if the Gorgon's head had surveyed it, when it was finished, two centuries ago" (book 2, chapter 9).

The journey that is not a journey continues. And the pursuit Carker dreads, and longs for, seems not to occur. In his fancy he hears the sound of wheels. But the driver declares, "There is nothing coming" (chapter 55). To which Carker can only reply, "Nothing?" If he is not pursued by Dombey, if vengeance is not exacted, his existence has been denied in yet another way. Edith has treated him as a worm. The apparent failure of Dombey to appear on his track further confirms in Carker the sense of his own nothingness. Like Bradley Headstone in *Our Mutual Friend,* Carker demands retribution from the man he has sought to bring down. Without such retribution, his existence is not confirmed by an Other: he will cease to be. He takes refuge in the English country inn: "His object was, to rest, and recover the command of himself, and the balance of his mind. . . . He was stupefied, and he was wearied to death" (chapter 55). Carker's condition is similar to that of Eugene

Wrayburn in *Our Mutual Friend*, which is described by Dickens in his
Memorandum Book:

As to the question whether I, Eugene, lying ill and sick even unto death, may be
consoled by the representation that, coming through this illness, I shall begin a
new life, and have energy and purpose and all I have yet wanted:
  "I *hope* I should, but I *know* I shouldn't. Let me die, my dear."

The rhythms of this entry are close to the rhythms of the passage in
Dombey and Son, touching as it does upon the condition of yet another
son who may succumb to the power, real or imagined, of the father.[20]
     Carker's condition, unlike Wrayburn's, proves to be hopeless. He has
lost track of the hours and days of the week. "How goes the time?" he
asks. "My watch is unwound" (chapter 55). Time has stopped for him.
And, like the automaton he has long since become, he is incapable of
human life. The spring that has moved him is uncoiled and broken. He
wants to die and the railway engine lures him to his final fate: "For now,
indeed, it was no fancy. The ground shook, the house rattled, the fierce
impetuous rush was in the air! . . . A curse upon the fiery Devil, thundering along so smoothly. . . . He felt as if he had been plucked out of
its path, and saved from being torn asunder" (chapter 55). The fiery devil
is surely, in Carker's fantasy, a vision of Dombey finally in remorseless
pursuit of him, a Dombey driven by forces he cannot understand. But
the train also represents something within Carker, the impulse to death
and to mutilation now controlling his life. Terrified as he is, Carker is
irresistibly attracted to the train. He seeks it out as a mechanical instrument of retribution, an apt extension of a dehumanized Dombey and a
manifestation of his own inner condition. His need to expose himself to
the irresistible engine and to confront its "two red eyes" face to face—as
he has not confronted Dombey—suggests how paralysis and a sense of
impotence lead to a compulsion to repeat the past and to die from the
inability to be free of it. The power of the train is the power of the imagined father and of that unrelenting past for which he stands. Carker's self
collapses under the pressure exerted by the two. At the moment he sees
Dombey on the station platform "and their eyes [meet]," Carker steps
back into the path of an oncoming train: he "looked round—saw the
red eyes, bleared and dim, in the daylight, close upon him—was beaten
down, caught up, and whirled away upon a jagged mill, that spun him

round and round, and struck him limb from limb, and licked his stream of life up with its fiery heat, and cast his mutilated fragments in the air" (chapter 55).

For those who deny their own impetus to change, who reject the imperative to self-creation, there remains the Kierkegaardian fate, either of paralysis, of becoming like Dombey, a mere memorial to the past; or of fragmentation, the rendering of a self unable to accept that "It's a world of change" in which metamorphosis is the necessary, if threatening, condition of life. Dombey's habitual stiffness transforms him into a specimen of a frozen gentleman, into—in Susan Nipper's words—a graven image. Carker's almost feminine softness and voluptuousness produce a blurred image in the glass of his imagination. Within the mirror of his own consciousness, he never establishes the fragile but necessary outline of a living self. Because of his failure to come to terms with Dombey, and with those involved in Dombey's life, and with his estrangement from the medium of time (for the pilgrimage of being is an intersubjective one), Carker's fragile, paralyzed self disintegrates, as the St. Evrémonde château will later collapse in *A Tale of Two Cities*.

In *Dombey and Son,* Dickens forges a coherent vision of the self, a vision he will employ throughout the later novels to follow his heroes and his heroines on their respective pilgrimages of being. A romantic ontology of the self underlies this pilgrimage, a conception of the living self evolving its unity in and through time, a unity never fully achieved and always subject to revisions and regressions. Mr. Morfin's figurative use of the word *image* in all its permutations pervades the later novels. And familiar situations are endlessly repeated. It is a surprise, at once reassuring and unnerving, to recognize that the confrontation between Carker and Edith Dombey in the inner room of the apartment in Dijon has its echo in the last, uncompleted novel, *The Mystery of Edwin Drood*. When John Jasper offers his twisted love to Rosa Bud in the garden of the Nuns' House, he, too, is in a hall of mirrors created by the windows overlooking the garden. He, too, becomes a stone man, an effigy, lost in his own exotic fantasies. He converses not with the real Rosa Bud, but with his image of her, the image suggested by the unfinished sketch of Rosa hanging above the chimneypiece in Jasper's rooms. Jasper's language is passionate, if melodramatic: "In the distasteful work of the day, in the wakeful misery of the night, girded by sordid realities, or wandering through Paradises and Hells of visions into which I rushed, carrying

your image in my arms, I loved you madly."[21] Here Dickens the artist is
not merely repeating himself in the stone dead language of a character
like Major Bagstock. He is not fixed upon a single repressed theme dominating his imaginative life. But he is true to his own enduring preoccupations that give a unity to his works, to his exploration of the romantic self that he presents, again and again, in the context of the family
constellation. Dickens is not merely anticipating Freud, with his achievement to be affirmed only in retrospect by the hypotheses of psychoanalysis. Rather, Freud and Dickens participate in that tradition shared
with Rousseau and Goethe and those who follow them. The romantic
situation involves a self, in isolation, seeking to experience change, yet
always threatened by impasse: by the temptation never to escape the
past, but only to repeat it and to reproduce the family constellation in
which the self is forever the child and those it encounters forever exist as
graven images of the mother and the father, and not as the living, changing individuals each romantic self is impelled to be.

Chapter 2

"Ah!" said my aunt, rubbing her nose as if she
were a little vexed. "That's his allegorical way of
expressing it. He connects his illness with great
disturbance and agitation, naturally, and that's the
figure, or the simile, or whatever it's called, which
he chooses to use. And why shouldn't he, if he
thinks proper!"
—Aunt Betsey Trotwood, *David Copperfield*

I saw now that this was a new sort of method of
answering, and by pressing repeatedly I brought
out what seemed to be a meaningless series of
words: "Concierge"—"night-gown"—"bed"—
"town"—"farm-cart." "What does all this mean?"
I asked. She reflected for a moment and the
following thought occurred to her: "It must be
the story that has just come into my head."
—Sigmund Freud, *Studies on Hysteria*

The Autobiographical Imperative

No one should be disarmed by the quiet manner in which David Copperfield begins his personal history: "Whether I shall turn out to be the hero of my own life, or whether that station will be held by anybody else, these pages must show."[1] Behind the modest stance there plays a richly ironic awareness of the task at hand, of the true nature of the autobiographical enterprise for those following the example of the inimitable Rousseau. David, alone privy to his own consciousness and relying upon the power of the written word, seems destined willy-nilly to be the compelling center of his own narrative. But we have already encountered Dickens's Carlylean skepticism about the individual's capacity for self-knowledge. David, standing on the figurative shore of the self and gazing into its depths, may only glimpse the treasure and other things submerged there. He may not come to see the "natural lineaments" of the spirit mirrored within his own Work, as Carlyle's Teufelsdröckh urges. Others who appear in his pages may tug more compellingly at our imaginations, and at David's. He may fall under the spell of an Other, becoming alienated from that hypothetical self he seeks and failing to emerge as the authentic hero of his own life. In *The Confessions* Rousseau falls under the spell of the charming charlatan, Venture de Villeneuve; he takes it "into [his] head to play the little Venture at Lausanne, to teach music, of which [he is] ignorant, and to say that [he comes] from Paris, where [he has] never been."[2] Rousseau "venturizes" himself, changing his name to Vaussore de Villeneuve. He imitates the picaresque rogue Venture, and in the process he loses his head, his identity, his self. James Carker, in *Dombey and Son*, risks the same loss of self, becoming the victim of his own mocking imitation of Mr. Dombey. David Copperfield, in his attempt to be Ortega's "novelist of himself," will flirt with plagiarism as he emulates the most glamorous Other in his life, James Steerforth.

Within the tradition of romantic autobiography, the seductive appeal of such plagiarism remains a constant temptation. The self as imaginative construct, to be realized through the completion of the autobiographical project, always remains susceptible to the lure of the Other. Because knowledge of the self is elusive and the faculty of the memory is potentially unreliable, the Other beckons to offer refuge from confusion. The self is necessarily a fiction founded upon one's perception of another or informed by the structures and the personages of literature. Rousseau and David respond to the fictional works they read, emulating the characters they encounter in the pages of the religious progress or the picaresque novel. The structure of such works helps to order the account of one's life; each provides a fictional model for the "immaterial embellishment [used] . . . to fill a void due to a defect of memory" (p. 17). True to the spirit of *The Confessions,* David will allude to the fictive status of the self, to the self he is creating, within these pages. We have learned, through John Forster's *The Life of Charles Dickens* that Dickens incorporated, almost verbatim, fragments of the abandoned autobiography into

David's history.[3] The voice of David Copperfield, however, is not the voice of Charles Dickens musing upon his life, but that of a fully imagined character, a poet of the past, invested with Dickens's understanding of the nature of the autobiographical venture.

Through David, Dickens offers an allusion to *The Old Curiosity Shop*, and to Dick Swiveller, as a cryptic assertion of the tentative status of the self in autobiographies written by historical, or fictional, personages. With her announcement that she is ruined, Aunt Betsey settles into David's rooms, routs the landlady, Mrs. Crupp, and consolidates her victory by generally improving David's domestic arrangements: "She converted the pantry into a dressing-room for me; and purchased and embellished a bedstead for my occupation, which looked as like a bookcase in the day-time, as a bedstead could" (chapter 37). This passage celebrates a rather private victory of Dickens's own—unless, of course, David is hypothetically the author of *The Old Curiosity Shop*. For Dickens has transported this protean bedstead into David's pantry out of the very rooms of Mr. Richard Swiveller (truly, the pivotal Swiveller as Garrett Stewart calls him).[4] In speaking of his single room as his "lodgings" or "chambers," Swiveller is "assisted by a deceptive piece of furniture, in reality a bedstead, but in semblance a bookcase. . . . There is no doubt that, by day, Mr. Swiveller firmly believed this secret convenience to be a bookcase and nothing more. . . . No word of its real use, no hint of its nightly service, no allusion to its peculiar properties, had ever passed between him and his most intimate friends."[5] This is one of those pleasant fictions by which Swiveller lives. He escapes, or denies, the falseness of his illusory gentility through the power of his imagination and the efficacy of the potent word. Words are magical for Dickens, as they are for Freud. For Swiveller's fiction extends beyond the one room and the incriminating bedstead with its bolster and blankets. It encompasses Swiveller himself: he creates a self through the fiction. Swiveller's belief in that self, like his firm belief in the bookcase, is necessary to his survival.

But the fiction cannot be sustained by Swiveller alone without the help of others. No word of the bedstead's real use ever passes between Swiveller and his friends: "To be the friend of Swiveller you must reject all circumstantial evidence, all reason, observation, and experience, and repose a blind belief in the bookcase. It was his pet weakness, and he cherished it" (chapter 7). This is not unlike the social construction of reality of which James Carker speaks as he talks to Edith of Dombey: "We who are about him, have, in our various positions, done our part, I dare say, to confirm him in his way of thinking; but if we had not done so, others would—or they would not have been about him; and it has always been, from the beginning, the very staple of his life." It anticipates that conspiracy to make her happy of which Esther Summerson will speak in *Bleak House*. Richard Swiveller must sustain a conception of himself as a gentleman. His friends cooperate with him, out of their own need. They ignore the bedstead so that they may participate in a collective fiction. They confirm Swiveller's story; he, in turn, confirms theirs. They create an inhabitable, if fragile, world out of their comic discretion. Yet, as Swiveller begins to live out the profounder implications of his fiction, it becomes his truth. In conferring the title of Marchioness on the child whose name has been "Nothing," Swiveller affirms his true gentility and saves the Marchioness, and himself, from anonymity and degradation.

David's own embellished bedstead alludes to Swiveller's imaginative virtuosity in similar circumstances. David seems only amused by the quaintness of *his* bedstead. But its appearance in his pages stamps his autobiography as a fiction. Always, David's written memory must be seen by Dickens, and by David, as a story, the story David tells himself and by which he sustains himself. David, too, is creating a reality, an inhabitable world in which he becomes a character projected by his own imagination.[6]

This is David's enterprise, and it generates the ambiguity of his opening words. For its success or failure becomes central to his personal history as a whole. David embarks upon the attempt to create a viable reality, an inhabitable fiction. If the fiction departs radically from the facts or circumstances of the self's history, for some facts can be determined, it will founder as surely as Mr. Peggotty's boathouse fails to weather the tempest that takes the lives of Ham and Steerforth. Once again the romantic self confronts either fragmentation, before the gale force of events, or perhaps more significantly, paralysis before the gorgon's head of the past. For David the greater danger may prove to be paralysis, marked by an inability to complete even an account of a plagiarized self. In his personal history David introduces us to a number of characters who, significantly, never complete the written projects they begin. Micawber, an inveterate letter writer, seems never to accomplish anything

until he unmasks Uriah Heep and sets sail for Australia and the jour-
nalistic career that turns up for him there. Doctor Strong continues laboring unendingly at his interminable Dictionary, as David at one point
calls it; it is a labor that leads to no satisfactory birth. And Mr. Richard
Babley, or Mr. Dick, is last seen promising to "finish the Memorial when
I have nothing else to do."

Each of these characters is, in different ways, an autobiographer manqué. Mr. Dick's name connects him to Swiveller—Swiveller often toasts
himself as Mr. Richard. He is a radical version of a man defeated by a
reality so painful he can allude to it only figuratively. Mr. Dick's semi-
comic struggles to write his own history illustrate the difficulties inherent in the autobiographical project. In his effort to complete the Memorial, Mr. Dick inevitably finds himself referring to the beheaded King
Charles the First. The allusion stops him in his tracks. Traumatized by
his sister's unhappy marriage, Mr. Dick is compelled to write of it, but
always indirectly, never explicitly:

"Ah!" said my aunt. . . . "That's his *allegorical* way of expressing it. He *connects
his illness* with great disturbance and agitation, naturally, and that's the *figure*, or
the *simile*, or whatever it's called, which he chooses to use. And why shouldn't
he, if he thinks proper!" (Chapter 14, emphasis mine)

Mr. Dick's way of speaking is not perceived, by Dickens, by David, or
even by Aunt Betsey, as meaningless. It is a symptomatic form of expression, "the deformed language of symptoms," as Steven Marcus calls it.[7]
As long as he continues to speak or to write in such a language, Mr.
Dick will remain cut off from himself, incapable of telling a coherent
story of his life. The reference to the martyred King Charles becomes his
own "(highly condensed) autobiography," in the words of Thomas
Szasz.[8] In the language of symptoms, the allusion to King Charles is at
once a synecdoche and a metonymy. It stands, as Aunt Betsey shrewdly
notes, for personal and familial strife as well as for that national domestic
chaos culminating in the Civil War, with the ambiguities of the word
civil providing the basis for the trope. The execution of King Charles
suggests Mr. Dick's own figurative beheading, which has led to a state of
intellectual and sexual arrest. Mr. Dick is one of those "blockheads or
crazy people" of whom Freud wrote in his 1883 letter to Martha Bernays;
he becomes Dickens's version of the natural or the romantic idiot.

Mr. Dick has become "'fixated' to a particular portion of [his] past,

. . . alienated from the present and the future" (*SE*, 16:273). Freud's words from the *Introductory Lectures* reveal his awareness that the existentially healthy person is in contact with the continuing story of his life—with his past, present, and future. Mr. Dick remains alienated from his own story because he can neither construct it nor project its hypothetical ending. And only he can construct it; no one else can forge a story and offer it to him as a viable narrative with which he can live. Until the Memorial is properly finished, Mr. Dick remains lost in a world of dreams and symptoms. Aunt Betsey sagely objects to the reference to King Charles's head: "There shan't be a word about it in his Memorial." Poetic expression may be analogous to Mr. Dick's way of speaking; it shares structural similarities with it. But, unlike the poet, Mr. Dick is captive to his own mode of expression. The allusion, however full of meaning, remains too idiosyncratic, too obscure, not only for others but for Mr. Dick himself, who lives exiled from the community of discursive language.[9] He fails to gain understanding and freedom from the figure of speech he employs. His Memorial will never progress beyond the allusion that dominates, and impedes, his life. Aunt Betsey realizes, in her characteristically eccentric way, that nothing less than a full account, chronologically and causally ordered, can effect Mr. Dick's cure. She is a comic proto-Freudian, recognizing with Freud that an "incomplete story . . . produces no therapeutic effect" (*SE*, 2:79). Until he can provide a complete story accounting for his suffering, Mr. Dick will remain the simpleminded Richard Babley, forever writing his Memorial, forever flying kites, and communicating his apparently unintelligible story to the sky.[10]

Mr. Dick's history stands both as a warning and as a key to the structure of David's narrative. For, in the completion of his own story, David may escape that state of impasse in which a Mr. Dick exists. Aunt Betsey's account of Mr. Dick's life suggests potentially ominous parallels to David's. Mr. Dick, like David, is "a sort of distant connexion" of Aunt Betsey's. He enters her life shortly after David's hypothetical sister, Betsey Trotwood, has unobligingly refused to be born: in short, after David's own birth. Each is essentially fatherless. David has been raised by an unyielding stepfather, Mr. Dick by a thoughtless brother. And Mr. Dick, too, has been exposed to a domestic tragedy with Oedipal overtones. He has been undone by his sister's unhappy marriage, a variation on Clara Copperfield's marriage to Mr. Murdstone. In the civil wars experienced by Mr. Dick and by David, it is the father, not the son, who triumphs. The historical martyrdom of King Charles the First at the hands of rebellious sons is quite simply the reversal of the experiences of Mr. Dick and of David. Mr. Dick's history finally mirrors David's: it suggests, "allegorically," to use Aunt Betsey's word, the fact of David's own potentially fixated condition.[11]

For David has never successfully confronted his mother's death and his ensuing exile to the blacking warehouse. On one occasion David revisits his mother's grave and notes that his former home, Blunderstone Rookery, is occupied "by a poor lunatic gentleman, and the people who [take] care of him. He [is] always sitting at my little window, looking out into the churchyard" (chapter 22). The lunatic gentleman acts as a middle term connecting David and Mr. Dick. Part of David has never left that room, has remained within it, gazing longingly in dread and yearning at the graves in the churchyard. The bewildered Mr. Dick asks, "How could the people about [King Charles the First] have made that mistake of putting some of the trouble out of *his* head, after it was taken off, into *mine*?" (chapter 14). And David in the churchyard wonders whether the rambling thoughts of the lunatic "ever went upon any of the fancies that used to occupy mine" (chapter 22). Poor Mr. Dick identifies himself with the beheaded King Charles. David, more whimsically, identifies with the madman in his old room: there are within David the seeds of similar disruption.

But within the autobiographical enterprise there is the opportunity to skirt madness and the entrapping language of symptomatic speech. David seizes the opportunity and transforms the language of symptoms into a coherent story adequately expressing the truth of his life. Mr. Dick never moves beyond his elliptic reference to the martyred king and to his own impeding past. The story of his life begins and ends there. He has provided no narrative account of himself that may accommodate the realities of time and change: he is time's victim. David, too, has memories that threaten to overwhelm him. Sometimes he affirms them openly. He deals candidly with the humiliating experience in Murdstone and Grinby's warehouse; he acknowledges, however uneasily, his relationship to the embarrassingly déclassé Micawbers. But he alludes far more obliquely, even cryptically, to other events, for they involve the most serious threat to the completion of his narrative, to the authorship of his self.

Of all the figures in his personal history, only Steerforth pulls more potently at the imagination, ours and David's, than David himself. It is Steerforth who threatens to usurp our interest and David's inviolable self. Steerforth's shallow class attitudes are transparent, as many critics have observed. But these attitudes cannot obscure the charismatic qualities to which David understandably responds. As a tempting alter ego with whom David identifies, Steerforth repeatedly denies David possession of his own story, and of himself. It is Steerforth who poses the most serious challenge to the completion of David's personal history. David must incorporate his complicated relationship with Steerforth into the narrative he is fashioning. If he fails, he will not emerge as the hero of his own story. David's history may well end, as Esther Summerson's progress ends, with a dash and not with a true period. Or it may become that wall of words of which Freud speaks in *Studies on Hysteria,* the "wall which shuts out every prospect and prevents us from having any idea whether there is anything behind it, and if so, what" (*SE,* 2:293).

The origins of David's relationship to Steerforth lie, predictably, in childhood. David, the posthumous son, encounters an adult world teeming with threats to his emerging self. He is compelled to face the disturbing fact of the rage with which he sometimes responds to it. This is a tale Dickens never tires of telling, and retelling, in all of the major novels. To repel the Murdstones' campaign to subdue, if not to destroy him, David turns to imaginative escape and, when he bites Murdstone's hand, to an act of pure aggression. Throughout these experiences he is succored by Peggotty's love and by the one real legacy of the dead father: the small collection of picaresque classics, fairy tales, and adventure stories that provide a mode of imaginative survival. Under the spell of a "few volumes of Voyages and Travels," David becomes "the perfect realisation of Captain Somebody, of the Royal British Navy . . . . The Captain never lost dignity, from having his ears boxed with the Latin Grammar. I did; but the Captain was a Captain and a hero" (chapter 4). If fictions sustain Dick Swiveller, they also sustain David. He is truly reading as if for life. The stakes are high. His imaginative identification with Roderick Random and a properly Victorian Tom Jones informs his fragile idea of himself. In his imagination, if not in fact, he need not always be the victim, a nobody; he may be the morally unambiguous and uncompromised hero, "in despite of all the grammars of all the languages in the world, dead or alive."

This process of identification replaces the usual identification with the father: it is a prelude to David's idealization of Steerforth, hardly a child's Tom Jones, a harmless creature. In the midst of Salem House, a world of unrestrained adult exploitation, Steerforth is the only boy upon whom Mr. Creakle "never venture[s] to lay a hand." He poses the only alternative to the innocent passivity of Tommy Traddles, who is reduced to drawing skeletons, "symbols of mortality," upon his slate. Traddles, like Mr. Dick, speaks in figures expressing a longing for escape, and the threat of psychic arrest and symbolic death. As Traddles's antithesis, Steerforth exploits his privileged status through theatrical gestures, such as dipping "a match into his phosphorous-box on purpose to shed a glare over his reply" as he explains what he would do if Creakle dared to touch *him*. The younger boys sit in the dark, breathless, before Steerforth's self-dramatizing bravado.

In his posturing, Steerforth presents his version of himself, that fiction he seeks to promulgate for himself and others. I am not speaking of calculated hypocrisy alone, but of Steerforth's suspect conception of himself. The danger for David lies in a naive acceptance of Steerforth's fiction, and in his desire to model himself upon it. David succumbs to a dizzyingly complicated process of self-violation. He accepts Steerforth's theatrical presentation of himself and ignores the evidence belying it: Steerforth's skillful manipulation of younger boys and his inexcusable exposure of Mr. Mell, leading to the man's dismissal from Salem House. Only Tommy Traddles's voice is raised against Steerforth. David silences his own legitimate doubts. He wants to incorporate within himself that suspect version of gentility and manliness for which Steerforth stands. All of this is captured as David becomes the Sultana Scheherazade, a member of Steerforth's private seraglio, telling stories night after night to a demanding master. The episode raises the specter of public school homosexuality, but even more interestingly, it reveals the way in which David has become a mere object for Steerforth. David, as the novelist of himself, falls into the most dangerous kind of plagiarism, constructing himself upon a doubly false vision of an elusive alter ego. His fragile self is threatened with ultimate usurpation by another.[12]

This context makes all the more haunting the exchange between David and Steerforth on the night of the memorable feast of currant wine, cakes, and fruit:

"Good night, young Copperfield," said Steerforth, "I'll take care of you."

"You're very kind," I gratefully returned. "I am very much obliged to you."

"You haven't got a sister, have you?" said Steerforth, yawning.

"No," I answered.

"That's a pity," said Steerforth. "If you had had one, I should think she would have been a pretty, timid, little, bright-eyed sort of girl. I should have liked to know her. Good night, young Copperfield." (Chapter 6)

The casual yawn veils the pointedness of the query. Steerforth, on the way to becoming an accomplished rake, is accustomed to preying on the sisters of those he seems to protect. His desire to know David's sister, if he has one, foreshadows the seduction of little Emily. And it raises the question of David's relationship to himself, to the story he tells himself, and whether that story can sustain him in the midst of those competing, and compelling, fictions by which others live. In the story of Steerforth and little Emily, David's virgin person, no less than Emily's, is once again in peril, as it has been in the courtship and marriage of Mr. Murdstone and Clara Copperfield. Steerforth possesses Murdstone's force and energy, obscured by his capacity to enchant and by David's eager imagination. David is once more Brooks of Sheffield, caught up in a complicated moral and sexual drama. The past may, sooner or later, uncannily repeat itself. Steerforth's pursuit and violation of Emily's person may correspond to yet another violation of David's fragile integrity.

For Emily is, figuratively, the sister about whom Steerforth so casually inquires. Even the young David vaguely perceives the nature of his relationship to her. When Steerforth meets Ham and Mr. Peggotty at Salem House, inevitably charming them, David is "almost tempted . . . to tell Steerforth about pretty little Em'ly. . . . I remember that I thought a good deal, and in an uneasy sort of way, about Mr. Peggotty having said that she was getting on to be a woman; but I decided that was nonsense" (chapter 7). David prefers to remember Yarmouth, and Emily, in very different terms: "I never hear the name, or read the name, of Yarmouth, but I am reminded of a certain Sunday morning on the beach, the bells ringing for church, little Em'ly leaning on my shoulder, Ham lazily dropping stones into the water" (chapter 3). This is a Dickensian spot of time: a moment of tranquility when three innocent children stand united beside the eternal ocean, removed from time and the world.

David's memory of that Sunday morning is ominously static, suggesting a form of fixation potentially as serious as Mr. Dick's. It involves a denial of the perplexing realities of class and sexuality, of personal differentiation itself. On his first visit to Yarmouth, Emily confides her dreams of becoming a lady to him. But someone like Emily can become a lady only by marriage to a gentleman. And, at the moment, the only potential gentleman on Emily's horizon is David himself. When he returns to Yarmouth after his mother's death, David encounters a new Emily, a woman and a coquette: "A curious feeling came over me that made me pretend not to know her, and pass by as if I were looking at something a long way off" (chapter 10). Emily relishes the fact that she is no longer a baby, that she is grown. David feels discomfort because she seems "to delight in teasing" him. He cannot reconcile his unchanging memory of Emily, and himself, with the cherry-lipped woman he now sees. He is already holding on tenaciously to his precarious innocence and to the dangerous illusions inherent in it. Innocence about the facts of the adult world—the facts of class, of sexuality, of mutual exploitation—can lead only to vulnerability before those who eagerly abandon innocence for knowledge, power—and guilt. David's willed innocence establishes him as an eternal victim refusing to use his knowledge of the world to survive in it. The ethically complex adult world *demands* a response; sometimes the response is creatively active, sometimes it assumes the form of destructive aggression. Willed innocence suggests the fate of a Tommy Traddles or a Mr. Dick.

But David cannot acknowledge the lessons of his mother's remarriage to Mr. Murdstone and the implications of her death. He cannot apply them to the changed Emily or to the handsome Steerforth. In seeing Emily and Steerforth as they are, David would announce his own loss of innocence, his awareness of threatening realities, and his own capacity for culpability. David vaguely understands that class and sexuality have been Clara Copperfield's undoing: he understands, and flees from the burden of such knowledge. He passes Emily by as if he were looking at something a long way off, as indeed he is. It is the childish self from which he must become inevitably alienated.

Yet, on this second visit to Yarmouth, David, in his thralldom to Steerforth, introduces Emily to precisely the social and sexual realities he finds so threatening. Mr. Peggotty inquires about Steerforth and David enthusiastically pursues his favorite theme: "I was running on, very fast indeed, when my eyes rested on little Em'ly's face, which was bent forward over the table, listening with the deepest attention, her breath held, her blue eyes sparkling like jewels, and the color mantling in her cheeks" (chapter 10). Emily's eyes mirror David's, revealing her response to the Steerforth of his imagination. Steerforth is the gentleman of whom both David and Emily had dreamed: the person David wishes to become, the man Emily longs to possess. Emily responds with unmistakable ardor to the ardor of David's words and the two are curiously bound together by the image, if not the reality, of Steerforth. If there is contagion in Steerforth, the young David unconsciously bears it to Yarmouth, where it will touch and change the lives of his friends there.

David continues to ignore the womanly qualities of the new Emily. He persists in dwelling upon her as she has existed for him imaginatively the year before. He is determined to think of Emily and himself as children, "never growing *older,* never growing *wiser,* children ever, . . . and buried by the *birds* when we were dead!" (chapter 10, emphasis mine). He has even begun to associate Emily with his dead mother: "I remembered [my mother], from that instant, only as the young mother of my earliest impressions. . . . In her death she winged her way back to her calm untroubled youth [and to David's], and cancelled all the rest" (chapter 9). In each passage there is a muted reference to birds, as well as the explicit reference to death. The image in his mind of the dead mother and the picture of the living Emily, "with no real world in it," return David to his original conception of them, and of himself. The two become integrated into a single image of stasis, a curiously romantic image, whose logical culmination is death. The sleep of purity and peace for which David longs occurs, if at all, only in death itself.

Both Clara, the mother, and Emily, the sister, have come to pose the same dilemma. They are, in spite of David's refusal to acknowledge it, complex and ambiguous beings caught in an increasingly perplexing world. His inability to see them in the fullness of their contradictory natures drives him to a terrible falsification of them. It leads to a failure of vision akin to Mr. Dick's. David and Mr. Dick can accept neither the contradictions in those they love, nor in themselves; and they respond with an ambivalence that prevents them from accepting the moral ambiguities inseparable from the human situation. In the face of such ambivalence, Mr. Dick takes refuge in the domain of symptoms, in his private allusion to King Charles the First. David dwells upon memories of serenity that, by their very nature, must be evanescent. David, no less than

Mr. Dick, is potentially fixated "to a particular portion of [the] past, . . . alienated from the present and the future" (*SE*, 16:273). But, unlike Mr. Dick, the mature David has perceived, through an act of the imagination, a pattern in his life. Like Freud, in his case history of the "Wolf Man," David cannot give "either a purely historical or a purely thematic account" of his own story: he must, like Freud, "combine the two methods of presentation" (*SE*, 17:13). He has begun to perceive recurring motifs within the chronologically ordered events of his life. He is poised to exorcise, or to accept, the impeding past so that he may complete his Memorial in a businesslike way, and reestablish contact with the present and the future of his unfolding history.

David Copperfield dwells upon ambivalence and moves, however tentatively, toward the acceptance of ambiguity. David must confront the ambiguous nature of Emily, and of the dead mother of whom she reminds him. He must recognize the failings of Steerforth, without rejecting what is redeeming in him. He must acknowledge the ambiguity of his own moral condition in which good and bad intermingle. Within a fictive world marked by such ambivalence, the Double inevitably appears, a figure from the world of dreams and of symptoms. For ambivalence leads to splitting within the subject itself; it produces the splitting of those Others the subject encounters. Through the figure of the Double, ambivalence may be explored and may even be resolved. The potentially imprisoning fiction of the self or of the Other may become a liberating one with ambiguity, rather than ambivalence, at its center.[13]

Ambivalence so thoroughly pervades David's personal history, always threatening impasse, that the narrative necessarily involves recurrent new beginnings. It returns to the origins of ambivalence in a persistent effort to move through and beyond them. David becomes a new boy with his escape from the blacking warehouse and with his acceptance by Aunt Betsey. His dusty clothes are removed, he is bathed and "swathed" in a shirt and a pair of trousers belonging to Mr. Dick. He is renamed Trotwood and figuratively reborn. With the end of his schooling at Doctor Strong's, he embarks again upon his "'meandering' about the world." And he begins, as he once began the journey to Salem House years before, in a state of apparent innocence, burdened with his old sense of inadequacy. The innocence, by now, is pure illusion. For David has been initiated into the world of adult culpability. He has come to perceive Doctor Strong's wife, Annie, with the suspicious eyes of Mr. Wickfield. David, sensitive to Wickfield's uneasiness in Annie's presence, begins to assume she has been involved sexually with her cousin, Jack Maldon. Annie is, of course, truly innocent; is horrified that she is, after all, a sexual being and that others suspect her. David's failure to see that the womanly Annie need not be an adulteress in thought or deed involves him in a subtle violation of her integrity. And he must bear the responsibility for what Mr. Dick might call another instance of the trouble in one person's head finding its way, not inexplicably, into another's, into David's.

As he rides toward London, David is temporarily the child of old, the one so completely duped by the knowing waiter at the inn in Yarmouth. That incident served as a prelude to Salem House and the appearance of Steerforth. On this occasion, some ten years later, David loses his seat in the coach. At the Golden Cross in London he is served flat wine and dispatched to a room over the stable. He continues to avoid those acts of self-assertion necessary to his survival in a world coolly indifferent to the claims of a seventeen-year-old gentleman. The old dread of himself as someone who bites, the old association of self-assertion with criminality, still takes its toll.

David's inability to accept the ambiguities of his own nature in a thoroughly ambiguous world necessitates Steerforth's reappearance. It is a magical moment. David, still feeling "completely extinguished" from his journey, goes to Covent Garden Theatre to see a performance of *Julius Caesar:* the "mingled reality and mystery of the whole show" momentarily free David from himself. He leaves the theatre at midnight, the legendary hour of his birth, to encounter "a bawling, splashing, link-lighted, umbrella-struggling, hackney-coach-jostling, patten-clinking, muddy, miserable world" (chapter 19), the confusing reality of London so alien to the supposedly romantic world from which he has just come. Under the influence of the play as he has experienced it, David becomes disoriented, "a stranger upon earth," fated to encounter the past and to experience it anew. He is prepared to appropriate to himself some heroic figure like those in the novels he once read: "I was so filled with the play, and with the past—for it was, in a manner, like a shining transparency, through which I saw my earlier life moving along—that I don't know when the figure of a handsome well-formed young man . . . became a real presence to me" (chapter 19). The self-absorbed David has failed to see the play for what it is, a study, and in David's case, an omen of treachery and betrayal. Even Steerforth is not a real presence to him: he is a figure conjured up out of David's psychic and imaginative needs. David, in his refusal to see the real Steerforth, uses him as Steerforth will, in turn, use David. For David the boundaries of the self are at best ill-defined: he has no awareness of himself as an autonomous being, with his own story to live out. Others seem not to exist independently of him: he incorporates them all too easily into his own fiction, all the while risking usurpation by Steerforth's fiction of himself. He acts upon a naive egoism that becomes the basis of the renewed friendship and that blinds him to the faults Steerforth so casually advertises.[14]

David's encounter with Steerforth at the Golden Cross becomes a ritual of regression. Steerforth is a figure of ambiguous power who copes all too well with the world. David is drawn to his capacity for mastery and control. Their nocturnal meeting is as uncanny as the encounter involving Charles Darnay and Sydney Carton on the night Darnay is acquitted of treason. The uncanny involves not only the transformation of the familiar into the unfamiliar, but also the "factor of involuntary repetition . . . [that] forces upon us the idea of something fateful and inescapable" (SE, 17:237). David, as in a dream, experiences a loss of control; he submits to the compulsion to repeat the past as Mr. Dick involuntarily repeats his allusions to King Charles the First. Steerforth has seemingly rescued David in the past at Salem House: he will once again. He will act for David, while David remains passive and innocent. It is a dangerous stance to adopt, for it threatens to cut David off from adulthood and to subvert his capacity to generate a coherent narrative of his life.

The personal history has arrived at a critical point. David may succumb to the confusing reality of London. The city suggests a chaos to which the fragile self may respond by pursuing dissolution. David may lose his clear perception of himself or of others. Or he may acknowledge the threats to the self and come to terms with them within his narrative. The mature David, armed with his knowledge of the past and of the temptation to repeat it, is prepared to adopt Mr. Dick's allegorical way of speaking, which leads only to condensed and imprisoning autobiography, and to transform it into a fully developed story intelligible to himself and to his readers.

At this moment, David plays a curiously Dickensian trick, echoing the buried allusion to Dick Swiveller's protean bedstead: he offers a sign, fleeting but unmistakable, to illuminate what is happening in the text. Under Steerforth's aegis, David moves from the loft over the stable into seventy-two, next to Steerforth's own room. He falls asleep to dream "of ancient Rome, Steerforth, and friendship, until the early morning coaches, rumbling out of the archway underneath, [make him] dream of thunder and gods" (chapter 19). Ironically, the dream points to the betrayal of friendship. It foreshadows the thunder of cannon that will pervade David's dream at Yarmouth during the tempest. David has imagistically anticipated the shape of the narrative to come, quietly as ever asserting his mastery over the material at hand. The next morning David awakens to stand "peeping out of window at King Charles on horseback, surrounded by a maze of hackney-coaches and looking anything but regal in a drizzling rain and a dark-brown fog" (chapter 20). This amounts to an innocent act of plagiarism, but plagiarism nonetheless. The statue of King Charles the First—another of Mr. Morfin's images— alludes to Mr. Dick and his never-to-be completed Memorial. David's history explores highly charged material, but it will not suffer the fate of the Memorial. David, too, faces the possibility of the fruitless repetition of the same image in his narrative, of the same events in his life. The impetus to health informing the autobiographical project is always shadowed by the potentiality for impasse. The mature David is aware that Steerforth has threatened to dominate his life as the allusion to King Charles the First dominates Mr. Dick's. The narrative has returned to its opening sentence: "Whether I shall turn out to be the hero of my own life, or whether that station will be held by anybody else, these pages must show." Within these pages David must explore his relationship to Steerforth if he is to avoid an impasse like Mr. Dick's and a similar imprisonment both in time past and in a purely idiosyncratic, a stone dead, language. However obliquely, he must confront Steerforth as his Double. In the process, he will introduce the language of dreams into his linear narrative in order to render fully all that has happened. The reference to the embattled statue of King Charles, encircled by that maze of hackney-coaches, suggests how the remaining pages of David Copperfield's personal history must be read, and how David will avoid paralysis.

The young men's friendship began long ago at Salem House when

Steerforth existed for David only as a talismanic word carved into a wooden door. It runs its natural course at the Golden Cross in London, where Steerforth airily tells David, "I feel as if you were my property" (chapter 20), echoing earlier words at Salem House, "You belong to my bedroom, I find" (chapter 6). At Yarmouth the relationship enters upon a new and perplexing phase. Steerforth strolls the beach alone while David sleeps, and perhaps dreams: "He had seen, in the distance, what he was sure must be the identical house of Mr. Peggotty . . . and had had a great mind, he told me, to walk in and swear he was myself grown out of knowledge" (chapter 21). Steerforth seems to have stepped out of David's dreams as the dazzling figure David wishes, and fears, to become. The two seem curiously interchangeable. Even Peggotty fails to recognize her "darling boy." The confusion about identity indicates that David is no longer simply the aggressive Steerforth's property. In fulfilling desires David cannot fully acknowledge, Steerforth has, ironically, become David's property too.

But Steerforth never exists simply as a projection of an unacknowledged part of David's self. He remains an autonomous figure, serving ends beyond those of David's secret desires. The separation of the two begins precisely at the moment that the boundaries of the two selves seem to dissolve, to overlap. Steerforth says, "I'll come anywhere you like, or do anything you like. Tell me where to come to; and in two hours I'll produce myself in any state you please" (chapter 21). For the adolescent David this bravado transforms Steerforth into a willing Puck or Ariel, pledging unambiguous fealty to David's Oberon or Prospero. Steerforth seems to exist only as the agent of David's desire. But for the mature David, and for us, Steerforth's speech reveals the chameleon nature of a radically unstable sensibility. Steerforth possesses the capacity to produce himself in any state because he has no self at all. He is the Byronic Don Juan forever adopting new roles, new fictions, to inhabit. In this way Steerforth serves only himself, an amoral artist manqué reveling in his own virtuosity.

The narrative penetrates more deeply into a complex world, the maze that has defeated Mr. Dick and threatens to defeat David. The mature David, reflecting on the past, seeks to render that complexity. To do this, he must do justice to Steerforth, capturing his adolescent vision of Steerforth and piercing to the figure beyond the veil of his youthful imagination. David achieves a subtle double vision. When the two visit Peggotty and Barkis, Steerforth's powers are fully revealed: "I thought even then, *and I have no doubt now,* that the consciousness of success in his determination to please [them], inspired him with a new delicacy of perception, and made it, subtle as it was, more easy to him" (chapter 21, emphasis mine). Later, Steerforth dazzles Emily in the same way. He possesses the ability to bring people into a charmed circle of which he is the center. There is egoism here, the delight in mastery. There is class arrogance. But there is also genuine virtuosity. Steerforth's prodigality with the Byronic energy he possesses, and is possessed by, is part of his attractiveness. He may abuse his capacities and hurt others, but for David, as for Dickens, his artistry is real.

Even Steerforth's moral perceptions cannot be ignored. Ham *is,* as Steerforth claims, "rather a chuckle-headed fellow" in comparison to Emily. He possesses neither the sexual authority nor the moral complexity Emily needs and quite clearly deserves in a husband. As Mr. Peggotty observes, Ham has "take[n] care on her, like a brother," like the brother David has, in part, remained in his relationship to Emily. David responds ambivalently to the news of the engagement. The marriage of Ham and Emily, who shared that Sunday morning on the beach with him years before, will fulfill one of his deepest fantasies: brother and sister will be united in a relationship beyond time, beyond taint. Yet, the pleasure borders on pain. David has come to Yarmouth, in Steerforth's company, with the fancy that he might still be fated to love Emily. He has been poised on the verge of moving, however tentatively, however fancifully, into the adult world. Ham's engagement to Emily is a welcome reprieve; an opportunity lost; an occasion for a brief insight into the violation of Emily's integrity by her uncle and her cousin.

David's response to Emily continues to be ambivalent and vacillating. Steerforth's response, grounded perhaps in an even more radical ambivalence toward women in general, seems all too predictable. He has met that sister of whom he once inquired, the sister of whom David hesitated to speak, and he acts accordingly. Miss Mowcher, who so completely understands Steerforth's "noddle," repeats words David has heard before when she asks of Emily, "A sister of yours, Mr. Copperfield?" (chapter 22). She knows Steerforth's ways. And Steerforth, fully aware of his compulsion to seduce, constantly drops hints to David, looking for a sign that will, perhaps, compel him to stop. He speaks of his discontent, of his inability to learn "the art of binding [himself] to any of the wheels on which the Ixions of these days are turning round and round" (chapter 22). He mentions that he has christened his new boat The Little Emily, and continues to look steadily at David, waiting for some response. Even Martha Endell's presence in Yarmouth seems to Steerforth an omen to which David must react.

All of this is simply lost on the younger David, who remains fixed in the past, alienated from the present and the future, like Mr. Dick and the lunatic gentleman at Blunderstone Rookery. He persists in his refusal to see the moral and psychological drama of which he is a part. Even when he watches part of the drama enacted before him, when Emily weeps and says, "I am not as good a girl as I ought to be!" David will have none of it. He fails to tell Steerforth of "those domestic weaknesses and tendernesses" of which he has learned. It would violate a sacred confidence—and David's childhood vision of Emily, and of himself as an innocent for whom certain facts remain beyond comprehension. He remains silent. His silence gives "her image a new grace" while confirming his own image of himself. But the grace David confers upon Emily will guard her neither from herself nor from Steerforth. David, for reasons of his own, has withheld from Steerforth knowledge of the final sign that might have deterred him in his designs.

The warnings from Agnes; Rosa Dartle's conviction that Steerforth and David share some secret; even David's perception that Steerforth has "applied himself to some habitual strain of the fervent energy which, when roused, was so passionately roused within him" (chapter 28)— these various signs fail to alert David to Steerforth's plan. He thinks of remonstrating with Steerforth about his way of pursuing any fancy that he takes. But his mind conveniently glances off to the topic of the dying Barkis. David's perplexity has become a form of complicity, based on his unwillingness to accept his awareness of certain realities, and his own desire to have the seduction take place. Through it, he will secure both Emily, and Steerforth, to himself, in the realm of fantasy, if not of fact.

The fact of his complicity exists as something almost too painful to speak of. Barkis dies, going out with the tide, and David attends the funeral, once again in the churchyard adjacent to Blunderstone Rookery, where his mother is buried. Throughout, the mad gentleman looks on from the window of David's old room. David remains figuratively within the room, his condition analogous to that of Mr. Dick. But, the

reference to the mad gentleman occurs in a passage immediately preced-
ing David's prelude to Steerforth's seduction of Emily:

> A dread falls on me here. A cloud is lowering on the distant town, towards
> which I retrace my solitary steps. I fear to approach it. I cannot bear to think of
> what did come, upon that memorable night; of what must come again, if I go on.
>   It is no worse, because I write of it. It would be no better, if I stopped my
> most unwilling hand. It is done. Nothing can undo it; nothing can make it other-
> wise than as it was. (Chapter 31)

With these words David potentially becomes the hero of his own life.
He will not be unable, like Mr. Dick, to speak of certain painful events.
He will not retreat into the private world of symptomatic, and apparently unintelligible, language. He will demonstrate the truth of Aunt
Betsey's observation that "It's in vain, Trot, to recall the past, unless it
works some influence upon the present" (chapter 23). The past will not
defeat David if he can say, and mean, that it is done; nothing can undo
it. If he were to stop his unwilling hand, he would be forever alienated
from his own story. So David persists, in order to come into the possession of his destiny, and his self, even as he recognizes that facts and
events lie outside the power of narrative to transform them completely.
There remains the chasm between the narrative structure and the deed of
which it speaks. Yet, the coherent structure of narrative remains the only
means of David's personal salvation.

The marvel of this sequence lies in the profound awareness of this
chasm between fact and narrative; and in David's, and Dickens's, coura-
geous refusal to lapse into moral platitudes. David has fully explored,
however obliquely, the situation that compels Emily to respond to Steerforth's advances. She is not merely the victim of some dashing seducer.
Her own sexual nature and her social aspirations have prepared her for
Steerforth. Her engagement to Ham has made her only more susceptible to Steerforth's vitality. Marriage to Ham would have been as un-
satisfactory as Annie Strong's to the paternal Doctor Strong. David's account omits none of these circumstances. And it captures the undeniable
fascination Steerforth generates. Steerforth manifests a life force that is
blind, chaotic, as destructive as it is potentially creative. Steerforth's
motto, "Ride on! Rough-shod if need be, smooth-shod if that will do,
but ride on! Ride over all obstacles, and win the race!" (chapter 28), is

the romantic version of that will-to-power Lovelace displays in *Clarissa*. Steerforth and Lovelace share the same ardor and artistry that place them almost beyond good and evil.

In his formal lament for a "cherished friend, who was dead," David remains faithful to the complexities of the man he has introduced into the world of Yarmouth. The lament reveals at once David's sense of loss, and his awareness of the capacities Steerforth has employed so carelessly, so destructively: "What is natural in me, is natural in many other men, I infer, and so I am not afraid to write that I never had loved Steerforth better than when the ties that bound me to him were broken. In the keen distress of the discovery of his unworthiness, I thought more of all that was brilliant in him . . . I did more justice to the qualities that might have made him a man of a noble nature and a great name" (chapter 32). Steerforth has ceased to be a mere projection of David's unconscious self. David acknowledges Steerforth's autonomous existence and moves toward judgment without bitterness or repugnance. The ties are broken even as David recognizes his own unconscious part in all that has occurred. The full recognition of the meaning of Emily's seduction remains to assert itself during the great storm at Yarmouth. But this is David's first explicit step beyond his infantile ambivalence toward Emily and Steerforth that has, in part, contributed to Emily's fall. This is the first, tentative acceptance of the moral ambiguities of life and the psychological ambiguities posed by the unconscious self. And this occurs because David can write of a past that cannot be undone; because he can prepare for that future moment in which Steerforth's corpse washes ashore after the tempest. David's lament fuses into a coherent whole the adolescent and the adult vision of Steerforth with which David, the mature artist, has been working since the Byronic Steerforth offered to play whatever role was desired of him.

With Steerforth's seduction of Emily, one strand of David's story comes to its temporary end, awaiting its final working out within David's account of his life. There are, of course, other elements in David's account. Critics have discussed the extent to which Uriah Heep can be seen as another, far more repulsive version of David.[15] But Heep never poses the temptation of a Steerforth. David has no desire to emulate the writhing, self-deprecating Heep, for he is exiled from David's imagination by class and personal demeanor. Heep may inhabit David's dreams, even as

Steerforth does, but he never exerts the fascination of a Steerforth whose energy and sense of romantic estrangement from society pose questions to which Dickens will himself return in later novels.

The other strands in the complex narrative David weaves reflect the impulse to the past, to stasis, that figures so centrally in David's relationship both to Emily and to Steerforth. David's willed innocence causes him to fix Emily permanently on the shore beside the sea, with himself and with Ham. It fixes Steerforth in the pose to which David so often refers, asleep at Salem House "in the moonlight, with his handsome face turned up, and his head reclining easily on his arm." This innocence leads David to Dora, in his ineffectual, and finally destructive, effort to regain his lost relationship with his dead mother and with the Emily of the first visit to Yarmouth. It threatens to control David's vision of Agnes and to impede, permanently, his capacity to complete his *own* Memorial.

For writing—the heroic attempt to tell a coherent story—remains at the center of *David Copperfield* as a significant act and as a trope with the broadest implications. David's determination to become a Parliamentary reporter and, in the process, to master the shorthand necessary to the craft is another moment of clarification and illumination. On one level David is beginning again: he has embarked, yet another time, on the journey to financial success and psychological maturity. But David's description of his trials suggests other issues as well: "I bought an approved scheme of the noble art and mystery of stenography . . . and plunged into a sea of perplexity." He continues: "The changes that were rung upon dots, which in such a position meant such a thing, and in such another position something else, entirely different; the wonderful vagaries that were played by circles; the unaccountable consequences that resulted from marks like flies' legs; the tremendous effects of a curve in a wrong place; not only troubled my waking hours, but reappeared before me in my sleep" (chapter 38). Isolated from David's personal history, the passage seems far more appropriate to the novelistic world of *Bleak House*. It anticipates the bewilderment of the illiterate Jo, who is "unfamiliar with the shapes, and in utter darkness as to the meaning, of those mysterious symbols, so abundant over the shops, and at the corners of streets, and on the doors, and in the windows!"[16] Both passages suggest the purely arbitrary nature of language, of any system of signs. But Jo, like Esther Summerson, moves in a world full of other kinds of signs, those enigmatic events that constitute their lives. For Dickens, discussions of language ultimately serve as figures for life itself. They allude to the potential unintelligibility of the nonverbal signs his characters perceive, and in the midst of which they live. The signs range from the symptomatic gestures of a Mr. Dick, flying his kite and "diffusing" his words to the world at large, to David's curious inability to catch quite the meaning of Steerforth's actions. The Dickens world consists, always, of a bewildering number of signs, the enigmatic gestures of his central characters and of those who surround them. There exists, then, a continuum between Mr. Dick's eccentric mannerisms and the events in the life of David Copperfield.

Both Mr. Dick and David may experience the world as mad—"Mad as Bedlam, boy!" as Mr. Dick proclaims. But behind apparent madness lies potential meaning: "When I had groped my way, blindly, through these difficulties, and had mastered the alphabet, which was an Egyptian Temple in itself, there then appeared a procession of new horrors, called arbitrary characters; the most despotic characters I have ever known" (chapter 38). Like Freud in *Studies on Hysteria*, David stands "before a wall which shuts out every prospect and prevents us from having any idea whether there is anything behind it, and if so, what" (*SE*, 2:293). For Freud, the wall is composed of the patient's words; for David, it is the wall of the arbitrary characters of shorthand, and the seemingly arbitrary events of his own life. His life—contingent, chaotic, punctuated with dots, which in such a position mean such a thing, and in such another position something else, entirely different—is a potentially coherent world of meaning. The work David offers the reader, as Rousseau offers his work to his Sovereign Judge, is the ordering, in an implicitly causal chain, of the perplexing events of his life. His narrative involves the penetration of the Egyptian Temple, the mastery of those hieroglyphs of experience that defeat Mr. Dick, as the street signs of London turn Jo stone blind and dumb. Only when David simultaneously perceives and creates the structure of the inherently symbolic world in which he lives will he become free, both from the anguish of paralysis and the inadequacies of purely private speech.

In his experience with stenography, in his encounter with the most despotic characters he has ever known, David reveals the true nature of his project. If *Bleak House* is a document about the interpretation of

documents, as J. Hillis Miller suggests, *David Copperfield* is an autobiographical document exploring the meaning of the autobiographical
act.[17] Out of the welter of hieroglyphs comprising his life, David detects
repetitions, patterns, and meaning, just as he finally masters stenography. He fashions a coherent story that does justice to the multiplicity of
meanings immanent in the events, or the hieroglyphs, of his life. He lo-
cates them in a narrative that is itself a willed, arbitrary form, indebted to
the religious progress and the picaresque novel, which are as conventional and arbitrary as the stenography he studies. David moves from the
arbitrary characters on the written page so that he may be *delivered back*
into the realm of time and experience. Here he will once again confront
events that will appear first as both arbitrary and despotic until they, too,
are mastered through the labor of the imagination. The autobiographical form remains deeply ironic, just as the autobiographical impulse remains absolutely irresistible. Within his personal history, David becomes
the secular pilgrim journeying to a secular celestial city that proves, at
last, to be Canterbury: "What I had to do, was, to take my woodman's
axe in my hand, and clear my own way through the forest of difficulty,
by cutting down the trees until I came to Dora" (chapter 36): and, ultimately, to Agnes and to the riddles her marriage to David poses.

The success of this figurative pilgrimage depends both on the creation of a form that fully accommodates the ambiguities of David's experiences, and on the rendering of truth, however elusive it remains. The
narrative account must approximate the truth of David's life, although
the gap between fact and account may never be fully bridged: the two
realms are parallel and forever separate. Yet, they move toward each
other through David's own imaginative activity. His marriage to Dora
poses the same challenge as his friendship with Steerforth. In marrying
her, David finds he has become the Murdstone of Dora's life as he tries
to shape her mind. He is instrumental in crushing Dora's will to live
once she becomes aware of the painful distance between herself and her
"Doady." In retrospect, David seems to understand fully: "If I did any
wrong, as I may have done much, I did it in mistaken love, and in my
want of wisdom. *I write the exact truth.* It would avail me nothing to
extenuate it now" (chapter 44, emphasis mine). David navigates through
the Scylla and Charybdis of symptomatic speech in his attempt to speak
truthfully in a businesslike way. He skirts Mr. Dick's habitual manner-

isms of speech to avoid the fate of becoming "deaf, dumb, blind, and paralytic, to a million things" from that figurative habit of Mr. Morfin's which is fixation.

But the quest for truth remains shrouded in ambiguity: "I search my breast, and I commit its secrets, *if I know them,* without any reservation to this paper" (chapter 44, emphasis mine). David himself points, always in that characteristically subdued manner, to the impediments he faces. There exists, along with that impassable gulf between the thing and the word, the enduring reticence of the unconscious self. David writes with the same awareness Rousseau possesses in *The Confessions:* "Since I have undertaken to reveal myself absolutely to the public, nothing about me must remain hidden or obscure. I must remain incessantly beneath [the reader's] gaze. . . . Indeed, he must never lose sight of me for a single instant, for if he finds the slightest gap in my story, the smallest hiatus, he may wonder what I was doing at that moment and accuse me of refusing to tell the whole truth" (p. 65). For Rousseau, as for David, what is at stake is always more than the reader's belief in the truth of his narrative. Finally, each of them writes to affirm his belief in his continuing existence in and through time without those lacunae resulting from defective memory, or unconscious repression. Each seeks to establish, on paper, evidence attesting to that "unbroken consciousness of [one's] own existence" (p. 19) of which Rousseau writes.

Beyond the moral imperative of truth lies this deeper ontological imperative: for David, as for Rousseau, his very being must be affirmed. And so David is driven on with a sense of inevitability, but an inevitability he has conjured up through a narrative whose coherence has been fully realized. David visits the Steerforth house only to learn of Emily's flight from Steerforth and Littimer. As he leaves, he observes Mrs. Steerforth and Rosa Dartle, "how steadily they both [sit] gazing on the prospect, and how it thicken[s] and close[s] around them." He continues: "From the greater part of the broad valley . . . a mist was rising like a sea, which, mingling with the darkness, made it seem as if the gathering waters would encompass them. I have reason to remember this, and think of it with awe; for before I looked upon those two again, a stormy sea had risen to their feet" (chapter 46). And to David's also. The stormy sea, like the sea of perplexity that is stenography, gathers and threatens to engulf David only after Dora's death and Emily's reunion with Mr. Peggotty, a reunion preceded by Emily's figurative death and her ambiguous rebirth through the agency of Martha Endell. In escaping from Littimer, Emily "was took bad with fever." Then "the language of that country [Italy] went out of her head, and she could only speak her own," (chapter 51). Emily regresses into a language no one else can speak or understand. She emerges out of her fever and her isolation as she begins to make signs to those around her. Her experience echoes David's encounter with the mysteries of stenography. She has to learn the names for common things all over again, until finally, "it all comes back!" and she reenters the symbolic world inhabited by others. Her rebirth is apparently completed when Martha calls Emily back from her open grave. But Emily's return to life is suspect: in emigrating to Australia, she embarks upon a journey as final as the one Dora begins when *she* figuratively leaves David. Dora and Emily have both "died," and David has been inextricably involved in the death of each. He finds it impossible even to talk to Emily, to this woman now so different from the child he once knew: "Ever rising from the sea of my remembrance, is the image of the dear child as I knew her first, graced by my young love, and by her own, with every fascination wherein such love is rich. Would it, indeed, have been better if we had loved each other as a boy and girl, and forgotten it?" (chapter 53). The words serve as an ambiguous epitaph. For, although he is speaking of his dead child-wife, David might just as well be speaking of Emily, whose life has also been blighted through the agency of his will, and through his obsession with the "image of the dear child" as he first knew her.

These events and reflections, "rising from the sea of [his] remembrance," are the necessary prelude to David's return to Yarmouth. During the memorable tempest, David's experiences culminate in a moment of illumination and self-recognition, the now inevitable climax of his account of himself. As Mr. Peggotty, presiding over the death of Barkis, observes, "People can't die, along the coast, . . . except when the tide's pretty nigh out. They can't be born, unless it's pretty nigh in—not properly born, till flood" (chapter 30). Only at Yarmouth, in the midst of the tempest, when the sea literally rises to his feet, is David finally, properly born.

The storm occurs during a period of impasse, an impasse experienced by all the heroes and heroines of Dickens's mature novels. Dora's death, associated as it is with Emily's imminent departure, has a very specific impact upon David's sense of himself and his relationship to time: "I came to think that the Future was walled up before me, that the energy and action of my life were at an end, that I never could find any refuge but in the grave" (chapter 54). David's relationship to the past, the present, and the future becomes disjointed, fragmented. There is no continuity between them to give coherence to the story of his life that must work itself out in the medium of time. Once again David risks becoming, like Mr. Dick, time's victim.

For Mr. Dick, his sister's fate has led to confusion, to impasse, and to the cryptic language of symptoms. David's current disorientation, as an interview with Ham reveals, involves a multiplicity of sisters. Ham now lives with David's Peggotty, and with the memory of Emily: "There were times, [Peggotty] said, . . . when he talked of their old life in the boat-house; and then he mentioned Emily as a child. But, he never mentioned her as a woman" (chapter 51). But this childlikeness has been David's image of Emily, and of Dora. Ham speaks for himself and for David when he says, "I loved her—and I love the mem'ry of her—too deep—to be able to lead her to believe of my own self as I'm a happy man" (chapter 51). The memories of Emily and Dora, as they once were, not as they come to be in the complexity of their ambiguous maturity, trap Ham and David, and create the wall separating both of them from the present and the future. Once again, David has employed the structure of symptoms, and of dreams, to dramatize his own condition. Ham, who was present at Blunderstone Rookery on the night of David's birth, and who was as red on that occasion as the newborn David, becomes yet another Double. His desire to ask Emily's forgiveness is also David's. And the need for forgiveness is intensified with the death of Dora, the child-wife, who is as surely a sister as Emily herself has figuratively been for David. Both Emily and Dora become the logical successors to the dead mother. If Ham dwells upon the old life in the boat-house, David still dwells upon the old life at Blunderstone Rookery: upon his birth, his mother's remarriage, and her death.

David's illness at Yarmouth during the storm and the deaths of Ham and Steerforth become the necessary components of a movement away from impasse: David's relationship to time will be altered, so that, like the stoic Mr. Omer, he will be able to accept its inherent vicissitudes. The opening sentence of the "Tempest" chapter, with its implicit allusion to Shakespeare's play, indicates how the storm has figured in David's consciousness from the beginning of his story: "I now approach an event in my life, so indelible, so awful, so bound by an infinite variety of ties to all that has preceded it, in these pages, that, from the beginning of my narrative, I have seen it growing larger and larger as I advanced, like a great tower in a plain, and throwing its forecast shadow even on the incidents of my childish days" (chapter 55). David's reference to his narrative in this passage indicates the extent to which it and his life are one. *David Copperfield* confirms that man *is* a narrative being: man *is* that inveterate storyteller, weaving tales about his cosmos, his culture, and himself, incorporating into the story those obdurate facts that all too often threaten to undo its fragile coherence. The tempest gives David yet another opportunity to make his life intelligible: it becomes the event making his narrative possible, and he acknowledges it as such. During the tempest both temporal and thematic elements fuse: events are placed in their proper order, and they are assigned, at last, appropriate meanings. Life, like the noble art and mystery of stenography, has its meaning, but it is a meaning realized by man himself. For David the tempest becomes a sign, one of the arbitrary characters in the stenography of life. His narrative muses upon that enigmatic event and its relationship to other moments in his life, moments to which David as the hero of his own story will attribute both significance and meaning. When properly understood through an act of the imagination, each moment becomes a repetition, a variation, of other events. David's narrative, a sustained act of interpretation, will unite into a coherent whole the past, present, and future currently walled off from him. The "despotic characters," literal and figurative, will cease to tyrannize over David as he becomes their master.

The Yarmouth coach bears David toward a "murky confusion . . . of flying clouds, tossed up into most remarkable heaps, suggesting greater heights in the clouds than there were depths below them to the bottom of the deepest hollows in the earth, through which the wild moon seemed to plunge headlong" (chapter 55). This is a landscape out of Wordsworth, suggesting lyrics like "A Night-Piece," as well as revelatory moments in *The Prelude*. It suggests the nature of human consciousness, its heights and depths, its creative and destructive potentialities. The world into which David moves is disintegrating. People talk in awe of "great sheets of lead having been ripped off a high church-tower" and of "great trees lying torn out of the earth." This rending of nature is a rending of David's self: he loses "the clear arrangement of time and distance." The storm is acknowledged for what it is, a figurative expression of David's inner turmoil, the inevitable consequence of his participation in the fates of so many who have figured in his account of his life: "Something within me, faintly answering to the storm without, tossed up the depths of my memory, and made a tumult in them" (chapter 55). There is no evasion as in the case of Mr. Dick's reliance upon allusions to the Civil War and its attendant chaos. David understands *his* figurative way of speaking. The sea that he negotiates is his own consciousness. The tempest is his personal crisis and David places it at the center of his story.

If, throughout his autobiography, David has attempted to create a coherent story, and implicitly a viable self, here in the storm the project almost founders upon the rock of his own guilt. The disorientation he now experiences proceeds from his unacknowledged complicity in the seduction of Emily and the death of Dora. And this complicity has led to the violation of his own self. When he cannot sleep, David rises to look out at the storm: "[I] could see nothing, except the reflection in the window-panes of the faint candle I had left burning, and of my own haggard face looking in at me from the black void" (chapter 55). The boundaries of the self have, once again, dissolved. The romantic aura of the London evening on which he was reunited with Steerforth has been dissipated by time. Then David reconstituted himself through his implicit identification with Steerforth, by his submission to Steerforth's appropriation of his person. All that has now been transformed to nightmare, and to spiritual anguish: he is a mere spirit to the servant girl he frightens in the kitchen of the inn.

David is in the midst of a regressive movement to the stormy night of his own birth, to a moment prior to the earliest consolidations of identity, prior even to a demarcated self founded upon others.[18] The conventional self, with its usual healthy sense of its own unity and coherence, apparently at home in a body, disintegrates. David becomes only a face reflected in a glass, bodiless and unreal. His condition suggests the extent to which he has imaginatively dispersed his self through his identification with others, or with his vision of them. David has failed to consolidate an authentic identity, a viable fiction, up to this moment. Rather, he has existed through those alter egos, Steerforth and Ham, the masculine poles of his fragile self. Now the process of identification, with its evasions of life's ambiguities, takes it toll. The impoverishment

of David's self, estranged from the Doubles through whom he has tried
to live, but through whom he may no longer live, is captured by the
solitary, haggard face staring back at him from the mysterious void of
the self. To regain a sense of wholeness without which life is impossible,
David must encounter the secrets of his own breast: he must encounter
the arbitrary characters of his past, master them, and reconstitute himself
upon the knowledge he has gained.

The dream that follows involves such an encounter: "[I] fell—off a
tower and down a precipice—into the depths of sleep. I have an impression that for a long time, though I dreamed of being elsewhere and in a
variety of scenes, it was always blowing in my dream. At length, I lost
that feeble hold upon reality, and was engaged with two dear friends,
but who they were I don't know, at the siege of some town in a roar of
cannonading" (chapter 55). David relinquishes his hold upon reality
and the illusory sense of his own autonomous existence. The dream
gathers in those Doubles he has exiled from himself. For he does know
the identities of the two friends. David has been thinking of them in his
waking hours before the dream. He is apparently uneasy about Ham
who is returning from Lowestoft and risks being lost at sea. And he has
mused that if he were to go into the town, he "should not have been
surprised . . . to encounter some one who [he] knew must be then in
London," surely an oblique reference to the absent Steerforth. For on
his previous visit to Yarmouth David has been thinking of Emily, the
child who has enchanted him, and of Steerforth: "And a foolish, fearful
fancy came upon [him] of his being near at hand, and liable to be met at
any turn" (chapter 51). David has summoned Ham and Steerforth into
the dream so that they may reenact the siege of a town. The dream exploits a traditional trope for sexual assault. The three figures in the dream
assault not only Emily, but all of the women in David's life, each of whom
stands for the other. Clara Copperfield and Dora are implicitly fused with
Emily. They are all victims of a willed naiveté, joined hand in hand with a
principle of aggression. But the besieged town does not stand only as an
emblem of Emily's lost virginity. Emily is another of David's alter egos.
Steerforth's seduction has involved David in the violation of his integrity,
his own self. In failing Emily, he has failed himself. The dream acknowledges this. It is a sign of David's condition. The roar of the cannonading
connects the dream to the night in the Golden Cross in London. The

appearance of the dream at this point in the narrative suggests David's
awareness of its meaning; it consolidates his recognition and foreshadows
the process of reintegration David is about to experience.

David admits that he often dreams of the incidents occurring during
the Yarmouth tempest. But the recurring dream is not like Mr. Dick's
compulsive reference to King Charles the First. In writing of the tempest and the dream, David as autobiographer, like Freud's physician, has
behaved "as 'timelessly' as the unconscious itself" (*SE,* 17:10). He has
perceived the timeless, thematic dimensions of his experiences and has
accurately placed them within the chronological scheme of his life. He
recognizes the dream as an experience that illuminates his life, unifies it,
and prepares him for change. He has been saved from disintegration by
a moment of self-recognition. There is no conscious, analytic statement
of the understanding gained. There is only its manifestation in the language of dreams. By placing the dream in the narrative as he does, David
fixes its meaning. The events at Yarmouth may recur in his dreams, but
they do not produce impasse. They clear the path to the future so that
David may once more become a person in time, a character whose story
presents a past, a present, and a viable future.

David awakens from his dream as he has been awakened from the one
at the Golden Cross: the thunder within both dreams gives way to
someone knocking at the door. Then, David awakened to the fog, to
King Charles on horseback, and to Steerforth. Now he encounters "unspeakable confusion." The cannonading that has impinged upon his
dream continues, connecting events in the dream with the fate of the
stricken ship, "roll[ing] and dash[ing], like a desperate creature driven
mad." The stricken ship and the stricken self are one. David remains a
spectator, the dreamer in an ongoing dream, helplessly watching the
deaths he wills at some indefinable level of his being. The storm with its
turbulent waters suggests the process of disintegration through which
David's obsolete self is passing, and speaks of the possibilities of reintegration and rebirth: "The wreck, even to my unpractised eye, was
breaking up. I saw that she was parting in the middle, and that the life of
the solitary man upon the mast now hung by a thread" (chapter 55): as
Ham's life hangs by the rope "made fast round his body." The ship disappears, Ham and Steerforth drown. The flood tide of which Mr. Peggotty has spoken bears Ham's dead body to David's very feet. Then, David is led to that part of the shore where Emily and he "had looked for

shells, two children," to find Steerforth, "lying with his head upon his arm, as [he] had often seen him lie at school." Ham and Steerforth merge into the symbolic tableau of the storm, sacrificed to that sea standing both for death and life. Neither Steerforth nor Ham is simply obliterated, annihilated, in short, repressed. In his dream prior to their deaths, David has confronted their complicity in the fate of Emily. In the dream, David has acknowledged his identification with Ham and Steerforth. In the storm, he relinquishes them to the sea to regain himself. He abandons his static image of the past, his memory of Yarmouth, "of a certain Sunday morning on the beach, the bells ringing for church, little Em'ly leaning on my shoulder, Ham lazily dropping stones into the water" (chapter 3).

The images of the past sustaining ambivalence have been dispelled, the impasse broken, the self reborn out of the swollen sea. But the loss is great. The seemingly inexplicable mourning of the Yarmouth folk for the dead Steerforth indicates a universal sense of loss. There is no diminishment of the human spirit in Ham's death comparable to that implied in Steerforth's. The energy, the vitality, of the red-capped man clinging to the mast of the foundering ship is forever lost to the world of *David Copperfield*. The lure of romantic potentialities, of the expansiveness of the Byronic self, however destructive, gives way to the mature David's restrained voice. He is no longer a haggard face suspended in a void. He is demonstrably the hero of his own life: he has *survived,* with the awareness of a diminished self. David is not a Mr. Dick, or a Ham, time's cripples. But he is less than Steerforth. So David is left only with "the ashes of [his] youthful friendship." He has seen Steerforth fully, in his innocence and in his culpability. Rosa Dartle's frenzied outburst before Mrs. Steerforth fixes that ambiguity forever in David's imagination. He does not recoil, as he once recoiled from Emily: "I lifted up [Steerforth's] leaden hand, and held it to my heart; and all the world seemed death and silence, broken only by his mother's moaning" (chapter 56). In Dickens's novels reconciliation occurs, though all too often, as here, it occurs only through death itself.

David's written story moves, then, towards its inevitable end, his marriage to Agnes. The conclusion of *David Copperfield* poses a variety of perplexing issues that are clearly relevant to the reading of the work I have been offering. It can be argued that, in his marriage to Agnes, David does not move into the future, but artfully recaptures the past he has so persistently pursued. The timelessness of Canterbury is all too much like the timelessness of that Sunday morning in Yarmouth when three innocents, bathed in the music of bells, stood together by the sea. And Agnes herself, with her Victorian earnestness, her platitudinous observations about the "bad angel" in David's life, seems never to be in touch fully with the ambiguities David has explored so scrupulously. Yet, if David has been fixated upon a particular moment in his past, alienated from the present and the future, the marriage to Agnes makes psychological sense. Both Emily and Dora have been sisters for David, creatures to whom he responded because they seemed untainted by the complexities of adulthood. And he perceives that he has encouraged Agnes to feel only sisterly affection for him: "I could not forget that the feeling with which she now regarded me had grown up in my own free choice and course. That if she had ever loved me with another love—and I sometimes thought the time was when she might have done so—I had cast it away" (chapter 58). Of course, it is possible to consider this passage as a piece of cheap irony: we know, as Aunt Betsey knows, Agnes's real love for David. But David *has* "accustomed [himself] to think of her, when [they] were both mere children, as one who was far removed from [his] wild fancies" (chapter 58). David is genuinely penetrating the mystery of his heart, the subtle ways in which the individual experiences change. He does not know when his vision of Agnes began an unconscious transformation. But his new vision of her is now conscious. Marriage to Agnes has been unthinkable until David breaks free of one pattern of his life, the futile grasping for the uncapturable past. We may always doubt the reality of Agnes's womanhood. But the novel thrusts always toward David's altered perception of her. The will in Dickens's design is present, if the art is not.

"And now my written story ends. I look back, once more—for the last time—before I close these leaves" (chapter 64). The potentially deformed language of symptoms has given way to what Steven Marcus has called the "complete story . . . the theoretical, created end story. . . . At the end—at the successful end—one has come into possession of one's own story." [19] At the end David's life as written stands in its chronological and thematic coherence. We must not forget the opening sentence of the "Tempest" chapter: "I now approach an event in my life, so indelible, so awful, so bound by an infinite variety of *ties* to all that has preceded it, in these pages, that, from the beginning of my narrative, I have seen it growing larger and larger . . . like a great tower in a plain, and throwing its forecast shadow even on the incidents of my childish days" (chapter 55, emphasis mine). The shadow threatens to darken the life completely, and even to silence the narrative voice with its painful implications. But the events of the tempest serve not to block the life but to give it coherence. In the closing pages of *Studies on Hysteria,* Freud speaks of the "'defile' of consciousness" through which "complicated and multi-dimensional" materials must pass under the aegis of the word. Memories, mutilated or repressed, block the defile until the patient, with the physician's help, delivers them through "a narrow cleft." They appear in consciousness "cut up, as it were, into pieces or strips." According to Freud, "It is the psychotherapist's business to put these together once more into the organization which he *presumes* to have existed" (*SE,* 2:291, emphasis mine). Likewise, it is the autobiographer's business to arrange such pieces or strips into the organization *he* presumes to have existed. The events of the tempest cast a double shadow, one reaching back into David's childhood, one foreshadowing the events consequent to the storm at Yarmouth. The shadow unifies the life through the pressure of David's narrative imagination. His life is not a series of incoherent pieces. Rather, it is a web with no "ravelled end[s]," a web spun out of his memory, constituting that memory itself upon the printed page. In weaving the web that is his story, his self, David perceives and creates a pattern in his life. He engages in the Kierkegaardian repetition of himself, remaining true to the dominant themes of his life and evading the sterile, static repetition of himself to which a Mr. Dick is doomed. In his marriage to Agnes, David is true to this pattern, exercising the circumscribed freedom of the self in time.[20]

In *David Copperfield* a coherent poetics of the self emerges, a poetics based upon a vision of man as a narrative being. Dickens explores the magical power of the Word to effect or to stymie change, an issue to which he will return in later novels. David stands as the earnest Victorian successor to Rousseau's flamboyant picaro, the brilliant but always ironic egoist proclaiming, "I have resolved on an enterprise which has no precedent, and which, once complete, will have no imitator" (p. 17). The claim demands imitation, both in autobiography and in the novel to which *The Confessions* is so clearly akin. Rousseau's romantic certainty that others will perceive themselves both as different and as self-creating leads to romanticism, to Dickens, and to *David Copperfield*, and to David's own successors in Dickens's fictions.

The opening words of David Copperfield's personal history serve as an appropriate epigraph for the careers of those heroes and heroines who follow him: "Whether I shall turn out to be the hero of my own life, or whether that station will be held by anybody else, these pages must show." The heroic task of such characters, in both Dickens's first-person and omniscient narratives, is to survive through the creation of a story by which to live. Each character must work within the limits of those alternatives posed to him, not by a past that he has chosen, but by a past that has chosen him. The Marquis St. Evrémonde of *A Tale of Two Cities* speaks, with unconscious irony, of the natural destiny with which each Dickens character must engage. That destiny is the historical situation into which each character is born, a situation to be accepted or rejected. The character must inevitably attribute his own meaning to the past. The meaning he chooses will free him to grow, to evolve, to pursue the never-to-be fully realized integration of the self. The meaning attributed to the past may turn it into a source of life-giving impetus; or into a gorgon's head, inducing paralysis and the figurative death of the self. Such is the nature of freedom in Dickens's later novels.[21]

Part Two

The Self Imagined:

Bleak House, A Tale of Two Cities, and Great Expectations

Chapter 3

> "—I will accuse the individual workers of
> that system against me, face to face, before the
> great eternal bar!"—Mr. Gridley, *Bleak House*

"Through a Glass Darkly"

With the completion of David Copperfield's personal history, Dickens
has consolidated the way in which he will continue to imagine the life of
the self in the novels to follow. The depths of a hypothetical self remain
unfathomable. The construct by which each Dickens character contrives
to live remains in time, influenced by those Others who exist as tempting models upon which to base the self; or by those Others who impose
their perception of that self upon a character inclined to succumb to an
alien image. Always, such a construct, however viable, remains subject

to obsolescence, to a refusal to change, which threatens the living self with figurative death. Ortega y Gasset's words in "History as a System" continue to point to the ontological assumptions at work in Dickens's creation of fictional characters: "It is too often forgotten that man is impossible without imagination, without the capacity to invent for himself a conception of life, to 'ideate' the character he is going to be. Whether he be original or a plagiarist, man is the novelist of himself."

The issue of originality or plagiarism—the need of the character to invent a legitimate version of the self or the tendency to acquiesce to an illegitimate version, falsifying the character's situation—remains one imaginative center of a Dickens novel. Esther Summerson, in the first-person account she calls a "progress," must concern herself not only with the fact of her literal illegitimacy, but with the legitimacy of that identity she chooses in her attempt to make her way in the fictive world of *Bleak House*. In inventing for herself a conception of life, in imagining the character she is going to be, Esther flirts with a terrible violation of her integrity as she moves between her aunt's twisted definition of her ward and her own, understandable, desire to take refuge in the role of a Dame Durden. Her challenge is to create a viable identity within the act of writing an account of her life so that she may come into possession of her story, of her self. The same challenge faces Charles Darnay. Even within the omniscient narrative of *A Tale of Two Cities,* Darnay offers an account of his life, not only to his uncle, the Marquis St. Evrémonde, and to Doctor Manette, but to the various tribunals before which he stands arraigned. He too must choose between versions of himself, between his role as Charles Darnay, self-proclaimed bourgeois and democrat, or his natural destiny as the surviving Marquis St. Evrémonde. Darnay must determine, if possible, the version of the self through which he will be true to a past he cannot altogether deny, while trying to escape the gorgon stare of the past embodied in the uncle's stony face. So must Pip, in *Great Expectations,* as he encounters the mystery of a past he must imaginatively reconstruct if he is not to be transfixed by it and made into an effigy to a dead past, be it the past of a Miss Havisham or of a Magwitch. Darnay and Pip will court the figurative, if not the literal, illegitimacy with which Esther also must contend. Like her, they encounter the paradoxical condition of innocence and guilt so puzzling to David Copperfield. They, too, will ponder the depths of the self by gazing into mirrors literal and figurative, perhaps to be engrossed by an image floating on a glassy surface. Each of them will seek refuge in a habitual self that hardens into a fixed pose, alienating one from the flow of time. Like Mr. Gridley, the man from Shropshire in *Bleak House,* they see as "through a glass darkly." Gridley tries to sustain himself in the labyrinthine world of Chancery with the desperate hope that he "will accuse the individual workers of the system" against him, "face to face, before the great eternal bar!"[1] But there may be no great eternal bar before which, in the words of St. Paul, one shall see face to face.

In *Bleak House, A Tale of Two Cities,* and *Great Expectations,* characters rarely experience more than partial knowledge. Esther, Darnay, and Pip must learn to see and to know in a world permeated by fog, dust, drizzle, and all that obscures their vision. They encounter, at best, detached and isolated signs and tokens, ambiguous clues to the potential meanings of their lives, looming at them through a pervasive darkness. They read signs as Esther reads the newspaper in the midst of a "London particular," without understanding what the words mean. They may not recognize, or understand, those tokens of their identities, of their selves, by which they are to orient themselves within disorienting circumstances. For now they see as through a glass darkly. There is no assurance they shall ever see face to face, to know, even as one is presumably known by God—if there is a God within the pages of Dickens's later novels.

It is precisely the absence of a transcendent Other who knows, of an eternal glass into which she may confidently hope to look, that gives meaning to the narrative Esther Summerson sets out to write. Esther is never the self-conscious artist that David Copperfield is, but she too engages in another essay of self-creation. She too responds to the autobiographical imperative and performs an analogous task as she tentatively, unwillingly, encounters those signs and tokens from the past to which she must respond if she is to become fully, and efficaciously, "acquainted with [her] personal history" (chapter 38).

But Esther's response to those signs that she must make a part of the progress of her life, her pilgrimage of being, become increasingly evasive and faintly self-righteous as she retreats into her habitual humility and self-negation: "I don't know how it is, I seem to be always writing about myself. I mean all the time to write about other people, and I try to think about myself as little as possible, and I am sure, when I find myself coming into the story again, I am really vexed and say, 'Dear, dear, you tiresome little creature, I wish you wouldn't!' but it is all of no use" (chapter 9). These words suggest that Esther is simply another earnest and self-effacing Victorian heroine, a failure of Dickens's literary imagination. In fact, her halting words, her desire not to write, not to think about herself take us to the heart of her dilemma: to her desire to avoid the creation of a self. If she fails to complete the writing of her account, she will remain not merely selfless, but without a self. She will have succumbed to the fate of becoming like Mr. Dick, a fate that David apparently avoids in the pages of his personal history. She will be another hostage to a painful past that can be dispelled only through the power of the written word.[2]

Esther is so deeply influenced by an understandable ambivalence toward her past that she recoils from it, seeking to flee it as best she can. But, in a novel beginning with a powerful evocation of a prehistoric era, informed by the geological perspective of the day, her flight can be seen as destructive, and doomed to failure. The recovery of the past, like the recovery of those fossils that Charles Lyell, in a letter to Gideon Mantell, spoke of figuratively as the letters of a foreign alphabet, *will* occur, perhaps without Esther's quite willing it.[3] And so it is that Esther, who is vexed to find herself coming into the story again, finally recognizes that it is all of no use: she does indeed have something to do with these pages.

The existence of the double narrative within the pages of *Bleak House* complicates matters. Esther may be seen to exist as a foil for the verbal and imaginative virtuosity of the present-tense narrator. The presence in the novel of a consciousness apparently so different from Esther's, whether this consciousness is Dickens's or the narrator's, serves to emphasize the limitations of Esther's perspective and the inevitability of such limitation for every character in the novel. Neither Inspector Bucket nor Esther, in mounting the high towers of their minds, can comprehend fully the murky complexity of the world in which they find themselves. Each offers an account of events that, at best, approximates an elusive truth.

The present-tense narrative may serve another, more subtle, function. Esther's personal history emerges finally out of signs and tokens often appearing first in the pages counterpointing her own narrative. The present-tense dominates the other narrative to suggest, not only the reticent omniscience of the Dickensian narrator, but also the timelessness of a form of consciousness alien to that appearing in Esther's account. The form of *Bleak House* anticipates the problem Freud confronts in the case history of the "Wolf Man": the physician and the artist must learn to "behave as 'timelessly' as the unconscious itself" and to create a literary form that can do justice to the historical and the thematic dimensions of a patient's and a character's story (*SE,* 17 : 10, 13). Esther's story emerges out of another realm of consciousness, a realm untrammeled by temporality; by notions of cause and effect; by the distinctions, either/or; by the power of the negative. The present-tense narrative, organized upon principles of association governing the world of dreams, and the activities of the unconscious, suggests the curious ways in which the past is always present. It reveals the extent to which personal history, like the act of creation in *Genesis* or *Paradise Lost,* imposes upon another, seemingly inchoate world, the laws of chronology and of cause and effect.[4]

Esther's "silent way of noticing what [passes] before" her becomes her characteristic response both to the external circumstances of her life and to the internal pressures the circumstances generate. The silence that so often accompanies the telling of her story suggests, not just a coyness bordering on the vacuous, but a failure to understand, a failure not fortuitous, but, in some way, willed. As early as her first visit to Krook's rag and bottle warehouse, it becomes clear that Esther's silences create an aura of mystery as important as any of the mysteries in *Bleak House.* As he ticks off the names of the families involved in Jarndyce and Jarndyce, "the great suit," Krook mentions the name Barbary—and nothing happens. Esther remains discreetly silent. There is no shock of recognition on her part at the mention of the name of her aunt (we learn only later it is an assumed name), the woman who has perhaps done more to define her being than even the mother whose disgrace she is. Like the letters that the illiterate Krook chalks upon the wall and then erases, leaving each one in a state of isolation and meaninglessness, until someone joins them to form the name *Jarndyce, Barbary* is left in suspension, unintelligible by itself until some consciousness is brought to bear upon it to give it meaning.

The macabre game Krook plays with Esther—he "went on quickly, until he had formed, in the same curious manner, beginning at the ends and bottoms of the letters, the word JARNDYCE"—serves as an emblem for the novel, as significant as David Copperfield's encounter with the noble art and mystery of stenography. The letters that form the name *Jarndyce* suggest the arbitrary characters of stenography "which in such a

position meant such a thing, and in such another position something
else, entirely different." Much as Mr. Venus in *Our Mutual Friend* is an
Articulator of human bones, David and Esther must connect the fragments of the past, those fossils of another time, itself timeless, and articulate those figurative letters into a coherent and meaningful whole. It is
Esther's task to recover the past—in the geological language of Dickens's time, to reconstruct it—and to articulate it through her progress,
her written memory emerging out of the sea of signs threatening to engulf her. Only at the end of *Bleak House* will all the mysteries converge
to reveal a meaning imminent in apparent chaos. If she ignores, consciously or not, the signs that may provide a clue to her identity, Esther
will remain a mystery to herself, and radically incomplete.

For Dickens, as always, understands that, in denying the past, one
becomes fixated upon it and estranged from the medium of time. Lady
Dedlock, bored to death behind the mask of her unchanging self, undergoes a process of disintegration, of internal combustion, as fatal as
that experienced by Captain Hawdon, who has chosen to acknowledge
his own annihilation through the pseudonym Nemo. Lady Dedlock believes in the story of the Ghost's Walk because she knows the past inevitably asserts itself. Like the Lady of Sir Morbury Dedlock whose history she relives, she never speaks "to any one of being crippled, or of
being in pain," but she is as deeply maimed psychically as her ghostly
predecessor was physically. In part, Esther's silence about the name *Barbary* is her attempt to deny the past, to shut out memories of her aunt's
denunciations and bitter resentment. She seeks to bury the past as she
buried the doll that was her only real companion in her childhood. But
the past cannot be buried, as her aunt's unexpected stroke reveals. With a
rather curious innocence, Esther implicitly challenges and condemns her
aunt by reading from St. John, "He that is without sin among you, let
him first cast a stone at her!" Miss Barbary's response is her desperate
attempt to justify herself, and to warn Esther: "Watch ye therefore! lest
coming suddenly he find you sleeping. And what I say unto you, I say
unto all, Watch!" (chapter 3). The lines from St. Mark remain forever
ambiguous. Perhaps Miss Barbary has been found "sleeping," or cul-
pable, in her treatment of Esther. But Esther herself may one day be
found "sleeping," under far different circumstances. The ambiguity must
be unresolved because Miss Barbary's paralysis becomes, like Lady Dedlock's, her refuge. Miss Barbary succumbs to a self immobilized into a

frightened, and suspect, rectitude. Her self-righteous condemnation of Esther's right to exist has hardened her, in Mr. Morfin's words, "from day to day"; it has left her as "susceptible as images [are] to new impressions and convictions." Mr. Morfin's words become a credo by which Miss Barbary lives and dies. Deaf, dumb, blind, and paralytic, to a million things, from habit, Miss Barbary cannot relinquish her unyielding rejection of Esther. Unable to respond to the child's plea, and to her muted rebuke, she chooses, or is reduced to, immobility—and the silence of a no longer figurative death.

Dickens is working here with a full awareness of the psychological predicaments of his characters. Miss Barbary's stroke is rooted in her own response to Esther's muted accusation. It is Dickens's knowledge of such experiences, reinforced by the objectivity potentially inherent in the double narrative, that permits him to maintain through much of *Bleak House* a remarkable detachment toward Esther. On that first night in London, as Ada sleeps and Caddy Jellyby rests her head in her lap, Esther's situation becomes clearly defined: "At length, by slow degrees, they [Ada and Caddy] became indistinct and mingled. I began to lose the identity of the sleeper resting on me. Now it was Ada; now, one of my old Reading friends from whom I could not believe I had so recently parted. Now it was the little mad woman worn out with curtseying and smiling; now, some one in authority at Bleak House. Lastly, it was no one, and I was no one" (chapter 4). Esther is not only a social nonentity because of her illegitimacy. She tends to perceive herself as a no one, and her dilemma is, in part, to become a *some one,* to say, with some kind of confidence and authenticity, either I or Me, as she apparently does in the final pages of the novel. If she fails to define, or redefine, herself in some viable way, she will run the risk of following in the steps of her father, Captain Hawdon, whose sign she encounters in the window of Krook's shop on the morning after her premonitory dream.

John Jarndyce and Bleak House provide Esther with an opportunity to define herself anew, to create an identity, however suspect. Like Edith Granger before her, though in an antithetical way, Esther is captured by the image Others have of her. She accepts the housekeeping keys and the names conferred upon her: Old Woman, Little Old Woman, Cobweb, Mrs. Shipton, Mother Hubbard, Dame Durden.[5] In the process, her "own name soon [becomes] quite lost among them" (chapter 8). Esther participates in a communal fiction that, in part, alienates her from herself and from her own name. She is submissive and eager to earn the love of others, on their terms. And she finds comfort in thinking of herself as "a methodical, old-maidish sort of foolish little person" (chapter 8). She seeks to deny or to evade the consequences of her illegitimacy by fixing herself psychologically in a time safely beyond that in which her own mother dealt, unsuccessfully, with the fact of her sexuality. For a Dame Durden, a Little Old Woman, a Mother Hubbard, there seems no threat of another dashing captain's appearing to set in motion a painful re-enactment of her mother's fate. But, in accepting this image of herself reflected in the kindly faces of those about her, Esther chooses an existence in limbo, beyond the entryway to a participation in life itself.[6]

Esther is also trying, however inadequately, to reconcile herself to her own humanity in a more general sense. All people inevitably feel, as Esther feels in her childhood, both guilty and innocent. This has nothing to do with illegitimacy or original sin. In Dickens's greatest novels, there is a full recognition of the ways in which we incur guilt and lose forever our precious innocence. In *David Copperfield*, the young David begins to perceive Annie Strong through the jealous, suspicious eyes of Mr. Wickfield, without at the time being aware that he is doing so. David becomes, however unwittingly, responsible for his misunderstanding of Annie. He is guilty *and* innocent. He has been unknowingly deceived by an adult. But later, when he becomes aware of what has happened, he must feel that his miscomprehension of Annie Strong has been a subtle violation of her integrity. This situation is not melodramatic in the way of Esther's illegitimacy, which tends to obscure the fact that, in *Bleak House,* Dickens is always getting at something more than Victorian sexual mores and their inadequacies.

Esther's dilemma is always both ontological and ethical. Her progress involves Dickens's, if not Esther's, emerging recognition that, sinned against as she may be, Esther is not fully the innocent victim. Her attempts to deal with her complex situation may involve her, like David, in the violation of others. Dickens suggests the inadequacy of the ways in which Esther chooses to know herself, and to be known by others, through her relationship with Ada and Caddy. She presides over, and is enchanted by, Richard's courtship of Ada. She is at least indirectly responsible for Caddy's marriage to Prince Turveydrop, for Caddy has sought dancing instructions to deal with the awkwardness she felt in the presence of Esther and Ada. Prince and Caddy meet secretly at Miss

Flite's and it is through Esther that she first encounters the mad old woman. Caddy's statement, "It began in your coming to our house" (chapter 14), possesses an ominous quality. Esther becomes involved, inevitably, in the sufferings of others, especially in those of Ada, through whom she tries to realize what she has denied herself. But these developments exist upon the periphery of Esther's story. It is through Esther's relationships to Jo, the illiterate crossing-sweeper, and to Lady Dedlock that Dickens explores more fully her situation and her response to it. Esther's visit to Boythorn's estate, in the company of Ada, Jarndyce, and Skimpole, leads to the inevitable meeting between her and Lady Dedlock and to a series of events culminating in her exposure to the diseased Jo and in her subsequent physical disfigurement.

The meeting occurs in the church near Chesney Wold and is introduced as the service begins, "Enter not into judgment with thy servant, O Lord, for in thy sight [shall no man living be justified]" (chapter 18). The verse from Psalm 143, with its explicit reference to judgment, returns us to the question of innocence and guilt and to that moment when Esther, however unconsciously, had challenged her godmother and precipitated the fatal stroke. As the priest reads, Esther encounters the eyes of the woman who will prove to be her mother:

Shall I ever forget the rapid beating of my heart, occasioned by the look I met, as I stood up! Shall I ever forget the manner in which those handsome proud eyes seemed to spring out of their languor, and to hold mine! It was only a moment before I cast mine down—released again, if I may say so—on my book; but I knew the beautiful face quite well, in that short space of time.

And, very strangely, there was something quickened within me, associated with the lonely days at my godmother's; yes, away even to the days when I had stood on tiptoe to dress myself at my little glass, after dressing my doll. And this, although I had never seen this lady's face before in all my life—I was quite sure of it—absolutely certain. (Chapter 18)

What Esther sees, of course, is a version of her own face. She knows the beautiful face as Guppy knew the portrait of Lady Dedlock. Upon seeing it, Guppy felt as if he "must have had a dream of that picture, you know!" (chapter 7). Esther is thrust back into the past, to her godmother's house, to her doll, and to herself on tiptoe before her little glass. It is a moment in time when she first sees herself in a mirror and becomes self-conscious. What Esther has seen in the mirror is not just a reflection of herself; rather, it is a vision of herself deeply rooted in her godmother's conception of her. Her vision of herself, even the reflection, is mediated by Miss Barbary's perception of the child. And Esther wills to be something quite different: good, industrious, contented. It is the image of herself by which she tries to live, in order to make life possible. But it is an image, however good, conditioned by the inescapable shadow of her illegitimacy. Hers is a self founded upon a twisted definition of innocence and guilt, and as such it is false.[7]

In Lady Dedlock she sees a reflection of her own face quite different from the face of one set apart by a nameless disgrace (she cannot know that Lady Dedlock is, in fact, secretly set apart as much as she). Esther encounters a potentiality quite beyond that she has imagined for herself. That lady's beautiful face becomes, "in a confused way, like a broken glass" to Esther, in which she sees "scraps of old remembrances." Appropriately, she thinks of a broken mirror. The fragments of her unintegrated past are assembling themselves mysteriously before her. The impact of Lady Dedlock's appearance is so disorienting that Esther ceases to hear the reader's voice: instead, she can hear the familiar voice of the dead Miss Barbary. Throughout this sequence, she links Lady Dedlock's face to that of the woman whom Esther thinks of not as her aunt, but as her godmother, as if to deny any real relationship to her. But the broken glass refers to the present, as well as to the past. Like Edith Dombey, before the picture-frame of her mirror but surrounded by glittering objects that, to Dombey, repeat Edith's beauty as "in so many fragments of a mirror," Esther has turned to an image mirrored in the reassuring countenances of those who surround her at Bleak House. But the image of herself fails her as it did once before in the dream in which she became "no one."

The broken glass of which she thinks suggests Esther's disintegration into so many parts, some quite terrifying and threatening. As she dwells upon the way in which Lady Dedlock has magically evoked her childhood self before her very eyes, Esther gradually becomes aware of the gaze of the French maid, Hortense. Dickens reveals in a stroke that curious triad for which he has already prepared. Hortense has been introduced as "a very neat She-Wolf imperfectly tamed," with "something indefinably keen and wan about her anatomy" (chapter 12). And, through the trope of the glass, a special relationship between Hortense and Lady Dedlock emerges, a relationship Lady Dedlock tries to deny:

One night, while having her hair undressed, my Lady loses herself in deep thought . . . , until she sees her own brooding face in the opposite glass, and a pair of black eyes curiously observing her.

"Be so good as to attend," says my Lady then, addressing the reflection of Hortense, "to your business. You can contemplate your beauty at another time."

"Pardon! It was your Ladyship's beauty."

"That," says my Lady, "you needn't contemplate at all." (Chapter 12)

The juxtaposition of Lady Dedlock's brooding face and Hortense's black eyes metonymically connects the two. But Lady Dedlock has already disguised herself in her maid's cloak to visit Captain Hawdon's grave. The merging of the two women is more or less complete. Whatever Lady Dedlock has suppressed by falling into a freezing mood—as her sister fell into the frozen immobility of paralysis—still exists within her, projected, however melodramatically, in the form of Hortense. The scene anticipates that in *A Tale of Two Cities* when Charles Darnay glances up at the glass fixed above the prisoner's box in the Old Bailey: it is like gazing into the ocean that is "one day to give up its dead."[8] The mirror does not simply reflect; it offers a glimpse into the self's depths. What Lady Dedlock sees are those eyes that always lurk within the depths of her habitually languid gaze. She characteristically rebuffs the Provence-bred Hortense and that teeming, fecund world for which Provence traditionally stands in British fiction.[9]

The triangular configuration Dickens has so deftly forged continues to haunt Esther during this visit to Boythorn's and through other episodes in *Bleak House*. For when she, with Ada and Jarndyce, takes refuge from the sudden storm in the keeper's lodge on the edge of Chesney Wold, Esther experiences a further reconfirmation of all the possibilities that the appearance of Lady Dedlock has already raised. The voice warning the girls not to sit near the window "in so exposed a place" is Lady Dedlock's, not Esther's. But Ada, responding not only to the concern in the words but to a familiar tone, turns to Esther, whose heartbeat quickens. "I had never heard the voice, as I had never seen the face," she says, "but it affected me in the same strange way. Again, in a moment, there arose before my mind innumerable pictures of myself" (chapter 18). Esther confronts, if not the intuition that this stern and beautiful woman is her mother, at least the sense that they are not so unlike. The innumerable pictures of herself that occur in her imagination suggest a world of possibilities as well as the swirl of remembered moments. And to initiate her further into the ambiguous energies and potentialities within herself and others, Esther is left, as the episode ends, with an unforgettable sight: the enraged Hortense, spurned by Lady Dedlock, removes her shoes and walks toward Chesney Wold, through the wet grass which, the lodgekeeper's wife speculates, she fancies is blood:

We passed not far from the House, a few minutes afterwards. Peaceful as it had looked when we first saw it, it looked even more so now, with a diamond spray glittering all about it, a light wind blowing, the birds no longer hushed but singing strongly, everything refreshed by the late rain, and the little carriage shining at the doorway like a fairy carriage made of silver. Still, very steadfastly and quietly walking towards it, a peaceful figure too in the landscape, went Mademoiselle Hortense, shoeless, through the wet grass. (Chapter 18)

The enchanted world of Chesney Wold and the people fortunate enough to inhabit it become fragile, delicate artifacts totally vulnerable to the implacable juggernaut moving toward them. Esther has been introduced to forces that have no place in *her* world, or so she thinks. Soon, she will, however mistakenly, become identified with these forces. She will have to deal with their implications for her own life.

Hortense's attempt to offer her services as a domestic to Esther is, in part, either a suggestion that the energies Hortense possesses exist in some form within Esther or that they may be conferred upon her magically through some proximity to the Frenchwoman. But Esther, true to her version of herself, recoils, especially from the ardor that Hortense so clearly possesses. Madame Defarge is foreshadowed by Esther's response to the maid: she "seemed to bring visibly before me some woman from the streets of Paris in the reign of terror" (chapter 23). Esther's response to Lady Dedlock remains more ambiguous and complex: it involves admiration, fear, and a yearning based on the "fancy . . . that what this lady so curiously was to me, I was to her—I mean that I disturbed her thoughts as she influenced mine, though in some different way" (chapter 23).

The three women become inextricably joined in Esther's imagination, and in the shape of the novel itself, when Jo and Esther finally meet at St. Albans. Jo has come from London in search of Jenny, the other woman in whose clothes Lady Dedlock will finally disguise herself. What happens in this meeting involves more than the inescapable taint of the disease that emanates from Tom-all-Alone's and from the cemetery where

Nemo is buried. The night is stormy and toward London "a lurid glare [overhangs] the whole dark waste." As she proceeds toward the brick-makers' cottage, Esther has "for a moment an undefinable impression of [herself] as being something different from what [she] then was" (chapter 31). This vague sense of her inauthentic condition is only confirmed by Jo's apparently delirious response to her. The boy has already seen both Lady Dedlock, disguised in her maid's cloak, and later Hortense herself in Tulkinghorn's chambers. He at first mistakes the veiled Esther for the "t'other lady" he has led to the "berryin ground." Even after Esther raises her veil and Jenny seeks to assure him that this is *her* lady standing before them, Jo remains unconvinced: "She looks to me the t'other one. It ain't the bonnet, nor yet it ain't the gownd, but she looks to me the t'other one." Jo's doubt, in the face of the assurances of Jenny and Charley, simply cannot be dispelled. At last, he makes the connection that is the most disturbing of all: "Then he hoarsely whispered Charley. 'If she ain't the t'other one, she ain't the forrenner. Is there *three* of 'em then?' Charley looked at me a little frightened. I felt half frightened at myself when the boy glared on me so" (chapter 31). The connection between Lady Dedlock, Hortense, and Esther has been established.[10]

Jo's confusion only mirrors Esther's own sense of her being different from what she has, until now, thought herself to be. To be mistaken for a Lady Dedlock or a Hortense is to be seen in some way as like them. It is not a question of how much Esther knows at this point in the novel, or the extent to which she associates herself in her own consciousness with these two women. Dickens has asserted, through plot and language, a relationship. Its full meaning may at best be working within Esther in an inarticulable way. But the moorings of her old self have been cut loose upon this stormy, disorienting night. Esther must begin to live with the possibility that, figuratively, Jo is right: there are "*three* of 'em then," floating somewhere behind the veil of Esther's public self.

The illness that follows is the natural consequence of the dilemma Esther now faces. The mask of Dame Durden no longer protects her from the complexities into which she has been pushed. She is responsible for Jo without having known him. On one level the responsibility is clearly social: no one can legitimately claim to be innocent of the horrors of Tom-all-Alone's that touch every one. But social guilt is only one element of the illness that follows. As Esther herself remarks, "It may be that if we knew more of such strange afflictions, we might be better able to alleviate their intensity" (chapter 35)—curious words to use in speaking of smallpox, but not at all inappropriate for the ontological and psychological affliction that is Esther's. The first stage of her travail is marked by blindness. In a novel obsessed with the interpretation of signs, blindness, like the illiteracy of Krook and Jo, is hardly the result of pure contingency.[11] Jo shuffles through the streets of London "in utter darkness as to the meaning, of those mysterious symbols, so abundant over the shops, and at the corners of streets, and on the doors, and in the windows!" (chapter 16). He is stone blind and dumb to the language of the written word. But Esther, too, has been accosted by mysterious symbols; she sinks into blindness through her inability, or her unwillingness, to see: to decipher and to give meaning to the signs that threaten her. Esther, too, has succumbed to the habitual self—"deaf, dumb, blind, and paralytic, to a million things, from habit."

Esther's literal and figurative blindness is a prelude to a sense of disorientation and her attempt to deal with everything she has so recently experienced. She has, in the broadest terms, been confronted with the terrible complexities of being human, complexities that transcend the fact of her illegitimacy. Her sexuality and her relatedness to others are involved. In her delirium, the stages of her life become confused and mingled "on the healthy shore," while she is separated from them by a dark lake: "At once a child, an elder girl, and the little woman I had been so happy as, I was not only oppressed by cares and difficulties adapted to each station, but by the great perplexity of endlessly trying to reconcile them. I suppose that few who have not been in such a condition can quite understand what I mean, or what painful unrest arose from this source" (chapter 35). Esther has lost a sense of unified being, and with it her usual relation to time. She perceives herself in fragments. Like the pieces of a shattered glass, each fragment mirrors back to her disparate and incompatible images of herself. The fragile self she has created, with the help of Jarndyce, Ada, and Richard, has momentarily ceased to be, broken by its contact with the very realities it was designed to evade. If she accepts the shattering of herself and the need to forge a new identity, Esther risks immersion in the world of sexuality, social injustice, and victimization inhabited by Lady Dedlock, Hortense, and Jo. This is both dangerous and frightening. It would also involve an act of disloyalty. To cease to be Dame Durden is a betrayal, implicitly, of the community that has sustained that identity through a mutual effort. And the community of Bleak House is comprised of all those for whom she most deeply cares. If the recreation of herself in new terms seems impossible, her present state of disunity offers no viable alternative: it is nonbeing.

Esther's disorder is reminiscent of that period of temporal disorientation in the life of David Copperfield after the death of Dora and prior to the events of the tempest when Ham and Steerforth drown. At that time David "came to think that the Future was walled up before [him], that the energy and action of [his] life were at an end, that [he] never could find any refuge but in the grave." Esther's sense of impasse is revealed in her frustrated yearnings for rebirth: "It seemed one long night, . . . I laboured up colossal staircases, ever striving to reach the top, and ever turned, as I have seen a worm in a garden path, by some obstruction, and labouring again" (chapter 35). This almost De Quincean labor that does not fulfill itself in birth leads Esther to that "worse time when, strung together somewhere in great black space, there was a flaming necklace, or ring, or starry circle of some kind, of which *I* was one of the beads! And when my only prayer was to be taken off from the rest, and when it was such inexplicable agony and misery to be a part of the dreadful thing" (chapter 35). The passage is almost unique in Dickens's novels. Perhaps only in *Great Expectations* does Dickens explore so fully both religious and ontological despair. Esther's prayer to be taken off from the rest is her denial of herself and the intersubjective reality that comprises the human condition. She wishes to escape from the incongruities inherent in her own humanity. There is the injustice of her illegitimate birth. There is the inevitable loss of innocence that occurs as one moves from childhood to adulthood. There is the unbearable fact that one's fate is joined, however mysteriously, with the fates of others. Esther is incapable of experiencing, at this point in her progress, an acceptance of herself and of her right to exist amidst the ambiguities of the human situation that David finally achieves within the pages of his personal history. In her illness she yearns for escape, for that refuge in the grave of which David has written. The fact of Esther's illegitimacy is now fundamentally figurative. Esther has confronted the contradictions underlying her conception of herself, contradictions that have led to the shattering of her fragile self into disparate, temporally discontinuous parts. She wants only to escape the contradictions plaguing her. When she awakens from her long night, she has failed to change significantly her idea of herself. She has been unable to accept the flaming necklace or starry circle of which she is a part.[12]

Esther seeks, in short, a simplification of the human condition through a return to that former self of willed innocence, and ignorance, to which she has become habituated. She accepts what she calls her "altered self" because it seems to offer the security she knew as Dame Durden. The absent mirrors do not go unnoticed. But when Esther speaks to Charley, there is a curious ambiguity in her question: "Yet, Charley, . . . I miss something, surely, that I am accustomed to?" (chapter 35). She can live without the old face that has marked her resemblance to Lady Dedlock, or so she thinks. Perhaps she can even live without her love for Allan Woodcourt. But to do this, she must think of the past, of the "childish prayer of that old birthday, when [she] had aspired to be industrious, contented, and true-hearted, and to do some good to some one, and win some love to [herself] if [she] could" (chapter 35). She repeats the prayer in an effort to fix herself, once again, in a state beyond temptation, a state that in some way will reconcile the various stages of her life and protect her from the shame of her unknown mother and from the ambiguous power embodied both in Lady Dedlock and Hortense. She acquiesces to the "old conspiracy to make [her] happy."

Esther knows that she has undergone some physical change. But it is only when she arrives at Boythorn's in Lincolnshire that she has the courage, finally, to look into the glass and face her altered self:

My hair had not been cut off, though it had been in danger more than once. It was long and thick. I let it down, and shook it out, and went up to the glass upon the dressing-table. There was a little muslin curtain drawn across it. I drew it back: and stood for a moment looking through such a veil of my own hair, that I could see nothing else. Then I put my hair aside, and looked at the reflection in the mirror; encouraged by seeing how placidly it looked at me. I was very much changed—O very, very much. At first, my face was so strange to me, that I think I should have put my hands before it and started back, but for the encouragement [of Jarndyce and the others] I have mentioned. (Chapter 36)

Esther moves through a number of veils, that of the muslin curtain and the veil of her own hair, toward a view of her self in the glass, a self that seems to look autonomously back at her. It is a moment of discovery echoing moments in the past, foreshadowing others in the future. It repeats her childhood emergence into self-consciousness when she first saw her face in her little glass. It calls up that moment in the church when Esther first sees Lady Dedlock and Hortense. Even poor Jo's sur-prise and terror at the sight of the veiled, and unveiled, Esther are evoked as Esther sees herself, though darkly, in the glass. All the characters in *Bleak House* are veiled, to some extent, to others and themselves. The muslin curtain and the dark hair through which Esther moves suggest levels of ignorance. The image she sees may be but another veil, another reflection floating upon the surface of the depths that Esther chooses not to plumb. She has not yet seen herself face to face: perhaps she only does so later in the novel when she pulls aside the long dank hair veiling the features of her dead mother.[13]

Gradually, the face before Esther ceases to be strange and grows more familiar. Esther pieces herself together by accepting the scarred face from which she originally pulls back; it becomes a Medusa's head, partly of her own creation, that will fix her in time and consolidate the identity Miss Barbary had tried so relentlessly to impose upon her. She submits to her aunt's perception of her as someone tainted, in preparation for the resumption of her role as "little housewife," the role forged for her by John Jarndyce. She chooses to diminish herself through this new iden-tity, altered, scarred, desexualized. But she feels a sense of loss. Her muted, "I had never been a beauty, and had never thought myself one; but I had been very different from this," and her allusion to Allan Wood-court's flowers reveal, in Esther's perhaps too quiet way, the protest ris-ing within her. But real or imagined disfigurement offers a sanctuary, even if an illusory one, from the agonies of the flaming necklace. Esther ceases to be a perfect likeness of Lady Dedlock, as her visit to Guppy will prove. No one will be able, apparently, to connect the two of them. When Lady Dedlock acknowledges her and fulfills something she has "pined for and dreamed of . . . [as] a little child," she feels "a burst of gratitude to the providence of God that I was so changed as that I never could disgrace her by any trace of likeness; as that nobody could ever now look at me, and look at her [as Hortense has done], and remotely think of any near tie between us" (chapter 36). Esther's gratitude is double-edged, to say the least. The tie binding the two, and seemingly sundered by Esther's illness, reaches beyond that between mother and daughter. The relinquished likeness is a relinquished potentiality. Esther will never encounter the situation that led to her mother's love for Captain

Hawdon and her own birth. *She* will never be humbled, as Lady Dedlock so gratifyingly is, before the living embodiment of a past indiscretion.

Esther's strange affliction becomes a denial both of her mother and herself. Her forgiveness of her mother is a terrible rebuke: "I told her that my heart overflowed with love for her; . . . [that] it was not for me, then resting for the first time on my mother's bosom, to take her to account for having given me life; but that my duty was to bless her and receive her, though the whole world turned from her" (chapter 36). How deftly the knife is turned in the wound! Esther's words to Lady Dedlock are full of Victorian rectitude. They are as suspect as the hauteur in Lady Dedlock's denial to Jo's innocent query, "You didn't know him [Nemo], did you?" (chapter 16). Dickens has captured the mother, and the daughter, in situations exposing the radical dishonesty of their lives. Lady Dedlock denies that she has known the dead law-writer. Esther implicitly denies her mother. Each response is morally and psychologically untenable. And Esther's sense of worthlessness and fear reveals how difficult it will be for her to live with the knowledge she now possesses. Lady Dedlock's letter to Esther undermines completely Esther's sense of her right to exist in the face of Miss Barbary's stern, "It would have been far better, little Esther, . . . that you had never been born!" (chapter 3). She realizes: "I had never, to my own mother's knowledge, breathed—had been buried—had never been endowed with life—had never borne a name" (chapter 36). Had never *been.* Esther is once again nameless, a no one, like Nemo. She weeps to think she is back in the world, bearing a load of troubles for herself and others. No wonder that, as she walks near Chesney Wold and the Ghost's Walk, with its stone balustrades, stone lions, and monsters, Esther imagines her echoing footsteps are those of the legendary ghost. Chesney Wold anticipates—as does the château in *Dombey and Son* before which James Carker pauses in his flight from Dombey—the St. Evrémonde château with *its* "heavy stone balustrades, and stone urns, and stone flowers, and stone faces of men, and stone heads of lions, in all directions. As if the Gorgon's head had surveyed it, when it was finished, two centuries ago" (book 2, chapter 9). Esther, running in terror from herself and everything, flees the past that exists, inert and unchanging, within the depths of her consciousness, the past as defined by her dead aunt and her mother, two others turned to stone by its relentless and pitiless gaze.[14]

Esther runs, of course, to Bleak House and to Jarndyce and Ada. She returns to her former role as Dame Durden and to her curious relationship with Ada, through whom she seems willing to live. But none of this is ever really satisfactory, for us, for Dickens, even for Esther, who remains far more knowing than even she is willing to admit:

It matters little now, how much I thought of my living mother who had told me evermore to consider her dead. I could not venture to approach her, or to communicate with her in writing, for my sense of the peril in which her life was passed was only to be equalled by my fears of increasing it. Knowing that *my mere existence as a living creature was an unforeseen danger* in her way, I could not always conquer that terror of myself which had seized me when I first knew the secret. At no time did I dare to utter her name. I felt as if I did not even dare to hear it. (Chapter 43, emphasis mine)

In retrospect it may matter little. But *then* it mattered a great deal. Nor is it simply the melodramatic plight of Lady Dedlock that is central. Rather, it is that Esther dares not to utter her mother's name, dares not even to hear it. And if it were possible, she would perhaps choose not even to think it. She resorts to a device that will drive Lady Dedlock out of her very consciousness. Perhaps the words she repeats to herself are her own nickname—Dame Durden, Dame Durden, Dame Durden. She remains in full flight from her mother and herself. To make the flight complete, to consolidate her loss into something permanent and irreversible—for the loss involves, really, a state of mind or being—she accepts John Jarndyce's proposal, knowing that in this act she is being untrue to herself.

Esther commits herself to John Jarndyce not out of love or passion but out of gratitude; she is aware that she will "become the dear companion of his remaining life" (chapter 44). She chooses to acquiesce once more to that conspiracy to make her happy that has in it the element of coercion even Esther can detect. But her decision to marry Jarndyce is, finally, her own doing. She is repeating her mother's fateful, and fatal, decision to marry Sir Leicester Dedlock. Esther will fall into her own version of a freezing mood, a condition of stasis only apparently beyond the realities of time and change, innocence and guilt. As she reads Jarndyce's letter of proposal, Esther girds herself for the one thing to do. She acknowledges, "Still I cried very much; not only in the fulness of my heart after reading the letter, not only in the strangeness of the prospect—for it was strange though I had expected the contents—

but as if something for which there was no name or distinct idea were
indefinitely lost to me. I was very happy, very thankful, very hopeful; but
I cried very much" (chapter 44). This is quintessential Esther. It reveals
not just the enduring, self-negating touchstone of goodness, but a woman
who is relinquishing something, however threatening to her, of real
value—the opportunity for passion in her life. Esther's choice leads to
the almost ghoulish act in which she kisses the sleeping Ada and presses
Allan Woodcourt's withered flowers to Ada's lips before she burns them
and they turn to dust: the same kind of dust existing within the com-
busting selves of so many in the novel. She will sacrifice her own legitimate desire for self-fulfillment and live vicariously through Ada and
Richard. But even this morbid act of self-sacrifice occurs only after Esther has conducted a curious dialogue with herself in her old glass. She
talks to her reflected face, even holds up her finger at it, in her determination to reestablish that "composed look you [the face in the glass]
comforted me with, my dear, when you showed me such a change!"
(chapter 44). She gazes again at the Medusa's head, her own scarred
face, and in effect turns herself to stone.

Dickens knows very well that this will not do, for a number of reasons. Apart from that Victorian commitment to the satisfying happy
ending, there is in Dickens's imagination a streak of integrity that modern readers continue to underestimate or to ignore. This integrity and
the equally fierce will to overcome the very paradoxes he has posed generate the fixated structures in so many of Dickens's novels, both early
and late. Time and again we see a hero or heroine reenacting the same
experience or a slightly transmuted version of it. This is true of the early
Oliver Twist, of *David Copperfield*, even of the last completed novel, *Our
Mutual Friend*. The novels begin with a paradox imbedded in the past,
recurrently involving someone burdened with that confused sense of innocence and guilt, inextricably combined. The novels proceed to unravel
the very Gordian knot that, by definition, seems impervious even to the
sword of Dickens's imagination. In *Bleak House* Esther's acceptance of
John Jarndyce's proposal is her attempt to deal with the old Dickensian
paradox. But her meeting with the returned Allan Woodcourt illustrates
how intolerable her situation has become. By now Esther is in dialogue,
not with herself, but with more than one self conjured up by her imagination and by the versions of her glimpsed, however darkly, in the faces
of others. Each self, each potentiality, is designed in one way or another

to obscure the traces of a deadening past. No matter how earnestly Esther may address the Esther in the mirror, the legitimate longings for life return: "I saw that he was very sorry for me. I was glad to see it. I felt for my old self as the dead may feel if they ever revisit these scenes. I was glad to be tenderly remembered, to be gently pitied, not to be quite forgotten" (chapter 45). Esther sees, in part, what she wishes to see in Allan Woodcourt's manner; she reads the signs and tokens he presents to confirm the wisdom of her decision and to keep her old self down. But that self is not dead: it exists beyond the face she sees in her glass, and even in the eyes of others who are equally mirrors for her. Like the ghost of the Ghost's Walk, the old self's footsteps can be heard in Esther's consciousness and in the consciousness of others. The willed deadness that Esther as Dame Durden feels must be confronted and dispelled. If not, it will become a permanent condition: she will be no less a sleeping beauty than her mother, Lady Dedlock.

The concluding episodes of the novel represent Dickens's efforts to resolve the impasse, to sever the Gordian knot he has himself so deftly tied. Through Sir Leicester Dedlock's stroke and the pursuit of Lady Dedlock by Esther and Inspector Bucket, Dickens seeks to resolve Esther's situation. Sir Leicester's continued loyalty to his wife, even after he has been felled by the news of her past and reduced to almost total silence, plays off revealingly against Esther's response to her mother. For he accepts and acknowledges his wife, as she is, in the presence of witnesses: "In case I should not recover, in case I should lose both my speech and the power of writing, . . . I desire to say, and to call you all to witness . . . that I am on unaltered terms with Lady Dedlock. That I assert no cause whatever of complaint against her. . . . Say this to herself, and to every one" (chapter 58). Sir Leicester does not succumb, in his suffering, to the habitual values of his dying class. He transcends his habitual self to perform a noble gesture and an act of love. There is no note of reproach in his words as there has been in Esther's response to her mother. Sir Leicester's compassion reminds us of Esther's failure to accept her mother, and herself.

So Esther and Bucket move through the snow into which the stricken Sir Leicester stares. "The giddy whirl of white flakes and icy blots" suggests—like the pages upon which Esther writes her progress—the ultimate inscrutability of the world in which these characters find themselves. Her previous illness, an abortive Carlylean "Baphometic Fire-baptism," has not produced a "Spiritual New-birth." The earlier experiences are reenacted, but this time the process of rebirth involves the more traditional baptismal process of immersion. The disorientation through which Esther passed during her "fever-paroxyms" returns. As she rides with Bucket, she feels that she is in a dream, that she is entering the labyrinthine world of streets, bridges, and serpentining river that is as much internal as external. She is losing herself once more, descending into a world in which she may again encounter the ambiguous self she has relinquished or finally succeed in exorcising its presence forever.

The "something wet" that Bucket and another man—described as "dank and muddy, in long swollen sodden boots and a hat like them" (chapter 57)—inspect proves not to be the body of a drowned Lady Dedlock. But Esther continues to fear, and perhaps to hope, that the tide in its rush toward her will cast her mother's body at the horses' feet. In her dreamlike state Esther's identification with her mother is now so complete that even the female figure flitting past the carriage is as much herself as Lady Dedlock: "In my memory, the lights upon the bridge are always burning dim; the cutting wind is eddying round the homeless woman whom we pass; the monotonous wheels are whirling on; and the light of the carriage-lamps reflected back, looks palely in upon me— a face, rising out of the dreaded water" (chapter 57). But whose face rises out of the water? The entire sequence is constructed upon the logic of dreams. Esther, Lady Dedlock, and the homeless prostitute are one. In this phantasmagoric setting, Esther gazes into the night, the water, or both, and looks into a watery mirror out of which rises not her mother's face, but her own: the face of the unquiet ghost that has not been charmed by the spell Esther has tried so vainly to cast upon it.

Dickens has transported Esther back into the past, to earlier events with which she has not come to terms. She is returned to the brickmakers' cottage and to Jo's unnerving query: "If she ain't the t'other one, she ain't the forrenner. Is there *three* of 'em then?" (chapter 31). Verbal parallels to Jo's words occur throughout the events following Tulkinghorn's murder. The arrested George Rouncewell recalls that on the night of the murder he "saw a shape so like Miss Summerson's go by [him] in the dark, that [he] had half a mind to speak to it" (chapter 52). Esther shudders at George's words: she thinks at once of Lady Dedlock. Within the larger structure of the novel, beyond Esther's consciousness, we see that, figuratively, all three women—Esther, Lady Dedlock, and

Hortense—are placed at the scene of the crime. George's observation becomes but another sign or token to be understood before the mysteries of Tulkinghorn's murder and Esther's identity can be fully resolved. When they arrive at the brickmakers' cottage, Esther and Bucket learn, in the words of Jenny's husband, that "one went right to Lunnun, and t'other went right from it." Once again Jo's words are echoed. The former confusion of identities is reinforced. Esther is back at the moment when she first *must* have perceived, however darkly, the implications of her similarity to Lady Dedlock and Hortense. The old triad reasserts itself once more, as it did when Esther gazed from the carriage window at the homeless woman in the dark. Esther and Lady Dedlock are fixed into an apparently eternal configuration, of which they are the two constants; only the third term alters: first Hortense, then the homeless woman of the streets, now Jenny.

Under the pressure of these most recent events, Esther retraces more and more closely the course of her earlier illness. She is blind to the signs at which Bucket so eagerly grasps. She begins to lose her sense of time and feels, "in a strange way, never to have been free from the anxiety under which [she] then [labours]" (chapter 57). But on this occasion the psychic laboring is designed to bring forth a more legitimate offspring. Esther has begun to be able to think of her mother, even if in death, and to speak of her, even if only in a whisper to Inspector Bucket. She is moving toward a gesture of loyalty and acceptance like that Sir Leicester made in speech and writing, in the presence of witnesses. Esther's moment of what should be authentic rebirth approaches. As it does, the falling snow continues to melt and finds its way into the moving carriage; the wetness penetrates her dress. Esther and Bucket descend further into the labyrinthine London streets, moving inexorably toward Nemo's grave and Lady Dedlock.[15]

The rhythms of Esther's previous suffering have come finally to dominate Dickens's imaginative conception of the search for Lady Dedlock. Once the parallels between these two critical episodes in Esther's life become established, Bucket's lecture to the near-maddened Mrs. Snagsby becomes curiously inevitable: "And Toughey—him as you call Jo—was mixed up in the same business, and no other; and the law-writer that you know of, was mixed up in the same business, and no other; and your husband, with no more knowledge of it than your great grandfather, was mixed up (by Mr. Tulkinghorn, deceased, his best customer) in the same business, and no other; and the whole bileing of people was mixed up in the same business, and no other" (chapter 59). Bucket's prosaic litany, with its persistent refrain takes us, and Esther, back to that "flaming necklace, or ring, or starry circle of some kind, of which [she] was one of the beads!" Bucket's matter-of-factness, his wry acceptance of the unthinkable, makes it all too clear that no one can cease to be a part of the dreadful thing. No process of physical or psychic disfigurement can free an individual, even an Esther, from participation in the many mysteries in the novel. The only viable response to such mysteries, though it need not be like Bucket's too easy professional acceptance, is one's immersion into the fictive world of *Bleak House*.

As she approaches the figure of the woman lying before the gate to the burial ground, in which her father's body has been placed, Esther experiences not just the melting and dissolution that her mother has undergone since the disclosure of the great secret: Esther melts within herself. She remembers "that the stained house fronts put on human shapes and looked at [her]; that great water-gates seemed to be opening and closing in [her] head, or in the air; and that the unreal things were more substantial than the real" (chapter 59). The unreal *is* more substantial than the real. The "clogged and bursting gutters and water-spouts" are within: her state of mind, associated with the breaking of the waters, is the real truth of this moment. The fixed and frozen waters of the self break apart, melt: the waters within her flow once more. Esther participates once more in the flux of time. The tide of the river rushes at her, to deliver the body of her mother at her feet: "I passed on to the gate, and stooped down. I lifted the heavy head, put the long dank hair aside, and turned the face. And it was my mother, cold and dead."

The death of Lady Dedlock is, of course, disturbing in many ways. Esther's inability to understand that it is *not* Jenny, the mother of the dead child, before the graveyard gate reveals her refusal to experience the truth directly: Jenny is a metonymy for Lady Dedlock, the dead child is a substitute for Esther herself. Esther wills that death—the only satisfactory punishment to the Victorian mind—for the sin that Lady Dedlock has committed. And Dickens—through Nemo, Krook, Tulkinghorn, Miss Barbary, and others—has asserted throughout the novel that certain ways of being constitute a corrosive death-in-life leading to literal death. Lady Dedlock has lived too long with her secret, with her bored and frozen self, to survive. The denial of time and of the ontological imperative to change takes its necessary toll.

But what remains most disquieting is that Esther comes face to face with her mother only in death; she sees her, in the presence of witnesses, only after her mother is no longer the kind of threat a living Lady Dedlock poses. When Esther pulls aside the veil of hair, as she once pulled aside her own hair before the mirror, to see that the heavy head is *not* Jenny's, the moment seems emptied of its full meaning. Cold and dead, no longer passionate, haughty, and alive, Lady Dedlock offers nothing really dangerous to encounter. And, in dying for her own sins, she seems also to atone for those that have accrued to Esther as an essentially innocent participant in the "dreadful thing" called the human condition.

The endings of Dickens's novels are rarely satisfactory. Inseparable from the imaginative integrity already mentioned is an equally powerful desire to eradicate much that is so effectively dramatized. No honest reader can be really comfortable with the concluding pages of the novel. Esther's marriage to Allan Woodcourt, their retreat to a virtual reproduction of the original Bleak House are, I think, discordant notes. But there is evidence that Dickens himself is aware of the falseness of the ending and works to emphasize the arbitrariness of it. For Esther's happiness is achieved in the midst of general misery. Richard Carstone dies. Ada becomes the captive of Jarndyce's coercive benevolence. Caddy Jellyby's baby is deaf and dumb, her husband an invalid. Even Mrs. Snagsby's jealousy reminds us that marriage is no final answer to the human capacity for the irrational: there will always be Mrs. Snagsbys convinced of their husbands' infidelities—and there will always be, in fact, unfaithful husbands and unfaithful lovers.

The double narrative itself helps us to retain a complex awareness of things. A final description of Chesney Wold precedes Esther's final words about herself and her felicity:

Thus Chesney Wold. With so much of itself abandoned to darkness and vacancy; with so little change under the summer shining or the wintry lowering; so sombre and motionless always—no flag flying now by day, no rows of lights sparkling by night; with no family to come and go, no visitors to be the souls of pale cold shapes of rooms, no stir of life about it;—passion and pride, even to the stranger's eye, have died away from the place in Lincolnshire, and yielded it to dull repose (Chapter 66).

It is a place inhabited by invalids with blighted dreams, an asylum for those who cannot deal with the new hell that Mr. Rouncewell, the iron-master, is now creating to replace the hell of the dying aristocracy. It is a place beyond time and change, with "no stir of life about it." Thus Chesney Wold. Thus Bleak House in Yorkshire. Perhaps Allan Woodcourt and Esther, surrounded by the blighted lives of their friends, are no less refugees from an alien world than are Volumnia, Mrs. Rouncewell, George, and Sir Leicester.

Bleak House ends, as it begins, in ambiguity. Esther seems to have gained the right to exist. She observes, "The people even praise Me as the doctor's wife. The people even like Me as I go about, and make so much of me that I am quite abashed" (chapter 67). Esther seems at last to possess an identity, even if it is primarily that of the doctor's wife. And, yet, this gentle affirmation is not the conclusion of Esther's narrative. Rather, Esther finds herself before a figurative glass, puzzling over the image that is reflected there:

> "My dear Dame Durden," said Allan, drawing my arm through his, "do you ever look in the glass?"
> "You know I do; you see me do it."
> "And don't you know that you are prettier than you ever were?"
> I did not know that; I am not certain that I know it now. (Chapter 67)

This is not simply Esther at her self-abasing worst. There is no reason to assume that the face she sees now in her glass is any more herself than the altered face that met her eyes after her illness. She lives in a relationship to the image of herself that she perceives in her glass, in her imagination, in the faces of others. But whether the image is truly herself can never be known. Even the words of others cannot be fully trusted. Allan Woodcourt has never known Esther completely. She has been quite forthright when she tells him quietly that during and following her illness she has had selfish thoughts. Woodcourt's response resonates throughout the final exchange of the novel: "You do not know what all around you see in Esther Summerson" (chapter 61). But what others choose to see in Esther, just as what Mr. Dombey chooses to see in Edith, may be no more than their own conception of her. Ultimately, neither Woodcourt nor Jarndyce can affirm the absolute validity of that face they see. Esther, after all, has found herself at the conclusion of her progress in but another conspiracy to make her, and others, happy. To be known as Dame Durden is not, finally, to be Dame Durden. This version of Esther may not be consonant with what she truly is. We are left, with Esther, as with Edith Dombey, not seeing face to face, but looking through a glass darkly, seeking the forever elusive self floating within the mirror's depths beyond the reflection on its surface. The veil between the self and self-knowledge is never fully raised.

Esther may not have succeeded in becoming truly the novelist of her self; she may well be, as Dame Durden, not an original, but a plagiarist, modeling herself upon the idea that others have of her. There is, however, no end, no period, to *Bleak House* or to the story of Esther's unfolding self. There is a dash, a hiatus, and no more: for the living self must continue to evolve. We encounter yet another mystery. Esther remains as enigmatic, to us and to herself, as the Roman figure of Allegory floating upon the ceiling of Tulkinghorn's chambers, a silent witness whose pointing hand is subject to the arbitrary suppositions of the excited imagination, and to endless interpretation.

Chapter 4

> "What the Father has made, the
> Son can make and enjoy; but has
> also work of his own appointed
> him. Thus all things wax, and roll
> onwards; Arts, Establishments,
> Opinions, nothing is completed,
> but ever completing."
> —Teufelsdröckh, in *Sartor Resartus*

> "In the beginning was the Deed!"
> —Goethe, *Faust;*
> Freud, *Totem and Taboo*

The Poetics of Impasse

A Tale of Two Cities has, for too long, been Sydney Carton's novel. The sheer melodramatic force of his last, unspoken words continues to obscure the significance of Charles Darnay's ethical and ontological dilemma. Of course, Darnay is all too often a prig, a bourgeois pilgrim en route, like David Copperfield, to a secular celestial city. But he is, however ambiguously, the novel's hero. It is Carton, not Darnay, who is the foil. In the popular imagination, their roles are commonly reversed. For who can resist either the novel's insistence in that cadenced conclusion,

"It is a far, far better thing that I do, than I have ever done; it is a far, far better rest that I go to than I have ever known"; or memories of Ronald Coleman as Sydney Carton? For Dickens himself, Sydney Carton exercises a powerful fascination, as did Carton's precursor, Richard Wardour, a character in Wilkie Collins's *The Frozen Deep*. Dickens helped to fashion the character of Wardour and then acted the part in private, and finally, public performances of the dramatization in 1857: Wardour, like Carton, is a man who chooses death as he saves the life of a rival. *A Tale of Two Cities* does not specifically emerge out of Dickens's suspicious identification with Wardour, but *The Frozen Deep* works its subversive influence upon a novel examining the French Revolution.[1]

Its ostensible subject, revolution and social change, suggests at once that *A Tale of Two Cities* is serious in ways *The Frozen Deep* is not. In the prophetic first chapter of the novel, Dickens seeks to invoke a revitalized historical imagination alert to the meaning of the past and alive to the need for social change in the present. But the incantatory phrases of the opening pages finally give way to a nightmare vision of social chaos and personal impasse. The French Revolution *becomes* the Carmagnole, a frenzied dance in which dehumanized revelers, their individual and even sexual identities obscured by their depravity, belie the original promise of the Revolution. The Carmagnole speaks of timeless, dionysian forces beyond history.

In a novel exploring the imperative of social change and the need to abandon obsolete systems of government, Dickens reveals his profound pessimism about such change. His pessimism also informs his exploration of the predicaments of the characters whose lives are influenced by the progress of the Revolution. The downfall of a decadent aristocracy becomes the context for the individual who must encounter the reality of the social situation into which he is born and of which he must make some sense. It is Charles Darnay, not Sydney Carton, who confronts the challenge to create personal history as defined by Maurice Merleau-Ponty in the essay, "Cézanne's Doubt": "The very decisions which transform us are always made in reference to a factual situation; such a situation can of course be accepted or refused, but it cannot fail to give us our impetus nor to be for us, as a situation 'to be accepted' or 'to be refused,' the incarnation for us of the value we give to it."[2] Merleau-Ponty's words are significant both for Dickens the artist and for Darnay the character, whose historical situation Dickens hopes to illuminate. Darnay, born into the French aristocracy, with its tradition of social repression and violence, must choose either to accept or to refuse the factual situation that is his father's legacy to him. He inevitably becomes responsible for the values he sees as incarnated in that legacy. But it is Dickens who will imagine the historical situation in such a way that a "terror of history," in Mircea Eliade's words, will pervade the social and the personal dimensions of the novel and generate a profound longing, on the part of Dickens and his characters, to move beyond time, to be released from the need to engender personal history as depicted in *David Copperfield* and *Bleak House*.[3]

When he claims, in *The Historical Novel*, that the French Revolution serves only as a romantic background to the fates of the central characters in *A Tale of Two Cities*, Georg Lukács is responding to the pessimism of Dickens's vision and to an ahistorical thrust in the novel.[4] Lukács, the subtle Marxist critic, senses the emerging lure of the archetypal for Dickens in the way in which he imagines change and renders the origins of the Revolution. Dickens, as a subtle bourgeois novelist, imagines historical situations in domestic, familial terms. Most readers of *A Tale of Two Cities*, and I include myself, tend to forget that the novel, literally and figuratively, originates in a rape. The dying woman whom the St. Evrémonde twins summon Doctor Manette to attend, on a December night in 1757, will prove to be the ravished sister of Thérèse Defarge. The episode is charged with social and historical implications: the rape points to the ruthless exploitation of one class by another, and to the consequences that must follow. But the rape has other, more volatile implications that come to dominate the novel. In their patriarchal relationship to their tenants, the St. Evrémonde twins prey upon those who stand, figuratively, in the place of sons and daughters to them. Unwittingly, Doctor Manette, himself a potentially rebellious son, finds himself in the midst of a primal scene in which the figurative father is engaged in dark and unspeakable acts.[5]

Dickens has returned to *Dombey and Son* and to earlier novels like *Nicholas Nickleby* and *Barnaby Rudge*. He invokes the "family constellation" of which Erik Erikson writes in his critique of Freud, with the "isolated individual forever projecting his infantile family constellation on the 'outer world.'"[6] In initiating a family drama, Dickens depicts a national struggle as a generational one, obscuring the significance of ideology and class. The conflict between generations presents itself as recur-

ring and inescapable, not subject to amelioration as social conditions
are, at least hypothetically, subject to change. Generation is forever pitted
against generation; sons and daughters writhe forever in the grasp of
unyielding fathers. And it is Charles Darnay, not Sydney Carton, whose
career reveals the son's complex, perhaps doomed, struggle to free himself from the father's tyranny.

The unyielding nature of the father, and the past for which he stands,
is embodied in the St. Evrémonde château. The building itself has been
anticipated in the stone château before which James Carker pauses in his
flight from Mr. Dombey; and in Chesney Wold, another stony monument to a dying class: "It was a heavy mass of building, that château of
Monsieur the Marquis, with a large stone court-yard before it, and two
stone sweeps of staircase meeting in a stone terrace before the principal
door. A stony business altogether . . . [as] if the Gorgon's head had surveyed it, when it was finished, two centuries ago."[7] The inertia of the
French aristocracy, its stony indifference to the needs of the poor, its ar-
rogant effort to deny time and to perpetuate itself forever are *there* in
Ruskinian terms. The present Marquis is no more than an extension of
the house, at best a living version of one of the stone faces adorning it.
He gazes at the world from behind his "fine mask" of stone, enduring a
self-inflicted paralysis as he speaks for his class, and the primacy of the
father and the past. His charge, as he sees it, is to transmit to his nephew,
Darnay, the gorgon's spell under which *he* has lived, the St. Evrémonde
legacy of social and personal repression. For the Marquis, "Repression is
the only lasting philosophy" (book 2, chapter 9). In denying the claims
of those beneath him and the fact of his own mortality, the Marquis is
almost as dead as the gargoyles his own face resembles. He is indis-
tinguishable from his château. The pile of stones, like the dust mounds
of Old John Harmon in *Our Mutual Friend,* expresses the father's determination to perpetuate himself, in defiance of time and his heirs, even
through life-denying forms.

The Marquis, as the twin of Darnay's dead father, stands in the place
of the biological father as his surrogate. His determination to make Darnay accept his "natural destiny" is the father's desire to establish the son's
dependence upon him and, thus, the father's mastery of the son.[8] Darnay's sense of the wrongs perpetrated by the family involves him in a
complex relationship both to the uncle and to the dead father. His defiance of his uncle's command that he accept his destiny is an attack upon

the past—the "father's time"—upon the father himself: "[I am] bound
to a system that is frightful to me, responsible for it, but powerless in it;
seeking . . . to have mercy and to redress; and tortured by seeking assis-
tance and power in vain" (book 2, chapter 9). Darnay speaks, far more
directly than usual, for all the troubled sons and daughters of Dickens's
later novels. They confront the father's authority, will, and legacy, which
bind them to the past, to sterile repetitions of the habitual stance of the
dead father. In *Our Mutual Friend*, the all too literal Harmon Will tempts
John Harmon into an acceptance of his father's twisted values, into becoming a mere instrument or appendage of his father. In acquiescing,
Harmon would forfeit his right to be a father on his own terms. To Darnay, the Marquis speaks of the primacy of the father's time—a chronicle
of social injustice, murder, and rape. In his defiance, Darnay renounces a
dead, and a potentially deadening, past: he affirms his right to create a
new, more viable tradition.[9]

On the night of Darnay's formal renunciation of his country, his
property, and his family name, Gaspard assassinates the Marquis St.
Evrémonde. The two events merge in the narrative line of the novel. But
this is not melodramatic coincidence. Darnay's renunciation is a form of
rebellion: he has dealt a fatal blow to his uncle, his family, and the repug-
nant values of the past. The Marquis's murder serves as a seal to Darnay's
decision, made five years before, to confer upon himself a new name and
a new identity as a good bourgeois. The implications of Darnay's act,
metonymically fused with Gaspard's, are all too clear. The mender of
roads, who brings the news of Gaspard's execution to the Defarges, has
heard the villagers whispering "that because [Gaspard] has slain Monseigneur, and because Monseigneur was the father of his tenants—
serfs—what you will—he will be executed as a parricide" (book 2, chapter 15). The bankrupt feudalism of Bourbon France still tries to assert the
validity of the patriarchal relationship between master and tenant that it
has itself subverted. The dead Marquis has failed in every way as the father of his peasants, even as the surrogate father of his nephew. But the
inviolable person of the father remains a cornerstone of the philosophy
of repression by which the Marquis lives, and dies. Assassins like Gaspard have been traditionally dealt with as parricides. Their punishment
is a warning to every restive son: "One old man says at the fountain, that
his right hand, armed with the knife, will be burnt off before his face;
that, into wounds which will be made in his arms, his breast, and his legs,

there will be poured boiling oil, melted lead, hot resin, wax, and sul-
phur; finally, that he will be torn limb from limb by four strong horses"
(book 2, chapter 15). The assassin's right hand, armed with the knife, is
mutilated so that no other hand or arm will be raised against the father.
The assassin's body is so completely violated that no one at the execution
may think even of his body as his own; it belongs to the father. The
body, the self, is subject to mutilation at the father's whim. To threaten
the father, even as Darnay does, is to commit the ultimate sin against the
society and the past for which the patriarchal figure stands.[10]

Gaspard's execution is less barbaric than those in earlier reigns: he is
merely hanged. But vestiges of the old ritual persist: "On the top of the
gallows is fixed the knife, blade upwards, with its point in the air" (book
2, chapter 15). The knife is symbolic by design, standing for the hand and
arm that wielded it, while conjuring up the old terror of the father's revenge upon the sons who challenge him. By bringing Darnay and Gaspard together upon the night of the Marquis's assassination, Dickens
figuratively unites them. Darnay, in his act of renunciation, has incurred
the guilt of the parricide.

The trial in the Old Bailey occurs before the Marquis's death, but it
serves, in spite of its mockery of justice, to raise the complex issue of
Darnay's guilt. Darnay's perception of the crowd in the courtroom anticipates the description of the executions of Gaspard and those parricides who were his predecessors: "The accused, who was (and who knew
he was) being mentally hanged, beheaded, and quartered, by everybody
there, neither flinched from the situation, nor assumed any theatrical air
in it" (book 2, chapter 2). Treason and parricide are one, the punishment
for either crime the same. Darnay is figuratively on trial for his continuing rebellion against France (not England) and the father. But surely evil
fathers, like corrupt regimes, *must* be defied. The son is not obligated to
acquiesce to a tyrannical father or to the past he embodies. But if the
son's defiance, regardless of its form, is perceived by father and son as
parricide, the son's own sense of his necessary act becomes shrouded in
guilt. If the need to create new personal and social forms leads to the
original sin against the father, it becomes a task from which most men
shrink. Self-assertion, viewed always as parricide, becomes impossible.

Darnay's muted heroism lies in his effort to change and to become
free of the father through the creation, ex nihilo, of a new identity. In
this he incurs the parricide's guilt. Nonetheless, his remains a flawed re-

nunciation, a suspect rebellion. His dying mother, in imploring him to redress existing wrongs, has committed him to a Sisyphean labor. Darnay falters before his all-too-accurate perception of the misery and ruin about him. He speaks of a "curse" on the land, and thinks only of placing the St. Evrémonde property "into some hands better qualified to free it slowly (if such a thing is possible) from the weight that drags it down" (book 2, chapter 9). But there are no hands better qualified than his own. He may not delegate his responsibilities to others, to minor functionaries like the befuddled Gabelle. In his renunciation Darnay reveals a tendency to self-deception. He wants to obliterate the past, to elude the responsibility he has acknowledged as his alone.

The significance of Darnay's revolt is undermined by other factors. Through his spies the Marquis has learned of his nephew's relationship to Doctor Manette and Lucie. The Marquis is a cynic, reveling in ironies of which Darnay cannot be aware. But cynics more than occasionally touch the raw nerve of truth: "A Doctor with a daughter. Yes. So commences the new philosophy!" (book 2, chapter 9). For the Marquis, Darnay is fulfilling his destiny, repeating a version of that act to which Doctor Manette became an unwilling witness. The Marquis also senses that Darnay is a little *too* eager to accept the idea of a curse upon the St. Evrémondes. Darnay calls England his refuge. But it is not England as much as the Manette household in Soho that lures Darnay away from his native France. The "new philosophy" of which the Marquis speaks with such disdain may, after all, be founded primarily on Darnay's selfish desire for Lucie and the tranquility over which she presides. The son's rebellion, with all its inherent risks, has been almost emptied of meaning. Darnay faces a new risk that his act of rebellion, incomplete as it is, will have no real significance for his personal history. In proclaiming the Deed, of which both Faust and Freud speak, Darnay has not entered into the performance of those acts implicit in his words. As an historical being who must realize himself through the Deed, he becomes alienated from the medium of time. He is unable to move onward, to continue the pilgrimage of being. Only later will Darnay fully encounter the unreality of his claims for himself. He is a parricide who has not accepted, for various reasons, the implications and the consequences of his actions: he has defied a primal taboo, and achieved nothing.[11]

In fleeing the social and personal paralysis embodied in the St. Evrémonde château, Darnay unwittingly embraces it. He moves from an un-

yielding past toward a tentative future with Lucie that is, itself, but an-
other encounter with everything he has denied. He is Oedipus fleeing
Corinth, only to find himself on the road to Thebes. The trial in the Old
Bailey, quite apart from its chronological place in the novel, introduces
Darnay to the fate with which he dimly struggles throughout *A Tale of
Two Cities*. His guilt is multiple and paradoxical: he is the would-be parricide and the man for whom the act has had no historical meaning. He
is fixed in an untenable situation, aware of a sense of guilt that is finally
ontological in nature: he is in a treasonous relationship to himself and
others.

The trial of Darnay in the Old Bailey crystallizes his situation. Over
Darnay's head "there [is] a mirror, to throw the light down upon him":

> Crowds of the wicked and the wretched had been reflected in it, and had passed
> from its surface and this earth's together. Haunted in a most ghastly manner that
> abominable place would have been, if the glass could ever have rendered back its
> reflections, as the ocean is one day to give up its dead. *Some passing thought of the
> infamy and disgrace for which it had been reserved, may have struck the prisoner's mind*
> . . . . he looked up; and when he saw the glass his face flushed. (Book 2, chap-
> ter 2, emphasis mine).

This is a uniquely Dickensian moment. It echoes the moment when Esther Summerson moves through a series of figurative veils to confront
the reflection of the strange face in the mirror. It anticipates those violent episodes in *Our Mutual Friend* when John Harmon and Eugene
Wrayburn break through the light reflected upon the surface of the
Thames, to enter the river's depths. Darnay's reflection mingles, if only
in his own imagination, with the reflections of the wicked and the
wretched who once stood where he now stands. The experience defines
Darnay's unconscious relationship to himself and to others. Momentarily, Darnay has looked into the hidden currents of himself, those currents suggested in Dickens's brooding meditation in the third chapter of
the novel: "No more can I look into the depths of this unfathomable
water, wherein, as momentary lights glanced into it, I have had glimpses
of buried treasure and *other things* submerged" (book 1, chapter 3, emphasis mine). The face floating beneath the mirror's surface cannot be
effaced because it exists at some level within Darnay's consciousness and,
he senses, within the consciousness of others. In ways he does not yet
acknowledge, he shares in the guilt of all those who have stood in the

prisoner's dock and who have been condemned rather than exonerated. The Marquis St. Evrémonde has failed to turn Darnay into another stone figure like himself. But, the ambiguities of Darnay's flawed rebellion have, ironically, fixed Darnay's guilt-ridden image of himself. During his trial Darnay pulls back from his moment of intuitive self-knowledge. But this vision of himself lurks within Darnay, waiting to return from the depths, as the ocean is one day to give up its dead.

Dickens has suggested forms of culpability and their consequences, unacknowledged by any court of law, but present in the court of one's own consciousness. Yet, for much of *A Tale of Two Cities,* he avoids a direct exploration of the impact of Darnay's bad faith upon his life. Rather, he explores Darnay's condition indirectly. Even Sydney Carton, as the "Double of coarse deportment," only cryptically signals that beneath the façade of Darnay's conventional self there is a deep-seated dislocation of the spirit. As the jury deliberates, Darnay and Carton stand side by side, reflected in the glass above them. A process of displacement occurs, as it does later in the novel in the metonymic relationship of Darnay and Gaspard. The mirror fleetingly contains two identical reflections. But only fleetingly, for Carton's reflection usurps Darnay's, at least that reflection Darnay has glimpsed buried in the mirror, and in the self. Detached from its origin, it gains an autonomous existence of its own. Carton suggests Darnay's passive and guilty self, the self that can tell Lucie, "I am like one who died young. All my life might have been" (book 2, chapter 13). He attests to the state of paralysis in which the respectable Darnay will, in fact, be living until the outbreak of the Revolution.[12]

This relationship between counterparts underlies all that happens when Darnay and Carton are left alone together in the darkness outside the Old Bailey. Darnay is still "frightfully confused regarding time and place"; he feels "hardly . . . to belong to this world again" (book 2, chapter 4). Under such circumstances, before the reprieved conventional self has managed to reestablish its primacy, the shadow self asserts its existence. Carton, only now, and perhaps never again, speaks freely of his own self-abhorrence and warns his Double of the dangers facing him. Carton, an artist of despair, knows the subtle ways in which the will may be subverted. His own sense of the blight on him, to which he has resigned himself, has attuned him to the same blight secretly at work in others. He tries to pierce the complacency of Darnay, who may eventually misuse his own talents, but he fails. The episode ends with Carton in earnest discourse with *his* image, reflected in a glass upon the tavern wall. He has perceived a version of himself from which he is irrevocably cut off: he is as alienated from conventional potentialities within himself as Darnay seems to be from those darker potentialities he has implicitly denied.

Curiously, this meeting never leads to an evolving, complex relationship. Dickens knowingly exploits the theme of the Double in his most successful psychological fiction. But in *A Tale of Two Cities* none of the dramatic intensity of David Copperfield's friendship with Steerforth or of Eugene Wrayburn's obsession with Bradley Headstone emerges from the interview between Darnay and Carton. Darnay dismisses the evening with Carton from his consciousness, repressing any understanding of the man who has saved his life. He can speak of Carton only as an example of carelessness and recklessness; he chooses to see no more. Dickens has decided to make Carton's life as shadowy as possible, in part a consequence of his similarity to the character of Richard Wardour in *The Frozen Deep*. Carton, unlike Darnay, seems to lack a significant past. There are vague references to a youth with great promise, to student days in Paris, and to his father's death. But Carton remains in the shadows, a literary blank cheque to be called upon at the novel's end to resolve the apparently irresolvable.[13]

However, Darnay and Carton are linked by a shared experience, by the common fate of every son. Their lives are significantly shaped by dead fathers and the father surrogates they encounter. Darnay defies his uncle, the Marquis; Carton contends with Stryver, "a man of little more than thirty, but looking twenty years older" (book 2, chapter 4). Old enough in appearance to be Carton's father. Stryver even bullies Carton in a parental way: "You summon no energy and purpose. Look at me." Carton's response implicitly condemns Stryver: "You were always somewhere, and I was always—nowhere" (book 2, chapter 5). This is the son's eternal complaint against the father who refuses to give him space in which to exist.[14] It is the only challenge to Stryver that seems potentially telling. In his self-destructive manner, Carton defies Stryver's summons to a conventionally energetic life of "driving and riving and shouldering and pressing" that denies the integrity of others. Stryver, the pale English version of the Marquis St. Evrémonde—and a later version of

Mr. Dombey—asks Carton to model himself upon *him*, to shoulder his way through the world. But Carton prefers not to.

Fathers and forms of parricide remain at the center of *A Tale of Two Cities*. Dickens chooses to dwell occasionally upon Darnay's experience in England as a bourgeois hero. But Darnay's economic strivings are really only of secondary importance. His relationship to Lucie, and especially to her father, is far more significant. Darnay has come to England to fulfill his destiny through his encounter with the Manettes. Lucie and the Doctor have taken lodgings near Soho-square. The courtyard of the house in which they live brandishes "a golden arm starting out of the wall of [a] front hall," the emblem of a mysterious giant, an invisible worker in precious metals who shares the building with the Manettes by day (book 2, chapter 6). The detail points to the true nature of Darnay's evolving relationship to Manette. The presence of the seemingly anomalous golden arm is related to Dickens's conscious pun upon Manette's name, *la main*, French for hand, and becomes a part of the parricidal matrix in the novel. The golden arm has a specific and telling antecedent in *David Copperfield*. When he first meets Mr. Spenlow in Doctors' Commons, David notices Spenlow's gold watch-chain: it "was so massive, that a fancy came across me, that he ought to have a sinewy golden arm, to draw it out with, like those which are put up over the gold-beaters' shops."[15] The similarities between David Copperfield's and Charles Darnay's situations are clear enough: the play with Dickens's own initials simply emphasizes them. Like David and Mr. Spenlow, Darnay and Manette are fated to become rivals, not only for Lucie's love, but for supremacy in their own relationship. Lucie only appears to be the center of the "tranquil bark" anchored in the quiet corner in Soho. The golden arm of the mysterious giant does not proclaim Lucie's maternal love, but Manette's potency, the father's potency of arm and hand. In his new life, Manette has become "a very energetic man indeed, with great firmness of purpose, strength of resolution, and vigour of action" (book 2, chapter 10).

Darnay has fled his natural destiny in France, only to encounter it in England. He has denied one father in the form of the Marquis; now he meets in Manette the father he might have chosen for himself. Quite apart from the issue of the St. Evrémonde legacy and Manette's imprisonment, there occurs the mythical meeting of the son seeking to become a parent in his own right and the father who may thwart his efforts. Dickens has returned unerringly to the family constellation. And, as in *David Copperfield*, the fate of the father becomes problematic: must Manette, too, die, as Mr. Spenlow does, to make way for the son?

Manette is a far more complex and powerful father surrogate than the others abounding in Dickens's novels: the golden arm, the emblem of force and potency, attests to that. Manette has experienced real suffering and has managed a precarious recovery. He is neither ineffectual nor childless. His love for Lucie competes with Darnay's, as Darnay himself vaguely recognizes: "I know," observes Darnay, "that between you and Miss Manette there is an affection so unusual, so touching, so belonging to the circumstances in which it has been nurtured, that it can have few parallels" (book 2, chapter 10). Darnay's language suggests Cordelia and Lear, Dickens's own little Nell and her grandfather. It also hints at the ambiguity of Manette's love for his daughter, who has entered his life not as an asexual child but as a young woman. Darnay's persistent, and unnerving, scrupulosity takes him closer and closer to the truth: "I know that when [Lucie] is clinging to you, the hands of baby, girl, and woman, all in one, are round your neck" (book 2, chapter 10). Darnay thinks he understands the sanctity of Manette's and Lucie's love for each other. He has, however, defined Manette's relationship to Lucie as a marriage to the idealized Victorian bride.[16] Inevitably, he and Manette are rivals. But Darnay vows not to displace the father, not to lay hands upon him: "I look . . . [not] to divide with Lucie her privilege as your child, companion, and friend; but to come in aid of it, and bind her closer to you, if such a thing can be" (book 2, chapter 10). But such a thing cannot be. Poor Manette can answer only with silence, and a "look which [has] a tendency in it to dark doubt and dread." He suspects Darnay is a St. Evrémonde and recognizes the various threats his future son-in-law must pose to himself.

Darnay continues upon an increasingly labyrinthine process of self-deception. He cannot fulfill his vow to Lucie's father. Darnay has promised loyalty to the father that, if he is to become both husband and father himself, he cannot honor. Eventually, he must raise his own hand and arm against Manette, if only figuratively. He must, in time, assert himself and his own rights and deny those of Manette. Once again, Darnay is flirting with fixation and arrest. Even the benign father must finally give way before the legitimate claims of the young. Perhaps, for once, the transfer of power from father to son will necessitate neither the father's death nor the son's defeat.

Darnay continues to court impasse as he persists in falsifying his situation and his self. His love for Lucie is informed by his need to identify with Manette as someone who has defied the ancien régime. Manette's mediating presence influences Darnay's love and encourages him in a subtle form of plagiarism, not unlike that of David Copperfield in his relationship to Steerforth, as he speaks of himself as a "voluntary exile from France; like [Manette], driven from it by its distractions, oppressions, and miseries." Darnay exclaims, "I look only to sharing your fortunes, sharing your life and home, and being faithful to you to the death" (book 2, chapter 10). This speech can be accepted at face value only by ignoring the ominous ambiguity of the word *death* and by failing to make important ethical distinctions. Darnay's experience has not been Manette's. He has been victimized by his own class in the sense that he feels repugnance for the moral and political heritage he is expected to uphold. But Darnay has not been persecuted as Manette, Thérèse Defarge, Gaspard, and countless others have. The only legitimate basis for Darnay's identification with Manette lies in his renunciation of his title: he has refused to perpetuate the crimes of the past. But he has also abdicated his responsibilities to his own class and to the peasants who continue, as he knows, to suffer. France remains unchanged in spite of Darnay's gesture of revolt.[17]

As son and social rebel, Darnay clings to the fragile and radically false conception of himself formulated in his interview with Manette. The interview ends upon a masterstroke of rectitude designed to consolidate Darnay's identity. Darnay asks Manette to speak to Lucie neither in his favor nor against him. The doctor is effectively stymied. He has no real choice but to say that if there were "any fancies, any reasons, any apprehensions, anything whatsoever, new or old" against the man she truly loved for which he was not directly responsible, "they should all be obliterated for her sake" (book 2, chapter 10). Manette's words fail to arouse curiosity or foreboding in Darnay, although they indirectly allude to all the facts that Darnay's account of himself has skirted. But Manette has conferred that absolution Darnay has been seeking: absolution not from crimes he has committed, but from crimes of his class and his family. It is an absolution devoutly to be wished, but one which no man, not even a victim of the St. Evrémondes, may confer. In *A Tale of Two Cities,* there is no absolution for the father's deeds, no refuge from generational conflict, and no escape from the past.

Darnay's marriage to Lucie Manette resolves nothing. It leads only to another act of parricide on Darnay's part. His revelation of his true identity, confirming what Manette already suspects, causes the doctor's relapse. After the ceremony, "Mr. Lorry observed a great change to have come over the doctor; as if the golden arm uplifted there, had struck him a poisoned blow" (book 2, chapter 18). The golden arm no longer stands for Manette's paternal strength alone. Now it announces the son's emerging power. The phrasing in the passage recalls the murder of the Marquis and the punishment inflicted upon parricides like Gaspard, whose corpse has been left hanging from the gallows, poisoning the village well below it. Once more Darnay is the unwitting parricide, subject to the guilt and punishment that is the parricide's timeless fate. This time Manette recovers after regressing to his pathetic condition as the shoemaker of the North Tower. But he remains vulnerable to future, more final, blows from the son's arm.

A Tale of Two Cities, like so many of Dickens's novels, has led to impasse, to a sense of the impossibility of normal change and growth. Darnay seems condemned to a perpetual repetition of that parricidal act he has committed in France. It undermines all that he does. He may prosper in London. He may marry and have children. But his life remains false, based upon a denial of his guilt and his responsibility. In their nocturnal interview Carton has warned, "Don't let your sober face elate you, . . . you don't know what it may come to" (book 2, chapter 4). The face with which Darnay meets the world masks that *other* face he has glimpsed in the Old Bailey mirror. As usual in Dickens's novels, the issue is defined in an indirect way. The news of Darnay's impending marriage reaches the Defarges in Saint Antoine through John Barsad, now a spy for the French monarchy. "And speaking of Gaspard," says Barsad, "it is a curious thing that [Manette's daughter] is going to marry the nephew of Monsieur the Marquis, for whom Gaspard was exalted to that height of so many feet; in other words, the present Marquis" (book 2, chapter 16). Barsad's apparently casual observations connect Manette's persecution, the Marquis's murder, Gaspard's execution, and Darnay's marriage. Darnay would protest that he is not the present Marquis, that he has relinquished his title. But one figurative father has been slain. The son, his heir, lives in self-imposed exile while the peasants of the St. Evrémonde estate endure their scarecrow existence in the midst of a France that is now a wasteland. Darnay, the father, has left unchanged the lives of those to whom he is directly responsible. He lives unknown in England, where he is "no Marquis." He is unknown to his tenants in France; unknown to his wife; unknown, finally, to himself.

Darnay's trial for treason has never ended. It pursues its subterranean course during the years of domestic tranquility in Soho. But the outbreak of the Revolution in 1789 brings this period of serenity to its necessary end. The failure to produce change in France, in part, Darnay's failure, leads to violent upheaval. A "living sea," an "ocean of faces," sweeps across France, engulfing the old order. In Saint Antoine its scarecrows raise a "forest of naked arms," struggling "in the air like shrivelled branches of trees in a winter wind: all the fingers convulsively clutching at every weapon or semblance of a weapon that was thrown up from the depths below" (book 2, chapter 21). Arm, hand, blade join in the final, convulsive assault upon the father. The day of judgment has come at last. This ocean of faces, with its unfathomed depths, returns us to the mirror in the Old Bailey: "Haunted in a most ghastly manner that abominable place would have been, if the glass could ever have rendered back its reflections, as the ocean is one day to give up its dead." In Paris the ocean yields up its dead. In their lust for retribution, the revolutionaries incur the guilt of "the wicked and the wretched" who once stood in the prisoner's dock. Dickens's language indicates that they exist in the relationship to Darnay which he has so long denied, that he participates in the events of the Revolution.

Once begun, the national orgy of retribution becomes a frenzied vegetation rite, an attempt to placate the gods and to rid France of its moral pestilence. The ritualistic element in the Revolution expresses itself in the capture and execution of Old Foulon, who has "caused himself to be represented as dead, and [has] had a grand mock-funeral" (book 2, chapter 22). The people of Saint Antoine resurrect Foulon, whose crime has been to tell a starving people that they might eat grass. They resurrect and punish him: Foulon's severed head is impaled "upon a spike, with grass enough in the mouth for all Saint Antoine to dance at the sight of" (book 2, chapter 22). Old Foulon becomes a version of Frazer's corn-god effigy, standing simultaneously for the king and the father. In a dionysian frenzy, the women of Saint Antoine chant, "Give us the blood of

Foulon, Give us the head of Foulon, Give us the heart of Foulon, Give us the body and soul of Foulon, Rend Foulon to pieces, and dig him into the ground, that grass may grow from him!" (book 2, chapter 22). Foulon is mutilated and returned to the earth, so that the nation, the people, and the wasted land may be renewed.

In a remarkably compressed sequence of events, Dickens merges the social and personal dimensions of the novel. Foulon's ruse is only one of a series of feigned deaths to which others have resorted. The most extravagant example is the mock funeral of Roger Cly, informer and cohort of John Barsad (himself dead to his original name, Solomon Pross). But the Marquis St. Evrémonde has been dead to the suffering of the people. Even Charles Darnay has died: he has entered a limbo of complicity in which he still exists. Events sweep over Foulon, Darnay, and France itself. Water transforms itself into fire in this period of elemental chaos and reaches out to destroy the St. Evrémonde château that has stood for both social and personal paralysis throughout the novel. The revolutionaries' naked arms, earlier compared to the shrivelled branches of trees, cease to be atrophied and ineffectual. As a living forest of smoke and flame, they now attack the château, which seems "as if it were the face of the cruel Marquis, burning at the stake."[18] We are very close to the world of *Totem and Taboo* here. The assassination of the Marquis, repeated in the ritualistic execution of Old Foulon, is performed once more, as if a single act of parricide is not enough. The château, and all it represents, disintegrates: "Molten lead and iron boiled in the marble basin of the fountain; the water ran dry; the extinguisher tops of the towers vanished like ice . . . and trickled down into four rugged wells of flame" (book 2, chapter 23). The father's effort to perpetuate himself through a tyrannical social system, impregnable stone, and subservient progeny has come to this. The gorgon's spell seems broken at last. Revolution has become the only way to alleviate social and personal impasse. It inundates France with blood and flame: it is one parricidal act that seeks to run its full course.

The patriarchal forces encouraging impasse and denying change and evolution succumb to the Revolution. Sustained tyranny causes and demands retribution, which may itself be subverted by the intensity of its fervor. Even Charles Darnay, who has futilely tried to elude his responsibility through exile and marriage, finds himself resurrected into the flux of events. The identity, the self, he so carefully shaped more than four-

teen years before when he appeared on the packet-ship, in the dead of
night, must yield, like the St. Evrémonde château, to the chaos of time:
Darnay must relinquish his present identity or become its victim.

The opportunity for change first presents itself to Darnay at Tellson's
in London. With the Revolution the bank functions as the meeting
place of the French emigrés who have taken to their collective heels,
abandoning France to her fate. Darnay inevitably finds himself talking to
Mr. Lorry in the midst of the vain chatter and complaints of people to
whom he is still related in ways he prefers not to understand: "And it
was such vapouring all about his ears, like a troublesome confusion of
blood in his own head, added to a latent uneasiness in his mind, which
had already made Charles Darnay restless, and which still kept him so"
(book 2, chapter 24). The disorientation Darnay once felt on the night
of his trial for treason returns. All the repressed doubts about the legitimacy of his past acts are aroused. Through Gabelle's letter, addressed to
"Monsieur heretofore the Marquis St. Evrémonde, of France," Darnay's
natural destiny inescapably confronts him.[19] The disparaging observations by the emigrés and Stryver about the Marquis who is not to be
found ironically hit the mark. Each malicious comment possesses an element of truth he can't ignore: he *is* "a craven who [has] abandoned his
post"; there *is* "contamination in such a scoundrel" (book 2, chapter 24).
However unwittingly, Darnay, like Old Foulon, has in effect told his
tenants to eat grass. He has struck Manette a poisoned blow by his very
presence in England. Gabelle's letter, his plea to the emigrant to whom
he has remained loyal in his way, almost to death itself, transforms a latent uneasiness into a crystallized realization.

Darnay moves out of Tellson's into the quiet of the Temple, near
which the heads of executed felons, impaled upon spikes, were once exposed as a warning to a curious public. Temple Bar alludes to the trial in
the Old Bailey and to the fates of the Marquis and Old Foulon. It is the
appropriate place in which Darnay's uneasiness can finally express itself:
"In his horror of [his uncle's murder] . . . , and in the aversion with
which his conscience regarded the crumbling fabric that he was supposed to uphold, he had acted imperfectly. . . .in his love for Lucie, his
renunciation of his social place . . . had been hurried and incomplete"
(book 2, chapter 24). In these reflections, Darnay confronts the common
omissions and failures of men everywhere, in all ages. He has succumbed
to the temptations time always offers: "The events of this week annihi-

lated the immature plans of last week, and the events of the week following made all new again; . . . to the force of these circumstances he had
yielded:—not without disquiet, but still without continuous and accu-
mulating resistance" (book 2, chapter 24). Darnay's life in England has
hardened into an imprisoning conception of himself that no longer
seems valid. He has become yet another victim of a paralyzing habit.
The cynicism of the dead Marquis has been confirmed by events. And
Darnay must now live with the wreckage of an obsolete self.

Darnay is struggling with a sense of disorientation like that experienced by Esther Summerson on the stormy night, before her first meeting with Jo, when she has "for a moment an undefinable impression of
[herself] as being something different from what [she] then was." Such a
moment of intuitive insight into one's most tenaciously held illusions is
inevitably disquieting. Once again, Darnay recoils in an effort to convince himself of his innocence: "He had oppressed no man, he had imprisoned no man; . . . [he had] thrown himself on a world with no
favour in it, won his own private place there, and earned his own bread"
(book 2, chapter 24). But in earning his own bread, in the best bourgeois manner, he has permitted others to starve. He has failed to unify
his private and his social obligations. He remains, in spite of his protests,
"the Marquis who was not to be found." The barren fields of the St.
Evrémonde estate and its peasants' gaunt faces belie his right to a private
place, with its negation of broader responsibilities. Darnay's illusion that
he may "guide this raging Revolution that was running so fearfully
wild" lacks a real basis. His sense of superiority to the revolutionaries,
along with his confidence that he is "better than they," reveals how easy
and necessary it may be to repair the broken web of one's existence with
threads of fancy. Darnay, but not Dickens, fully expects his intentions to
be accepted in France as if they were achieved realities. Such thoughts
reveal the extent to which good but misguided men have shared in the
making of the Revolution, and their inability to perceive clearly their
guilt.

Darnay succumbs to his own half-truths and to the lure of Paris, the
Loadstone Rock at the center of his consciousness: "In seasons of pestilence, some of us will have a secret attraction to the disease—a terrible
passing inclination to die of it. And all of us have like wonders hidden in
our breasts, only needing circumstances to evoke them" (book 3, chapter 6). Darnay's failure to comprehend his true situation, and how he

will be seen by those in France, is *his* disease, corresponding to the leprosy of unreality that has struck down the ancien régime. His journey to Paris becomes a ritual shaping the endings of Dickens's mature novels. David Copperfield travels to Yarmouth through the violent storm, to find Steerforth's body washed ashore, almost at his feet. Esther Summerson pursues Lady Dedlock through the London maze until she discovers her, dead, near Nemo's grave. Pip returns to the haunts of his youth in response to an anonymous note. Eugene Wrayburn seeks out Lizzie Hexam in the mill town on the Thames, where he is attacked and nearly drowned. In each case the physical journey is an inner, psychic one, a descent into a personal maelstrom. An unresolved dilemma comes to pose a threat to the character's existence. The identity by which each has tried to live proves inadequate to the realities of a changing situation. Darnay's choice of a new identity, in his renunciation of the St. Evrémonde name, has not led to personal autonomy and integrity, not even to authentic fatherhood. Unknown even to his own family, he is a true father neither in England nor in France.

But relinquishing that identity to which Darnay has become habituated proves harrowing, if not impossible. Darnay's journey to France involves a return to that moment in which he has tried to deal with the past by denying its claims upon him. Like David Copperfield and Esther Summerson before him, he remains "'fixated' to a particular portion of [the] past, as though [he] could not manage to free [himself] from it and [is] for that reason alienated from the present and the future" (*SE*, 16:273). The future is, in David Copperfield's words, "walled up before" Darnay who reenacts not only David's travail, but also Esther Summerson's long night of psychological and spiritual disorder. He labors up figurative staircases, "ever striving to reach the top, and ever turned, as [Esther has] seen a worm in a garden path, by some obstruction, and labouring again." Darnay's journey becomes *his* labor upon which he has embarked, as he at first claims, of his own will. But, at last, he must see that he has no choice, that he responds to magnetic forces within himself not fully understood. As one revolutionary cries, "His cursed life is not his own!" (book 3, chapter 1). The ride toward Paris through the soggy darkness is a personal nightmare. He is compelled to recognize that "all here is so unprecedented, so changed, so sudden and unfair, that [he is] absolutely lost" (book 3, chapter 1). The circumstances are not even primarily Dickens's comment upon the chaos and injustice of the Reign of Terror. Through them he reveals not only universal flux and discontinuity, but the further erosion of Darnay's conventional notions of himself.

The miry roads and the darkness lead to the prison, La Force, a place figuratively under water. Darnay enters the watery depths of the Old Bailey mirror, of himself, to encounter an aristocratic version of the wicked and the wretched faces once reflected there. The prisoners, spectral in the squalid chamber of La Force, rise ceremoniously to greet him, as the imagined faces in the mirror greeted him before. Darnay's sense that the prisoners are "Ghosts all!" confirms his own deadness and culpability. He belongs with them. The unreal ride, like "some progress of disease," has culminated in this crisis of a will infected with paralysis. Darnay has been plunged into the depths from which he has pulled back, just as so many sons and fathers in Dickens's novels are plunged into the baptismal waters of the Thames. His confidence in his own innocence has proved false. Now he finds himself among those who, like himself, confront the paradox of innocence and guilt. Darnay relives David's experience in the tempest when he comes upon Steerforth's corpse washed up upon the shore; and Esther's experience in *Bleak House* when, in pursuit of her mother, she encounters "a man yet dank and muddy, in long swollen sodden boots," who has fished something wet, a woman's body, from the waters of the Thames. With the appearance of the gaoler, "so unwholesomely bloated, both in face and person, as to look like a man who had been drowned and filled with water," Darnay finally knows despair: "Now am I left, as if I were dead" (book 3, chapter 1). It is never clear that Darnay perceives there is a certain justice in a fate that he has partially forged for himself.

The root of Darnay's despair remains the falseness of his relationship to himself and others. Dickens captures this, as always, through oblique allusions to Darnay's condition. The revolutionary Tribunal addresses him as Charles Evrémonde, called Darnay, denying that he has established in England an identity worthy of its recognition. The novel, in its subplots, plays repeatedly with this issue. Even Miss Pross's encounter with her long-lost brother, Solomon, echoes this central concern. The exposure of Barsad's double identity with its moral duplicity poses a real threat to his life. Jerry Cruncher's comic wonder about Pross's true name, combined with his first-hand knowledge of Roger Cly's mock funeral, deftly connects the issues of identity and responsibility, authenticity and bad faith. Darnay, like Solomon Pross, could be subjected to a version of Jerry Cruncher's interrogation about *his* two names. St. Evrémonde was not his name over the water in England: which of the two names has priority—the family name of St. Evrémonde or the self-conferred name, Charles Darnay? Darnay insists that he has ceased to be a St. Evrémonde, that he is innocent of crimes against the French people. But his first acquittal by the Tribunal is followed almost immediately by his subsequent arrest on new charges. This second arrest is true to Darnay's condition, to a state of psychic arrest, growing out of his failure to cope with the suspect nature of his claims to innocence.

As usual, the father, in his various aspects, presides over these events. Doctor Manette arrives in Paris with Lucie, ostensibly to save Darnay's life. As a former victim of the ancien régime, he returns to Paris as one of the few sons who has raised his hand against the father and survived to become a father. Manette feeds upon the disorder of the Reign of Terror. He passes through maddened men and women sharpening their weapons at the grindstone and pushes "the weapons aside like water." He is a Mosaic figure, determined to lead his family safely out of France: "For the first time he felt that in that sharp fire [of captivity], he had slowly forged the iron which could break the prison door of his daughter's husband, and deliver him" (book 3, chapter 4). He is once more the mysterious giant of the golden arm. Lucie and Mr. Lorry turn to a Manette transfigured by the change and rely upon him. He has successfully displaced Darnay as the father, reasserting the claims to ascendancy he has apparently relinquished for so many years.

With this transformation, Manette exists as a formidable threat to Darnay. He secures Darnay's acquittal by the Tribunal during the first trial. And a thrill of exultation resonates in his words to Lucie: "You must not be weak, my darling . . . ; don't tremble so. I have saved him" (book 3, chapter 6). Manette has won a victory in court—and a victory over Darnay. For Darnay will always be in debt to Manette, will always owe him his very life. The father may triumph in many ways: the hostility of the Marquis St. Evrémonde may, finally, be less potent than the benevolence of Manette. Darnay may once again be effectively cut off from fatherhood and the right to father forth himself in the presence of the now truly patriarchial Manette.

Dickens's uneasiness on this very point informs the conclusion of

A Tale of Two Cities. Manette's renewed ascendancy is fleeting. With Darnay's return to prison, Manette's new life, set in motion like a clock after years of dormancy, ends. For even the benevolent father must be felled, preferably not by the son's hand, but by another Gaspard or by the force of circumstances. Manette becomes one of Darnay's accusers. His written account of the events leading to his imprisonment is *his* legacy, *his* will: a curse upon the St. Evrémondes and "their descendants, to the last of their race." It is a son's curse upon the father and the decadent patriarchy of which Darnay, as the present Marquis, is a part; it is a father's curse upon the son-in-law who threatens the father's dominance. As son to Darnay's father, as father to Darnay's son, Manette has never fully granted the absolution Darnay sought. Impelled by an habitual resentment that he has never cast off, Manette has reached out to point an accusing finger at his son-in-law. His word could send Darnay to La Guillotine, which the revolutionaries jestingly speak of as "the best cure for headache[:] it infallibly [prevents] the hair from turning grey" (book 3, chapter 4). La Guillotine is the gorgon's head of the Revolution; its impact reaches out to touch everyone. It cures the headache caused by time by inflicting upon its victims either the stasis of death or psychic trauma. The tormented man who is still imprisoned by the past and who has denounced the St. Evrémonde race becomes not so unlike the dead Marquis who once urged Darnay to accept the curse of his natural destiny. And, as a victim of the past, he suffers a similar fate: he becomes one of Mr. Morfin's images. With Darnay's second arrest, Manette, "paralytically animated" by the past, is turned "into stone . . . as if he were a statue."

By now Darnay's destiny is clear: he is always to be the parricide. Manette, again the broken prisoner of the Bastille, wanders the streets of Paris aimlessly, only to return to Mr. Lorry's chambers, whimpering for the shoemaker's bench that once sustained him. Surely, the golden arm has descended once again to strike another poisoned blow. But, as in the murder of the Marquis, the significance of Manette's undoing is obscured. Manette seems the victim of poetic justice: his curse upon the St. Evrémondes includes his own daughter and grandchild and justifies his own ruin. For Dickens the struggle between father and son never leads to unqualified victory for one or the other. Instead, it produces yet another impasse. Manette is overcome by his seemingly gratuitous act of vengeance. Darnay's triumph, if it occurs, will inevitably involve the near-destruction of Lucie's father. There is no simple way, perhaps no way at all, to resolve the impasse. The victory of the father or the son entails a price few would willingly exact. Finally, Dickens chooses to circumvent the logic inherent in his own fiction. Characteristically, he seeks a resolution, one which seems to acknowledge the son's claims. The author calls upon Darnay's "Double of coarse deportment" to avert Darnay's fixation in his role as unwilling parricide, and to rescue him from death.

Sydney Carton has also responded to the pull of the Loadstone Rock, to the secret attraction of the pestilence raging in France. The siren call of death touches him, as it has Darnay. The two share in a single venture involving despair, figurative death, and the possibility of a rebirth. As Doubles they may participate in a process that frees them from the father and the past. But one of them may have to die so that the other can survive. In *Beyond Psychology*, Otto Rank offers an interpretation of "twin-traditions," more literary than anthropological, that may illuminate some of the dynamics at work not only in *A Tale of Two Cities* but in the literature of the Double in general: "In our modern conception of the Double, the killing of the alter-ego invariably leads to the death of the hero himself, that is, suicide; at earlier stages [in history], on the contrary, the sacrifice of one of the twins was the condition for the survival of the other. Hence, in twin-mythology the typical motif of fratricide turns out to be a symbolic gesture on the part of the immortal self by which it rids itself of the mortal ego."[20] The twin who dies stands for the mortal self; the surviving twin, freed from his mortal part, becomes immortal, no longer subject to time and death. But the significance of twins goes beyond a simple dualistic conception of the self: "Twins were considered self-created, not revived from the spirit of the dead, but generated through their own magic power, independent even of the mother. In the totemistic system . . . no fatherhood was acknowledged. The twins have dispensed with the mother, too, and are dependent only upon each other." Mothers are strangely absent from *A Tale of Two Cities*. The idealized Lucie remains ineffectual other than as the guiding angel both of Darnay and Carton. It is the masculine Miss Pross, a later Betsey Trotwood, who suffers deafness in her effort to save Lucie and the others from Thérèse Defarge, a truly sensual creature who has foresaken her sexuality for the pleasures of retribution. If there is a potential mother in the novel, it must be the sister of Thérèse Defarge: the woman whose death sets in motion the complicated events surrounding Darnay's heroic saga. The novel, having dispensed, somewhat violently, with the mother, moves to dispense with the father too. The hero, whom Otto Rank sees as the historical successor to the twin in those myths dealing with fratricide, possesses the unique ability to create himself. The immortality of the surviving twin leads to that "utter independence which makes the twin the prototype of the hero."[21] The hero has no need to acknowledge, or to turn against, a progenitor—male or female—who threatens his primacy and autonomy. He becomes the father, even the mother, of himself through the agency of the twin who dies for him. Dickens's use of the Double becomes his way of resolving that which is irresolvable on a realistic level: the relationship between parent and child, the dead and the living, the past and the present.

Sydney Carton, as Charles Darnay's mortal self, has been dragged for years "in [Stryver's] wake, like a boat [or a corpse?] towed astern" (book 2, chapter 21). He is the son who has not defied the father, but who has settled into what he calls rust and repose. He surfaces in Paris at the moment Miss Pross and Jerry Cruncher are badgering Solomon Pross about Pross's true identity. When he strikes in to identify Barsad, Carton solves the riddle of identity for Darnay as well. His death will serve to unify the split within Darnay's consciousness and resolve his perplexing duties as son and father. In the process, Carton will both dispense with the father, by saving Darnay, and propitiate him, as Gaspard has done before him. It is clear to Miss Pross that he has undergone a transformation: "There was a braced purpose in the arm and a kind of inspiration in the eyes, which not only contradicted his light manner, but changed and raised the man" (book 3, chapter 8). The reference to the arm is fleeting. But it suggests, once more, the parricide's arm and the hand wielding the avenging blade. In his altered state Carton is no longer dissipated, irresolute. He has become a son capable of raising his hand against the father. He is the son who has rebelled against the slain Marquis, the son who has inadvertently struck down the apparently benevolent Manette. And as Darnay's mortal twin, Carton also embodies the unacknowledged failure of Charles Evrémonde, who is called Darnay. Carton's death will free Darnay from the social guilt of the St. Evrémondes as a family. It will also serve to placate the dead father, the murdered uncle, and the stricken Manette. For in Dickens's imagination the hero-son must be spared any of the consequences for asserting his right to exist.

As he wanders through Paris, awaiting the verdict of Darnay's last trial, Carton thinks of his own father: "These solemn words, which had been read at his father's grave, arose in his mind. . . . 'I am the resurrection and the life, saith the Lord: he that believeth in me, though he were dead, yet shall he live: and whosoever liveth and believeth in me, shall never die'" (book 3, chapter 9). The Christian implications of the passage are powerful and moving. But they should not obscure the central preoccupations in the novel: the dilemma posed by the father's death; the yearning for absolution and rebirth through self-creation; the desire to be freed from the paradoxes of being in time. None of these complex issues is satisfyingly resolved by Carton's death or by allusions to the Crucifixion.[22] Rather, they are swept away just as everything Carton sees before he dies flashes away with the fall of the blade. The crowd that "swells forward in a mass, like one great heave of water" (book 3, chapter 15) baptizes Carton unto death, and delivers Darnay back to life.

But that life will remain as specious as the other life he has lived prior to his return to France. In prison Darnay has dreamed of being free and happy, "back in the old house in Soho. . . . A pause of forgetfulness, and then he had even suffered, and had come back to [Lucie], dead and at peace, and yet there was no difference in him" (book 3, chapter 13). The dream reveals Darnay's strong will to live. But the nature of that life he envisions is, in fact, a form of death. For only death may confer upon Darnay forgetfulness and peace. Carton's prophetic vision at the end of the novel is irrelevant. There is no life without conflict; without moral ambiguity and divided loyalties; without the unrelenting pressures of the father and the past. The whole of *A Tale of Two Cities* is a testament to this fact. But Darnay's dream denies all this: it is a return to an imaginary time prior to the father. Darnay wants to be restored unchanged to Lucie, whose proper abode is the world of dreams. And, yet, the Marquis St. Evrémonde has been assassinated. Doctor Manette has been destroyed, reduced to a helpless, whimpering old man. The fires of the Revolution still burn. The peasants on the St. Evrémonde estate continue to assert their legitimate claims within the context of Dickens's own paternalistic imagination. With Carton's death these realities flash away as if they were, after all, only a dream. Darnay's obligations to the living and to the dead are severed by the ironically "innocent atonement" that Darnay's mother has prophesied: Carton, actually though not figuratively innocent, dies so that the guilty Darnay may survive.

Within *A Tale of Two Cities* the structure of the poetics of impasse emerges in almost crystalline form. The death of Sydney Carton, the twin, makes at best only ritualistic sense since it evades and obscures the other issues posed by the novel. Dickens imagines with remarkable clarity the recurring encounter between father and son: the son's impetus to become a father requires the setting aside of the good or the bad father, with the inevitable claims he makes upon the son through his very existence. Dickens simply cannot imagine a viable resolution to the conflict, the voluntary stepping aside of the father to make way for the son.[23] There is no imaginable way, other than that of ritualistic sacrifice, to effect the transfer of authority and power from one generation to the next. Such a transfer becomes, for Dickens, inseparable from the act of parricide. This vision of the son's dilemma leads to the ahistoricism of this apparently historical novel. For parricide is both an inevitable and an intolerable crime: the father remains sacrosanct in the face of the son's most legitimate claims to be free of him. The only resolution is to die, to gain access to that better land of which Sydney Carton speaks before his execution: "There is no Time there, and no trouble there." The world of *A Tale of Two Cities* remains one of intolerable impasse or unthinkable chaos. Not even Carton's sacrifice, the act that has made the novel so ineradicably *his,* can end the recurring struggle between generations.

In the closing pages of *A Tale of Two Cities,* impasse reigns. Allusions to the filial heroism of Christ's atonement, muted parallels to the mythology of twins, do not convincingly depict that passing on of authority from father to son that Dickens wishes to effect. Doctor Manette's condition at the end of the novel captures the paradox Dickens has posed. His is the defeat of a legitimately rebellious son at the hands of a St. Evrémonde (who, in spite of his protests, stands in the father's place, after all, in his relationship to Manette). Yet, the defeat is also, clearly, that of the father who has sought control of the son's destiny. The broken Manette, the quintessential Double in the novel, suggests the fate of every son, of every father. It is a fate that Dickens as son, father, and artist cannot imaginatively accept. In *Great Expectations* and in *Our Mu-*

tual Friend, Dickens will once again explore the eternal encounter of fathers and sons. For if Jerry Cruncher is, at last, only a comic and ineffectual Resurrection-Man, Dickens the artist is the Resurrection-Man in earnest, striving to recall to life those thwarted sons and fathers whose natural destiny, like Charles Darnay's, threatens finally to overwhelm them.

Chapter 5

> The interval between that time and supper,
> Wemmick devoted to showing me his collection
> of curiosities. They were mostly of a felonious
> character; comprising the pen with which a
> celebrated forgery had been committed, a
> distinguished razor or two, some locks of hair,
> and several manuscript confessions written under
> condemnation—upon which Mr. Wemmick set
> particular value as being, to use his own words,
> "every one of 'em Lies, sir."—*Great Expectations*

The House of the Self

Great Expectations opens upon a moment of ambiguous self-creation as a young Philip Pirrip, standing before the tombstones of those he has been told were his parents, attempts to free himself from a threatening past. As an infant, he has mispronounced both his family and his Christian names, in effect, naming himself: "So I called myself Pip, and came to be called Pip."[1] But the act of self-naming becomes fully meaningful only in his encounter with the tombstones engraved with the hieroglyphic traces of his parents, convincing him "that Philip Pirrip, late of

this parish, and also Georgiana wife of the above, were dead and buried." Pip's childish mispronunciation of his own name, and of his father's, originally accidental and meaningless, now becomes an intuitive
denial of his parents, an attempt to avoid the fate of the five dead brothers who, in Pip's imagination, "had all been born on their backs with
their hands in their trousers-pockets, and had never taken them out in
this state of existence" (chapter 1). In his construction of the meaning of
both the tombstones and the letters engraved on them, Pip sees life as a
universal struggle to which his parents and his dead brothers have succumbed, perhaps through a shared passivity. He chooses not to emulate
them, not to repeat the past as fixed in the letters engraved on the stone
tablets. On the day that Pip first becomes aware of the identity of things,
and of himself, the tombstones become signs and tokens of literal and
figurative death. Pip chooses life, unwittingly seeking to become the father of himself, someone freed from the conditioning realities of social
class, of place, of time.[2]

The denial of time and the past becomes a crucial center of *Great Expectations,* as it has been in *A Tale of Two Cities*. The elder Pip, engaged in a
manuscript confession written under the condition of self-condemnation,
circles around this center, often resorting to the platitudes of high Victorian earnestness. The writing Pip can be curiously alienated from his
younger self at important moments in his narrative, subtly misleading
the reader, and himself. The humanistic essays of Humphry House and
G. Robert Stange, exploring what House called the "snob's progress,"
emphasize the ethical dimensions of the novel in an inevitable response
both to the moralizing voice of the elder Pip and to the apparent re-
liability of the account he offers: "It is at first as though we were standing before a wall [of words] which shuts out every prospect and prevents
us from having any idea whether there is anything behind it, and if so,
what" (*SE*, 2:293). Freud's observation on the problematic status of autobiographical accounts, in *Studies on Hysteria,* again serves as a warning
to be alert to instances of discontinuity in Pip's narrative. Early on, the
confusion pervading his manuscript reconstruction of his past is revealed as Pip recalls the splendid whoppers he told after his first visit to
Satis House. The dread of being misunderstood leads Pip to withhold
from Mrs. Joe and Pumblechook his response to Satis House and Miss
Havisham. With an intuitive delicacy he lies to protect Miss Havisham

in her bizarre plight and to preserve for himself the meaning of that shaping imaginative experience.

But, in the account of his attempt to explain to an uncomprehending Joe his complex reasons for his lies, the elder Pip unconsciously reveals the discontinuity in perception that informs his rendering of many of his experiences. He tells Joe of the beautiful young lady who has said he was common and confesses his anguished desire not to be common: "The lies had come of it somehow, though I didn't know how." Pip goes on: "This was a case of metaphysics, at least as difficult for Joe to deal with, as for me. But Joe took the case altogether out of the region of metaphysics, and by that means vanquished it" (chapter 9). In his use of the word *metaphysics,* the elder Pip raises, as in the case of Mr. Morfin in his musings on *habit* in *Dombey and Son,* serious ontological issues. At Satis House Pip's conception of himself and of the identity of things has again been profoundly altered: he has experienced the ineluctable reality of a self conditioned by the perspective of others. And to this, Joe, who will himself later lie about *his* experiences at Satis House, can only reply "that lies is lies." Such an observation does not vanquish ontological issues; it obscures them, rendering their full significance almost inaccessible to us, and more significantly, to the writing Pip who all too often, without an ironic awareness, acquiesces to a shift in perspective from the ontological to the reassuringly ethical.[3] The writing Pip, like his Victorian brethren, takes refuge in the ethical platitudes of a Joe Gargery or a Biddy, for they too cast a spell upon Pip as significant as any spell cast by the inaccessible Estella. The elder Pip uses their language as he attempts to understand his former feelings: "I know right well that any good that intermixed itself with my apprenticeship came of plain contented Joe, and not of restless aspiring discontented me" (chapter 14). The language of conventional morality condemns the Faustian career of self-creation as mere ingratitude, offering a tempting refuge from the vicissitudes accompanying the ontological imperatives of the romantic self.

The guilt pervading Pip's narrative is not only fostered by Mrs. Joe and Mr. Pumblechook, who unite to treat Pip as if he has "insisted on being born in opposition to the dictates of reason, religion, and morality, and against the dissuading arguments of [his] best friends" (chapter 4); nor is it primarily the guilt of a remorseful and chastened adult aware of his callous treatment of those most dear to him. Rather, his guilt is

that of an Esther Summerson or a Charles Darnay, of someone who has
set out upon the pilgrimage of being, only to abandon it. On the "memorable raw afternoon towards evening" when he first becomes aware of
himself, Pip tries to free himself of the family history grimly recorded
in the tombstones before him. He acts upon a natural desire to reject
his parents and the past memorialized in the graveyard—what Darnay
called his father's time—perhaps even upon the desire to reject time itself. Inevitably, he finds himself inescapably in time, dealing with a new
situation that will significantly influence his conception of himself. The
man who, Lazarus-like, rises up from among the graves, will become
a figurative father, a living rebuke to the act of figurative parricide in
which the trembling boy has been innocently engaged. The convict attests to the fact that time is not to be denied, that the creation of the self
ex nihilo is doomed from the start.

   Time has begun for Pip, not with his introduction to Satis House,
but with the apparently contingent joining of his individual history with
that of the convict. The scene in the churchyard initiates a complex chain
of historical events and another equally complex chain of psychological
associations: "That was a memorable day to me, for it made great changes
in me. But it is the same with any life. Imagine *one selected day struck out
of it,* and think how different its course would have been. Pause you who
read this, and think for a moment of *the long chain* of iron or gold, of
thorns or flowers, that would never have bound you, but for the forma-
tion of *the first link* on *one memorable day*" (chapter 9, emphasis mine). In
this passage Pip muses upon his first day at Satis House. But the phrase
"one memorable day" also alludes to the memorable raw afternoon
when he was confronted by the escaped convict. The language of the
passage, like the language David Copperfield uses to discuss the mysteries of stenography, points to something crucial to his unfolding
narrative: Pip chooses to see his first meeting with Miss Havisham and
Estella as the shaping event in the narrative that is his life. He seeks consciously to strike out, to censor, the other memorable day, one year earlier, in order to deny its place in the long chain that would never have
bound him but for the forging of the first link. Pip's attempt to forge a
self in defiance of the self's historical situation, as if it might exist independently of the events that, in part, constitute its structure, leads to impasse, to the figurative death awaiting so many of Dickens's heroes and
heroines.

The timid boy who stands before the gate of Satis House remains a small bundle of shivers: he is, at best, an inchoate self precariously bounded by the monosyllabic and prophetic name "Pip." There is, as yet, no center to that fragile self, for neither Mrs. Joe, with the Tickler and her "square impregnable bib . . . that was stuck full of pins and needles," nor Joe, who surreptitiously spoons gravy upon Pip's plate, has nurtured that self. Pip stands in need of the experiences awaiting him to gain knowledge of possibilities of which he cannot yet be aware. The encounter with Miss Havisham and Estella will intensify his existing discontent with his lot; it will provide, however ambiguously, a way of imagining the self he resolves to be. Within the darkened rooms of Satis House a version of René Girard's "'Triangular' Desire" is enacted. Pip finds himself in a triadic situation through which his subjectivity will be shaped. The process begins with the contemptuous use of the word "boy" by Estella who will, later in the day, comment disdainfully on Pip's coarse hands and thick boots. Pip now sees himself, more acutely than before, as another sees him, inspiring within him a self-consciousness that reveals an excruciating sense not only of social, but of ontological, inadequacy. In "the smart without a name" Pip experiences a sense of nonbeing; as much as Esther Summerson, he runs the risk of becoming a "no one." Yet the painful rebuff he perceives in Estella's face and words provides further impetus to Pip to fashion a self. When he later cries that Estella is part of his character, his very existence (chapter 44), Pip speaks the truth. She is indispensably part of his conception of himself.

But Pip never sees the real Estella. She exists for him through the mediating consciousness of Miss Havisham, who lives in the past. If Estella is the "embodiment of every graceful fancy" for Pip, she is forever the embodiment of lost youth for Miss Havisham. Pip comes upon Miss Havisham in a room lighted with wax candles from which the light of day has been excluded: "It was a dressing-room, as I supposed from the furniture. . . . But prominent in it was a draped table with a gilded looking-glass, and that I made out at first sight to be a fine lady's dressing-table" (chapter 8). Once again, as in *Bleak House* and *A Tale of Two Cities,* a real mirror is at the center of a scene of self-formation. Miss Havisham, with her half-arranged veil, is seated before the looking-glass, one of the many objects "all confusedly heaped about [it]." She has been transfixed, not only by Compeyson's premeditated denial of her existence, but by her own visage in the glass. Pip sees her as "some ghastly waxwork at [a]

Fair": she is, like Mrs. Skewton in *Dombey and Son,* like the Marquis St. Evrémonde in *A Tale of Two Cities,* a grotesque revenant, paralytically animated by her memories. And she casts a spell of arrest upon those who enter her house: for Miss Havisham, who knows nothing of days or weeks, time and change no longer exist.

Commanded to call Estella, Pip is momentarily confused: "As she was still looking at the reflection of herself, I thought she was still talking to herself, and kept quiet" (chapter 8). Miss Havisham is communing with her self, and continues to do so until the episode of the fire, when she will see in Pip "a looking-glass" showing her what she once felt herself (chapter 49). Estella becomes Miss Havisham's reflection, not of the person she once was, but of someone she wishes she had been, impervious to the inducements of the gentleman who duped and abandoned her. She has created a figure out of her own fantasies who will break the hearts of men and beggar their selves as her own self has been beggared. Pip begins to desire Estella under the influence of Miss Havisham's mediating gaze, seeing in her only what Miss Havisham sees: "Miss Havisham said, 'Let me see you two play at cards; . . . .' I was beggared, as before; and again, as before, Miss Havisham watched us all the time, directed my attention to Estella's beauty, and made me notice it the more by trying her jewels on Estella's breast and hair" (chapter 11). In this macabre and erotic ritual, Miss Havisham invades the center of Pip's fragile self, remorselessly empties it, and then compels the boy to gaze upon Estella, reduced metonymically to the jewels she wears, an object deservedly beyond the boy's reach.

Ironically, the ritual is curiously meaningless for Miss Havisham. Pip is a makeshift substitute for an absent gentleman. In Miss Havisham's scheme of things, Pip has no self worthy of being beggared. But beggared he is: Pip acts upon the need to fill the emptiness within him. He will begin to reconstitute a self by emulating a shadowy figure of the imagination, that "him," the absent gentleman for whom Miss Havisham perversely grooms Estella. In Pip's life there is no legacy of novels whose heroes serve as models to be copied; there is no Steerforth upon whom to fashion an ambiguous self. Pip will commit an act of plagiarism, in imitating Miss Havisham's, and thus Estella's, idea of a gentleman. He absorbs Miss Havisham's destructive snobbery, a snobbery inseparable from the contempt she feels for herself, the result of the events of her aborted wedding day. Her self-hatred becomes contagious, a form of René Girard's "ontological sickness." It is a disease of being passed on both to Estella and to Pip: "In the heavy air of the room, and the heavy darkness that brooded in its remoter corners, I even had an alarming fancy that Estella and I might presently begin to decay" (chapter 11). And they do decay, subtly and irreversibly, from within. At the center of the self that Pip begins to create lies the seed of a self-hatred only intensified by his inability to speak of it other than in the form of a displaced guilt he later feels for his shabby, but not unsurprising, treatment of Biddy and Joe.[4]

After his apprenticeship to Joe, Pip will continue to yearn for Estella, "far out of reach, . . . admired by all who see her"; he will continue to hope that he might win her if he were only like those vague admirers with whom he is taunted by Miss Havisham. He can, at best, only imagine their nature, assuming them to be the antitheses of the "little coarse monster" Estella has called him, the monster he still secretly believes himself to be. Through it all, Estella beckons, "like a star," unattainable and unreal, with "her back towards [him], and . . . her pretty brown hair spread out in her two hands," never looking back at the boy (chapter 8).

He pursues an abstraction, a reflection in a figurative glass in which he himself is reflected. These images have been conjured up through the perverse wizardry of the woman he casts as the fairy godmother in the fairy tale of his imagined life. The "poor labyrinth" that is the figurative edifice of his self has as its cornerstone a dead thing, as inert as the jewels with which Estella is so often adorned. Another family constellation, another triad emerges in *Great Expectations*. Without the intersubjective exchange involving both Miss Havisham and Estella, Pip would not become the tortured youth and man he is: "What could I become with these surroundings? How could my character fail to be influenced by them? Is it to be wondered at if *my thoughts were dazed, as my eyes were,* when I came out into the natural light from the misty yellow rooms?" (chapter 12, emphasis mine). Figuratively, Pip does not leave the rooms of Satis House. He remains dazed within them, carrying with him the gorgon's spell cast upon him by Miss Havisham. Satis House, with its brick walls, iron bars, walled-up windows, and stopped clocks, is the St. Evrémonde château transported to England. It has fallen under the spell of Miss Havisham's dementia. Transfixed by Miss Havisham, Pip betrays the meaning of his self-conferred name, to become interred with Miss Havisham, another mummy in a house memorializing a past event of which Pip, for the moment, is ignorant.

Pip's ontological sickness will manifest itself primarily in his uneasy relationship to his past. But other signs mark the effects of the spell cast by Miss Havisham. In his fight with the pale young gentleman—identifiable as a gentleman by his manner, his speech, and his grey suit—Pip comes face to face with a version of the person he wants to be. When the nameless youth issues his comic challenge, Pip feels as if he has no choice: "What could I do but follow him? . . . His manner was so final and I was so astonished, that I followed where he led, as if I had been under a spell" (chapter 11). For the inexperienced Pip, the youth embodies the image of the gentleman inspired in his consciousness by Miss Havisham and Estella. Pip, after the fight, sees himself as the "village [boy] . . . ravaging the houses of gentlefolks and pitching into the studious youth of England": he is at once a rebel and a slave to the figure before him, who only apparently possesses the qualities he desires. The fight dramatizes Pip's alienation from whatever self may at one time have been germinating within him. He has been captured by the specular image of the gentleman discerned in the mirroring faces of others. The reality behind the image is exposed through the ease with which Pip dispatches the wonderfully inept youth, who is playing by those laws of the game that are not only pugilistic but also designed to make Pip feel guilt as an upstart. But social guilt obscures a vague, inarticulated awareness, akin to the smart without a name, that he has lost an earlier, aborning self to become a slave to an abstraction. Pip senses this, yet continues to model himself upon the ideal that must betray him.[5]

The writing Pip is no less alienated from his earlier self. He fails to capture the meaning of his youthful experience, remaining blind to the falsifying shifts in perspective that mark his narrative. In confiding to Biddy that he wants to be a gentleman, the young Pip externalizes the quarrel with himself so perplexing to him. Their exchange not only captures his unthinking condescension towards Biddy, purportedly the moral point of the episode, but also the dilemma inseparable from his aspirations. Biddy, like Joe, has a knack for transforming a case of metaphysics into a case of common sense, inevitably missing the real point. It is not enough to argue that lies are lies, or that Pip would be happier in the station to which he has born. Even if the life at the forge were to

offer satisfactions commensurate with his imaginative and intellectual
capacities, as it does not, Pip cannot abandon the desire to be a gentleman for Estella's sake, even as he senses that she may not be, in Biddy's
words, "worth gaining over."[6] But to abandon the pursuit of Estella involves abandoning that imagined self by which Pip contrives to live, a
self apparently offering invulnerability to the vicissitudes to which he
has been exposed at home and at Satis House. However, behind the aura
of her beauty, Estella is figuratively "stock and stone! . . . [a] cold, cold
heart!" as Miss Havisham finally proclaims (chapter 38). From childhood, she has been turned to stone much as Edith Granger has been by
her mother, Mrs. Skewton. Estella observes, "I . . . have sat on this same
hearth on the little stool that is even now beside you there, learning your
lessons and looking up into your face, when your face was strange and
frightened me!" (chapter 38). The gorgon's stare has performed its cus-
tomary task. The cool indifference to the passion of Miss Havisham, and
to Pip's ardor, so carefully instilled within Estella, has been mistaken by
Miss Havisham and Pip as a sign of a desired autonomy, an invulnerability to attacks upon the self by others. But Estella's is only an illusion
of autonomy, fostered through her relationship with Miss Havisham,
who sees in her the freezing indifference she desires for herself.[7] For the
autonomy that Miss Havisham and Pip desire cannot, and should not,
exist. The self is never invulnerable to intersubjective violations and usur-
pations from without because the self cannot exist without others. This
fact underlies Miss Havisham's crazed definition of love: "It is blind devotion, unquestioning self-humiliation, utter submission, trust and belief against yourself . . . , giving up your whole heart and soul to the
smiter—as I did!" (chapter 29). This is a nightmare vision of a self necessarily conditioned by intersubjective relationships. The self may never
attain the autonomy it desires to preserve it from such a vision. There is
no invulnerability to the potentially ravishing Other: the intersubjective
reality persists throughout the life of the self, unless such life is denied.

    Biddy's common-sense advice, transforming an ontological dilemma
into an ethical one, obscures the complexity of Pip's situation. Her conventional pieties implicitly deny the imperatives to self-creation. They
fail to acknowledge the perils of alienation and paralysis such an imperative poses. Pip already courts both fates in his pursuit of Estella. He has
come to distrust his very real sensitivity to others, an imaginative capacity revealed in his response to the convict and to the mysterious world of

Satis House. In his desire to deflect the power others exercise over him, he "essays [a] form of life, attempts to realize this imaginary character he has resolved to be," only to imagine a self as potentially dead as that of Estella.[8] For Estella is cunningly misnamed: she is not the distant star, generating her own light, but a cold moon reflecting the desires of those who gaze upon her.

Estella, bred and educated to be loved, but not to love, acts the part of the automaton: "I must be taken as I have been made. The success is not mine, the failure is not mine, but the two together make me" (chapter 38). Her disavowal of moral agency involves a form of amnesia. She cannot remember the day when she first met Pip and made him cry. Her stance serves as a sign at once of her complicity and her victimization. For though she chooses forgetfulness to evade responsibility, there is also much that she does not know about herself. Estella lives without any knowledge of her parents, aware only of her utter dependence upon Miss Havisham. Living within a temporal limbo, she is denied another dimension of herself. She must live with the gaps and lacunae of which both Rousseau, in *The Confessions,* and Freud, in *Studies on Hysteria,* write. She can only scrutinize the face of the imperturbable Jaggers with curiosity and distrust, knowing that he alone holds the clues to her past. Estella has been denied those facts, subject to interpretation, that might enable her to place her life within a context and to break the gorgon spell of Miss Havisham. With a face like a statue's, she becomes yet another of Mr. Morfin's images.[9]

Estella has been denied her personal history, even a family name, if one were to exist. Pip chooses to relinquish his history, willfully misreading events in his life so that he may possess a past consonant with the future he imagines for himself. He has invented for himself, in Ortega's words, "a program of life, a static form of being." Pip proceeds to strike out from the chain of his life those days that tend to subvert the idea of the gentleman acquired at Satis House. As in the beginning, in the churchyard, Pip will seek to annihilate the past. He wants time to start with the announcement of his expectations, obliterating much that has occurred before. But he cannot annul time, for the past will assert itself—not simply through a series of apparent coincidences to remind him of it, but also through the resurrection of the past within his own

consciousness, stirring within him a vague, unarticulated awareness of
the true source of his expectations, and the identity of the nameless pa-
tron he wants to evade.   ✓ Magwitch's meeting ch 1

Pip's past first resurrects itself with the appearance of the stranger
with the handkerchief tied over his head and the mysterious file at the
Three Jolly Bargemen on a Saturday night. The event is significant because it reminds Pip of a "feature in [his] low career that [he has] previously forgotten" (chapter 10). It attests to the way in which the past will
manifest itself as a series of signs and tokens demanding his attention.
The episode properly begins when Biddy lends him a "large old English
D which she [has] imitated from the heading of some newspaper." Pip at
first mistakes the copied letter as a design for a buckle. The events of
Pip's life are analogous to those characters to which he has turned, "in a
purblind groping way," as he teaches himself to read, write, and cypher.
Like the long chalk scores on the wall near the door of the Jolly Bargemen, they act as hieroglyphic signs, repeating those which confront Esther Summerson in her encounter with Krook: Pip is about to encounter signs of his past; like Esther, he may choose to recognize them, or to
be blind to their presence and their significance.

The stranger has already determined that he is drinking with the local
blacksmith, and carefully elicits Joe Gargery's name, for Joe is as nameless to the convict of old as *he* is to Joe and Pip. On the alert for Pip,
whose name he does know, the stranger cocks his half-shut eye "as if he
were taking aim at [him] with an invisible gun." He rubs his leg, "in a
very odd way," as it strikes Pip—the first of a series of enigmatic signs
that must be connected in much the same way that Pip's relationship to
Joe, to whom he is neither son nor nephew, must be sorted out and ex-
plained. Pip and Joe are, at best, metonymically connected in a fragile
chain of signification. Finally, the stranger makes his shot, not a "verbal
remark, but a proceeding in dumb show . . . pointedly addressed" only
to Pip. The man stirs his rum-and-water with a file, so that no one else
but Pip may see: "I knew it to be Joe's file, and I knew that he knew my
convict, the moment I saw the instrument. I sat gazing at him, spell-
bound" (chapter 10). There is, of course, no evidence the file is Joe's file
since it may have been lost or confiscated by the soldiers. Pip, possessing
a visionary capacity upon which Herbert Pocket will later remark, imaginatively connects this file with another, placing it into a fragile, met-

onymically associated, chain of meaning. Momentarily, Pip is capable of acknowledging his past, even perhaps of accepting it as he thinks of *his* convict. He does not yet suffer from Estella's symptomatic amnesia.

All too soon the past will come to haunt Pip in his dreams and in his life: "A dread possessed me that when I least expected it, the file would reappear. I coaxed myself to sleep by thinking of Miss Havisham's next Wednesday; and in my sleep I saw the file coming at me out of a door, without seeing who held it, and I screamed myself awake" (chapter 10). The file connects Pip to the events in the churchyard, fitting him into another triad—that of a trembling boy, a semihuman convict, and an unseen young man with "a secret way pecooliar to himself, of getting at a boy, and at his heart, and at his liver." This triad is another family of the imagination, the young man a version of the monster that Pip, with Estella's encouragement, suspects himself to be. He coaxes himself to sleep that night by dwelling upon Miss Havisham and Estella, the other family of the imagination continually beckoning to him. It is his way of censoring his past, of denying that he is a prisoner of time. Ironically, the act of suppression makes him even more a prisoner as he resists those facts that he cannot simply will away.

For Pip the file will continue to act as a sign, both a metonymy and a synecdoche. Any person or event associated, however obliquely, with the world of convicts will, like the file in his dream, allude to the denied events on the marshes, generating a sense of guilt at once both social and ontological in its implications. When the unknown assailant fells Mrs. Joe from behind, Pip at first feels he has had a hand in the attack since she has now been punished for her rampages in a way he might secretly desire. But the presence of a convict's leg-iron that had been filed apart long ago soon leads to different thoughts: "Knowing what I knew, I set up an inference of my own here. I believed the iron to be my convict's iron—the iron I had seen and heard him filing at, on the marshes—but my mind did not accuse him of having put it to its latest use" (chapter 16). Pip cannot know this is the manacle once worn by his convict, just as there is never definitive proof that the stranger at the Jolly Bargemen wielded the file he once stole. Pip connects the file, the leg-iron, and the convict partly to acknowledge a sense of guilt, but also to create meaning out of facts that may well be unrelated and meaningless. He must piece together potentially chance links into the chain of a coherent narrative. The individual life remains for Dickens a series of repetitions, like the large old English *D* copied from another sign in a newspaper. The repetitions may be real or imagined, but they are necessary, for without them the individual life is meaningless, a "tablet upon which time writes every instant a new inscription," as Kierkegaard's persona muses. Repetitions, real or imagined, provide the structure of the human life through the integration of the past into the unfolding narrative of a character's career; they are the signs to which the individual must attribute meaning.[10]

Pip finds he cannot speak of the narrative he has imaginatively forged. The faces and the voices of Miss Havisham and Estella are always with him, imposing upon him *their* interpretation of the events in his life. The inferences he has drawn establish a link to a past event he wishes to forget, yet an event so "grown into [him] and become a part of [himself]" that he cannot tear it away (chapter 16). He will ignore it only at his peril: "It was horrible to think that I had provided the weapon, however undesignedly, but I could hardly think otherwise. I suffered *unspeakable trouble* while I considered and reconsidered whether I should at last *dissolve that spell of my childhood* and tell Joe *all the story*" (chapter 16, emphasis mine). There is no need to be unconscious of the past; there is only the need to be unable to speak of it for dislocation to occur. Pip may piece together a coherent narrative to account for perplexing events. But if he does not speak of it openly, acknowledge it, and integrate it into the conception of himself by which he tries to live, that self will founder as surely as it has in the case of Esther Summerson or Charles Darnay. The only way to dissolve the spell of the past is to speak of it. But he fails to speak of the memorable event that has taken root in his emerging self. Pip runs the risk of becoming like the incapacitated Mrs. Joe, suffering from a traumatic event that has affected her speech and memory. Mrs. Joe communicates only through mysterious signs chalked upon a slate. She creates her own sign system, "again and again and again" tracing upon "the slate, a character that looked like a curious T." It is not a *T*, but a hammer (or so Biddy infers) standing for Orlick: "She had lost his name, and could only signify him by his hammer" (chapter 16). Like Mr. Dick, with his repeated references to the beheaded King Charles, Mrs. Joe alludes figuratively to her assailant and to the attack that has affected her memory. Pip, too, loses his capacity to speak of the past. He will, in fact, try to deny the past altogether by avoiding even those indirect references to it that seem to plague him. He

continues to suffer from the unacknowledged past, referring to it symp-
tomatically, until he can speak or write of it, and integrate it into his
conception of himself.

His suppression of the past, motivated by his desire to become a gentleman, provides the context for Pip's response to Jaggers's sudden appearance at the Three Jolly Bargemen. Almost four years have passed
since Pip's apprenticeship to Joe. The meaning of Miss Havisham's decision to pay his indentures is unambiguous. The ritual is performed before the watching Estella, who is to learn the power of money and class
as Miss Havisham turns Pip over to his master, consigning him forever
to the world of the forge. She even calls Joe back to tell him in an em-
phatic voice, "The boy has been a good boy here, and that is his reward.
Of course, as an honest man, you will expect no other and no more"
(chapter 13). As Joe understands, Pip is to be forever exiled from Satis
House: "Which I meantersay, Pip, it might be that her meaning were—
Make a end on it!—As you was!—Me to the North, and you to the
South!—Keep in sunders!" (chapter 15). The fragile link to Estella is
meant to be sundered as even Pip ruefully has understood. He begins
the annual visits to Miss Havisham, on his birthday, in a pathetic effort
to maintain some connection to Estella, to a part of his imagined self,
only to be greeted with the words, "I hope you want nothing? You'll get
nothing" (chapter 15). Pip lives in the midst of perplexities, caught between a desire to accept the honest working life to which he has been
born and the "confounding remembrance of the Havisham days." Such
a memory would fall upon him "like a destructive missile, and scatter
[his] wits again." His mind "would be dispersed in all directions by one
stray thought, that perhaps after all Miss Havisham was going to make
[his] fortune when [his] time was out" (chapter 17). Pip is, once again,
no better than the "small bundle of shivers" in the churchyard, trying his
best to avoid the dispersal of a fragile self.

Pip cannot relinquish his desire for Estella without abandoning the
idea of himself, fostered through Miss Havisham's mediating influence,
that currently sustains him. He becomes so deeply committed to this as
yet unrealized conception of himself that he refuses to perceive clearly
any sign or token that might subvert it. Choosing to ignore the implications of his own experiences, he suffers, in effect, a loss of memory, a
willed denial of his past. He experiences what, in his discussion of the
case of Miss Lucy R., in *Studies on Hysteria*, Freud calls the "blindness of

the seeing eye," by averting his glance from "something which [does] not fit in at all with [his] expectation" (*SE*, 2 : 117, n. 6). When Jaggers materializes at the Three Jolly Bargemen on a Saturday night, Pip is confronted with a repetition from the past, but willfully connects Jaggers not to the stranger with the file, and thus with the convict on the marshes, but to Satis House and Miss Havisham. For, if he were to acknowledge to himself, on the basis of the evidence before him, the true source of his expectations, Pip would be compelled to a wrenching reimagining of himself, an act for which he is utterly unprepared.[11]

As the convict's emissary, Jaggers follows instructions that cause him to retrace the stranger's steps and to reenact a version of the ritual with the file. His actions repeat the events of that earlier Saturday night. Wopsle is once again there, reading newspaper accounts of assorted crimes, doing the police in different voices. Jaggers interrupts to harangue the listeners about the interpretation of evidence, and the dangers of a hasty verdict—an apt, if indirect, prelude to his asking if "there is a blacksmith among you, by name Joseph—or Joe—Gargery" (chapter 18). His words echo those of the stranger with the file; he assumes that where Joe Gargery the blacksmith is to be found on a Saturday night, as he has been found before, the boy Pip is sure to be. Pip, with the visionary capacity to see in files and leg-irons signs and tokens of his past, can only identify Jaggers as the gentleman he has seen on the stairs during his second visit to Satis House. Two quite different forms of repetition confront Pip with a choice. He ignores the more probable patterns of recurrence, and wills a causal connection where none exists, compelled by his own need to ignore the signs by which Jaggers, perhaps not inadvertently, tries to identify himself and the person he represents. The stipulation that he should bear the name Pip, the only name by which the convict knows him, is yet another sign misread. Miss Havisham, as benefactress, would seek to eradicate the stigma of a name linking Pip to his common origins, just as she obliterated Estella's connections to her origins by refusing to make inquiries of Jaggers.

Jaggers even hints at the identity of the nameless benefactor: "If you have a suspicion in your own breast, keep that suspicion in your own breast. It is not the least to the purpose what the reasons of this prohibition are; they may be the strongest and gravest reasons, or they may be a mere whim" (chapter 18). Jaggers equivocates in his legalistic way, but he thinks the clues are clear enough. The evidence, with its unnerving im-

plications, accumulates. Although he catches at the name of Matthew
Pocket, yet another sign apparently pointing to Miss Havisham, Pip, in
his final request to Jaggers, should at last see how this event does not fit
in at all with his expectations. For Jaggers is simply uncomprehending in
reply to Pip's query, "Would there be any objection to my taking leave of
any one I know, about here, before I go away?" (chapter 18). Jaggers's
"No" is another token Pip willfully misreads. As Jaggers is later to say, in
his self-serving manner, "not a particle of evidence" connects him to Miss
Havisham beyond a chance encounter with a nameless, unremembered
boy some ten years before. Pip becomes lost in "the mazes of [his] future
fortunes," in the labyrinth of the self he has constructed, brick by brick,
out of those facts he misinterprets to create a false strand of repetitions:
his manuscript confession, like Rousseau's, reveals its own miry maze in
which he may become lost. Though others share in his complicity, he
has made, in Miss Havisham's words, his "own snares," and he remains
responsible for them. The stranger with the file has come on a Saturday
night to deliver "two fat sweltering one-pound notes"; Jaggers comes on
a Saturday night to announce "Great Expectations." Pip refuses to make
the connection. He suppresses the past, knowing on some level of his
consciousness the source of those expectations, and wishing it were not
so. Pip seeks to sunder the metonymic chain—the leg-iron, the file, the
stranger with the half-shut eye, the one-pound notes—and to consign
the nameless convict, no longer represented even by a sign, to the graveyard of the past. He wills the convict literally and figuratively to his
death, and he apparently succeeds.[12]

   Pip now begins to move through a world of signs and tokens all of
which remind him, however darkly, of his condition. Throughout his
manuscript confession, Pip not only reconstructs events as he now understands them, but tries to capture the phenomenological truth of the
experiences as they occurred. From his present perspective he continues
to moralize, to take events out of the region of metaphysics into the regions of the ethical and the social. But he remains reluctantly in touch
with an earlier version of himself, the visionary youth who, like David
Copperfield, is still a poet of the memory with the capacity to "behave as
'timelessly' as the unconscious itself" (*SE*, 17:10) and to pierce the mist
of circumstance to revelatory moments. For both the younger Pip, as for
the authorial Pip, there exists a need to regain something that has been
lost. "Recapturing the past," as René Girard observes, "is recapturing

the original impression beneath the opinion of others which hides it; it is to recognize that this opinion is not one's own. It is to understand that the process of mediation creates a very vivid impression of autonomy and spontaneity precisely when we are no longer autonomous and spontaneous."[13] Pip, in his new suit, goes through "an immensity of posturing with Mr. Pumblechook's very limited dressing-glass, in the futile endeavour to see [his] legs" and to convince himself that the suit fits (chapter 19). He stands before his specular image to assure himself he *is* that image, that self he has desired to become. Wanting to believe in the autonomy and the integrity of the character he has imagined, he is implicitly reminded by the image in the glass of the necessarily fragmentary status of a self based upon an incomplete acknowledgment of the past. Pip has become the creature of those Others he hopes either to emulate or to please. His return to his hometown for his sister's funeral only reinforces his doubts about the status of the self incompletely reflected in Pumblechook's glass. Trabb's boy "[feigns] to be in a paroxysm of terror and contrition, occasioned by the dignity of [Pip's] appearance" (chapter 30). The tailor's boy mocks the pretense of gentility, "strutting along the pavement . . . , wriggling his elbows and body, and drawling to his attendants, 'Don't know yah, don't know yah, pon my soul, don't know yah!'" (chapter 30). Pip's sense of injured helplessness in the face of this dodging serpent is a symptom of his own unease, his implicit recognition of the lie that he is living: it is another mark of his ontological malaise, and his humanity.

Pip begins to encounter avenging phantoms, pointing always to the falseness of his current situation. In London, he engages a servant boy in top boots: "After I had made this monster (out of the refuse of my washerwoman's family) and had clothed him . . . , I had to find him a little to do and a great deal to eat; and with both of these horrible requirements he haunted my existence" (chapter 27). Pepper, "the compromising name of the avenging boy," is Pip's Frankensteinian creation, a diminutive Double reminding him of that human offal that is the true source of his expectations, the origin of his precariously established self. Pepper is Pip's allegorical way of acknowledging the unacknowledgable. On the journey to Satis House, where he is to be reintroduced to Estella, Pip accidentally confronts yet another token of the past. As he travels by coach, he shares the outside seat with two convicts, one of whom proves to be the stranger with the half-closed eye who has appeared at the Three Jolly Bargemen on a Saturday night. The man offers an account of that evening to his fellow convict as Pip, unrecognized, dozes, to awaken to "the words of [his] own thought, 'Two One-Pound notes.'" The gift of which the convict speaks and of which Pip has been dreaming, metonymically associated with Saturday night, refers simultaneously to the night of the convict's visit and to that other Saturday night when Jaggers appeared with the gift of Great Expectations. Pip refuses to acknowledge the significance of his dream even as he is "touched in the marrow [as if] with some pungent and searching acid" by the convict's presence, and his words. Pip remains determined to treat as pure coincidence events in his life that remind him, like Pepper, the Avenger, of the suppressed past.[14]

Pip's awareness of the significance of his earlier sensitivity to these apparently meaningless events reveals how fully he now, in writing, perceives them as tokens of his condition, posing a threat to the fragile conception of himself that he once bore to Satis House as a form of tribute to Estella. The younger Pip seeks always to deny the implications of these revelatory moments. But, "there is no such thing as *forgetting* possible to the mind; a thousand accidents may, and will interpose a veil between our present consciousness and the secret inscriptions on the mind; . . . but alike, whether veiled or unveiled, the inscriptions remain for ever." For Pip, as for De Quincey, "accidents of the same sort will also rend away this veil": the unnerving visit to Newgate with Wemmick compels Pip to free himself of the memory of the events on the marshes that seem to pervade his clothing, and his being, "like a stain that was faded but not gone" (chapter 32). Like De Quincey's stars that shine forever, the figurative stain fades only to return again unexpectedly.[15] So it does with the arrival of Estella, for whom Pip has been waiting: "I saw her face at the coach window and her hand waving to me." The nameless shadow, passing instantly, is Pip's memory of Jaggers's female servant, Molly, she of the streaming hair and the scarred wrists. Whenever he is visited by intimations of Estella's similarity to Molly, Pip is returned to Molly serving dinner at Jaggers's table and, curiously, to thoughts of a performance of *Macbeth* and the faces he "had seen [rising] out of the Witches' caldron." He confesses, "Years afterwards, I made a dreadful likeness of [Molly], by causing a face that had no other natural resemblance to it than it derived from flowing hair, to pass behind a bowl of flaming spirits in a dark room" (chapter 26). Pip produces his own romantic image, fusing Molly and Estella, with her luxuriant hair, into a single, demonic Medusa's head. Even years afterwards he seeks to degrade Estella, as he once created a past for her akin to his own denied past. The desire to establish connections between the two women becomes Pip's revenge upon Estella, and a displacement for his failure to decipher the hieroglyphic events of his own experience.

These varied experiences become the signs and tokens of Pip's dilemma, of his refusal to piece together and to acknowledge, to himself and to others, what he knows within the "marrow" of his self. Instead of experiencing a sense of autonomy and spontaneity, he is wracked by an awareness of dependency and uncertainty. Unable to name any one person as his benefactor, upon whom his expectations depend, Pip remains a victim of a past about which he fears to speculate. Until he fully possesses that past, as part of his story, his narrative conception of himself, he remains, like Estella, fixed in a temporal limbo. At Satis House, prior to the fateful night upon which the ghost of Hamlet's father will mount the stairs to his rooms, Pip sees his condition mirrored before him: "As I looked round at [the candles], and at the pale gloom they made, and at the stopped clock, and at the withered articles of bridal dress upon the table and the ground, and at [Miss Havisham's] own awful figure with its ghostly reflection thrown large by the fire upon the ceiling and the wall, I saw in everything the construction that my mind had come to, repeated and thrown back to me" (chapter 38). Nothing has changed since his first visit to the house. Pip sees, and does not see, the "perversion of ingenuity" in Miss Havisham's plans for Estella, and for him, and he still feels that "the prize [has been] reserved" for him. He chooses to become part of the fabric of Miss Havisham's crazy schemes. Knowing her story, he permits himself to become entombed, with Estella, in a house and a construct that is merely a memorial of the past. The three of them inhabit the figurative center of this labyrinthine edifice, paralytically repeating the past and inwardly eroding, as the mice and the spiders feed upon the wedding cake and their captive selves. Pip arrives at the construction of Miss Havisham's plans, even as he acquiesces to the structure of a self informed, he would believe, by them.

Pip has become identified both with the inhabitants of Satis House and with the fortunes of the house itself. The house and the self, both obsolete edifices, resist the passage of the seasons, the ebb and flow of the tides. As in *Bleak House* and *A Tale of Two Cities,* the dislocation of the self is revealed through architectural figures of speech. In her delirium Esther Summerson dreams of "[labouring] up colossal staircases, ever striving to reach the top, and ever turned, as [she has] seen a worm in a garden path, by some obstruction, and labouring again." Charles Darnay and his uncle become identified with the St. Evrémonde château, "a stony business altogether, ... As if the Gorgon's head had surveyed it, when it was finished, two centuries ago." The buildings, part of literal and figurative dreamscapes, suggest a self in stasis. They conjure up De Quincey's recollection of Coleridge's account of Piranesi's *Dreams,* a set of plates recording "the scenery of his own visions during the delirium of a fever." Some of the plates "represented vast Gothic halls: on the floor of which stood all sorts of engines and machinery, wheels, cables, pulleys, levers, catapults, &c. &c. expressive of enormous power put forth, and resistance overcome. Creeping along the sides of the walls, you perceived a staircase; and upon it, groping his way upwards, was Piranesi himself: follow the stairs a little further, and you perceive it come to a sudden abrupt termination, without any balustrade, and allowing no step onwards to him who had reached the extremity, except into the depths below" (p. 330). The staircase and the balked Piranesi are repeated endlessly, with "poor Piranesi busy on his aspiring labours: and so on, until the unfinished stairs and Piranesi both are lost in the upper gloom of the hall" (p. 330). De Quincey offers a vision of the arrested and the unfinished self, cut off from the process of self-creation as it hovers over the mysterious depths of its own origins.

So it is with Esther, Darnay, and Pip, each of whom struggles in an unproductive laboring. Pip has seen his condition mirrored back to him in Estella, Miss Havisham, and Satis House. Aware intuitively of his impasse, for introspection remains suspect in the Dickens world, Pip must will the fall of the edifice he has, with the help of others, constructed. As he writes of the "heavy slab" that is "to fall on the bed of state," Pip refers to the quarry, the tunnel, the rope, the roof, the iron ring, and the labor leading the sultan to his self-destruction as he wields the axe that parts the rope, causing "the roof of [his] stronghold [to drop] upon" him (chapter 38). The parallels to the *Confessions* point to the similarities between De Quincey and Pip, each at work on a manuscript confession, each striving to emerge out of impasse. But such a change demands the collapse of the house of the self into its own depths, and its reconstruction upon new foundations.

Pip wields the axe of fate in the dead of the night. He summons from the lower reaches of his chambers in Garden-court the nameless person buried in its figurative depths. Of course, the convict literally returns, but only when Pip's condition demands the self's transformation, or its death. The night of the return recalls the evening on which the disoriented David Copperfield travels toward Yarmouth and the tempest: "It was wretched weather; stormy and wet, stormy and wet; . . . high buildings in town had had the lead stripped off their roofs; and in the country, trees had been torn up, and sails of windmills carried away; and gloomy accounts had come in from the coast, of shipwreck and death" (chapter 39). Again, the chaos in nature reflects the chaos within Pip. As David has done before him, Pip looks out through black windows into a darkened courtyard and into a realm of surging water. Unlike David, who falls asleep to dream, Pip reads on until the clock strikes eleven. He experiences a waking dream as he hears a footstep on the stair that makes him start, and "awfully connect[s] it with the footstep of [his] dead sister." Presiding over the resurrection of the man he has wished dead, Pip even now cannot confront the figure from the past who will speak of himself as Pip's second father. The thought of the dead sister, felled by the leg-iron, alludes metonymically to the still nameless convict. The divided Pip recalls him to life even as he continues to will his death, as he once may have willed the death of his sister.

Pip's chambers, like "a storm-beaten light-house," become a fragile citadel of consciousness necessarily admitting the voice and the face "from the darkness beneath." With his recognition of the convict, Pip at last seems on the way to regaining the autonomy and spontaneity he has relinquished both to Miss Havisham and Estella and to that idea of himself to which he has become habituated. His response to the convict is telling: "If the wind and the rain had driven away the intervening years, . . . had swept us to the churchyard where we first stood face to face . . . , I could not have known my convict more distinctly than I knew him now" (chapter 39). Pip has returned to the moment time began for him, to the man he has always known to be his benefactor. He may also be returned to himself through his acceptance of the past that the faces of Miss Havisham and Estella, always with him in his imagination, have caused him to reject. But the process is difficult, its outcome forever in doubt. The repugnance Pip at first feels for the still nameless figure is social and ethical: it is also ontological. He has erected his conception of himself upon hypotheses designed to wall out disturbing facts. With the tendency of the self to be conservative, with its reluctance to abandon even an obsolete structure, Pip can only experience a loss of self-possession and a desire to faint: "For an hour or more, I remained too stunned to think; and it was not until I began to think, that I began fully to know how wrecked I was, and how the ship in which I had sailed was gone to pieces" (chapter 39). The old self founders: Pip momentarily yearns for the forge, for Joe and Biddy, though he knows he "could never, never, never, undo what [he has] done." At that moment, he ceases merely to be the puppet of his own desires and of the desires of others. He begins to accept responsibility for his suppression of the past, moving tentatively out of impasse, perhaps to rejoin the flux of time suggested by the elements raging outside his chambers.

But just as he only gradually overcomes his repugnance to the presence of Magwitch—whose actions, but especially whose story, humanize him—Pip only slowly begins to incorporate the denied past into his sense of himself. He cannot formulate a plan for the future because he cannot yet imagine what kind of future might proceed logically from the embodied past he now confronts. Nor has he yet conferred upon past events those meanings that will make action of any sort possible. He has encountered his past face to face; he has not yet fully understood it or interpreted it. Pip continues to act under the spell cast by Miss Havisham, even as he proceeds to free himself from it. To live without a self remains impossible, and Pip relies still upon the self conjured up through his face to face interaction with Miss Havisham and Estella. He cannot separate Estella, "in the past or in the present, from the innermost life of [his] life." The life he has imagined for himself, his "poor labyrinth" with his vision of Estella at its center, is that of the knight of romance whose trials will empower him "to restore the desolate house, admit the sunshine into the dark rooms, set the clocks a going and the cold hearths a blazing, . . . and marry the Princess" (chapter 29). The fairy tale of Sleeping Beauty is apparently the rich mystery of which Pip is the hero. The story has conferred meaning on his life and bestowed upon an iron age a sorely needed aura of romance. Finally, Pip, in pursuit of an elusive self, is a romantic hero engaged in an internalized quest-romance.[16] It is

an ironic quest: in admitting the sunlight into Satis House, Pip will
undo Miss Havisham and himself. Like the archaeologist who unearths
"bodies buried in ancient times," he will cause them to fall "to powder in
the moment of being distinctly seen" (chapter 8). Pip may prove to be
not the Prince of fairy tale, but the Theseus or Perseus of classical myth,
following a clue of thread to a monstrous encounter.

In his final meeting with Miss Havisham, Pip will live out the logic of
the romantic career he has envisioned for himself. He is true, if only
ironically, to the self he has created, and fulfills his destiny. He confronts
one gorgon figure in his life, now transformed, no longer all stone, as
she once has been. Miss Havisham has been touched into life by gazing
into Pip's face and seeing there, as in "a looking-glass," what she once
felt herself (chapter 49). Pip's anguish over Estella destroys Miss Havisham's false autonomy. She drops on her knees at his feet, presses his
hand, and weeps. The stony effigy to the past has melted, as Esther Summerson and Lady Dedlock have, through a process of empathy and self-
recognition. There is something gratifying in her plea for forgiveness, as
there has been in Lady Dedlock's similar plea at the feet of Esther. But
Pip, like Esther, wills a greater satisfaction: he once again fancies Miss
Havisham hanging from a beam of the abandoned brewery, as he has on
his first visit to Satis House. It serves as an omen, signifying his desire
for retribution not only against Miss Havisham, but against that obsolete self, influenced by her mirroring gaze, that he is in the process of
relinquishing. Miss Havisham, no less than Estella, is part of his existence, part of himself.[17]

The fire that consumes Miss Havisham, leading to her death, will
consume Pip's self in a Carlylean transformation through flame, if genuine transformation is to be his fate. In his attempt to save her, he pulls
the cloth from the table with the wedding-cake, dragging down "the
heap of rottenness in the midst." The two struggle on the ground, like
desperate enemies. As Pip puts it, "I still held her forcibly down with all
my strength, like a prisoner who might escape; and I doubt if I even
knew who she was, or why we had struggled" (chapter 49). He struggles
with a version of himself, with someone whose identity has been consumed by the course of events. Through the fire, the figurative darkness
of Satis House has been dispelled. Satis House still stands, only awaiting
the time when it is "to be sold as old building materials, and pulled
down." Miss Havisham's garments are ashes, the process of dissolution

apparently ended. She lies upon the great table, where the wedding cake once decayed, "covered . . . to the throat with white-cotton wool, and . . . with a white sheet loosely over-lying that, the phantom air of something that had been and was changed . . . still upon her" (chapter 49). Her bandages are her chrysalis, a sign that she may once again, if only briefly, be participating in that "world of change" of which Mrs. Chick speaks in *Dombey and Son*.

The swathed body of Miss Havisham suggests the possibilities and the perils of transformation if Pip is to emulate Mrs. Chick's silkworm who changes into all sorts of unexpected things continually. The concluding pages of Pip's manuscript confession record his effort to gather together the filaments of his past, as if he were seeking to weave the chrysalis of his own transformation. But it is not clear whether Pip follows the thread of Magwitch's narrative and the stories of Molly and Estella in order to prepare for a newly emerging self, or to twist them into the strands of a cable anchoring the old, foundering self, in order to sever them forever. Before the events at Satis House culminating in Miss Havisham's fiery accident, Pip has begun to gain some knowledge of Magwitch's past. He must understand the history of Magwitch, the self-proclaimed second father, if he is to understand his own history, so that he may live it out rather than be lived by it. He must interweave the thread of Magwitch's narrative, as well as those of others, known and unknown to him, into the fabric of his own story. If he does not, he will remain the victim of those complex influences that have informed his life. Pip must, in Hans Loewald's words, weave his history into a complex design, at once fascinating, and harrowing.[18]

As he reviews "the book of his remembrance," and offers his account of his life, Magwitch speaks of the gentleman thief, Compeyson, and the shadowy accomplice, Arthur, haunted by the specter of a woman, "Sally, . . . all in white." Herbert Pocket recognizes these figures as part of Miss Havisham's story. They are, inevitably, part of Pip's story too. He has encountered Compeyson not only on the marshes with Magwitch. The ghost of Compeyson has shadowed his every experience at Satis House. As the target of her hatred, Compeyson is the model of all the gentlemen against whom Miss Havisham seeks vengeance through Estella. As the "chance boy" who has been "a model with a mechanical heart" for Estella to practice upon, Pip unwittingly becomes a version of the absent Compeyson: the gentleman he aspires to be, perceived darkly in the mirroring glances of Miss Havisham's face, is a reflection of the man she most detests. Pip is stalked inevitably by a multitude of parental specters. Compeyson, no less than Magwitch and Molly, connects the episode on the marshes to apparently unrelated events at Satis House. Appropriately, Compeyson appears behind him when Pip attends the play in which Mr. Wopsle is performing. From the stage Wopsle stares "in [Pip's] direction as if he were lost in amazement"; he has been gazing at someone of whom Pip is "quite unconscious . . . , sitting behind [him] there like a ghost." Wopsle connects the figure, in a chain of associations, to the Christmas day of long ago, to the two escaped convicts, and finally to the one who had been mauled. Pip recalls his response to Wopsle's words: "I cannot exaggerate . . . the special and peculiar terror I felt at Compeyson's having been behind me 'like a ghost.' For if he had ever been out of my thoughts for a few moments together since the hiding [of Magwitch] had begun, it was in those very moments when he was closest to me" (chapter 47). Pip, consciously and unconsciously, has begun to make all the connections the various narratives suggest. Compeyson is yet another second father. He, too, has influenced the self Pip has willed into existence.

At Jaggers's house, after the night at the theatre, other connections emerge as Pip watches Molly and the movement of her fingers, so like the act of knitting, as if she were one of the three Fates weaving the destinies of others. Yet Pip is the true weaver, as he notes Molly's eyes, hands, and flowing hair, and he is returned to Satis House and the knitting Estella, listening, unmoved, to his anguished words: "I thought how one link of association had helped that identification in the theatre, and how such a link, wanting before, had been riveted for me now. . . . And I felt absolutely certain that this woman was Estella's mother" (chapter 48). As before, the unconscious is made conscious; the connections, sensed up until this moment but never acknowledged, are now articulated. But Pip never possesses conclusive evidence that Molly *is* Estella's mother. He weaves together the stories of Miss Havisham, Estella, and Magwitch; he listens to Wemmick's account of Molly's past and hears Herbert Pocket's version of the story Magwitch has told of his "Missis" and their daughter. Pip arrives at an hypothesis only indirectly confirmed by the imaginary case Jaggers offers of the daughter of a woman accused of murder and of an unnamed woman of wealth who wants to adopt a female child. Pip is convinced by the coherence between the stories and the second-hand accounts he hears as well as by the chronological correspondences between them. As Steven Marcus observes, "What we end with, then, is a fictional construction which is at the same time satisfactory to us in the form of the truth, and as the form of truth."[19]

But the truth need not reassure. What Pip observes to himself about Compeyson, during the episode at the theatre, applies to Magwitch, to Molly, to his entire past: "To think that I should be so unconscious and off my guard after all my care, . . . as if I had shut an avenue of a hundred doors to keep him out, and then had found him at my elbow. I could not doubt either that he was there, because I was there" (chapter 47). Pip carries his past with him, even when unconscious of it; the past, in the form of the specters haunting him, remains dangerous, "always near and active." The various figures of speech converge. Pip, the former blacksmith, has forged a chain of associative links to which he is, ironically, riveted. He has followed the narrative threads of different stories, weaving them imaginatively into an ensnaring web. As the hero of his own internalized quest-romance, he has become the archaeologist of his own past, excavating the labyrinth with its hundred doors in which he is trapped. He has discovered the medium of time, the regions of the mind, and the nature of personal history. And he seeks release from his discoveries, and freedom from any of the hypothetical selves to be founded upon those versions of the past he has imaginatively reconstructed. It is no wonder that he feels "as if [his] last anchor were loosening its hold, and [he] should soon be driving with the winds and waves" (chapter 52). Pip anticipates, as he wills, the foundering of the ark of the self, the dissolution of those potential selves that provide no escape from the shaping influence of personal history.

The Pip who could once imagine himself as the hero of a "rich attractive mystery" has completed his quest, only to stand, like Childe Roland, before the squat tower of disillusionment. Out of the past he has reconstructed, part willfully, part inadvertently, emerges a welter of surrogate parents whose stories speak of violence, betrayal, murder, and madness. Pip may well be fated to repeat a version of the past lived by these now spectral parents. And he chooses not to. With the return of Magwitch, Pip begins to feel a sense of disorientation that intensifies until he lapses into a state of literal and figurative arrest. The self he has constructed upon a false hypothesis is, nevertheless, lived out to its logical conclusion as he brings light into the darkened rooms of Satis House. In the months between the November of Magwitch's return and the onset of the final illness, Pip increasingly desires to be "driving with the winds and waves," to let the flux of events envelop his now obsolete self, and those other selves his complex past would seem to presage, as the elements engulf the St. Evrémonde château: he wishes no longer to be time's victim and to start anew, untrammeled by the past.

The anonymous letter, darkly posing threats to Magwitch, leads to the inevitable coach ride, returning Pip to the marshes and to the beginning of his story. Like David Copperfield, Esther Summerson, and Charles Darnay, Pip sets out upon yet another figurative journey during which his disorientation becomes delirium. He has "not been [himself] since the receipt of the letter"; he wonders "at [himself] for being in the coach"; he ponders his response to an anonymous communication, a communication from the depths of his own consciousness. At the inn, unrecognized by the landlord, he is entertained with his own story, and hears of his ingratitude to his benefactor, the worthy Pumblechook. There are too many figures from the past eager to claim Pip; he is instinctively drawn to the two, Biddy and Joe, who seem to make no claims at all.

In approaching the limekiln and the stone quarry near it, Pip moves into the landscape of a De Quincean dream: the dark night, the full moon, the mountains of cloud, the vapour of the kiln suggest a region of the mind. The voice from behind, actually Orlick's, becomes his own voice, displaced upon a dream figure. Orlick is a threat to his life, but it is the threat of dissolution that Pip seeks out. Orlick materializes as unexpectedly as Magwitch and Compeyson, each of them summoned to a terrible reckoning. Orlick's threats reveal Pip's own desires: "You're dead . . . . I won't have a rag of you, I won't have a bone of you, left on earth. I'll put your body in the kiln—I'd carry two such to it, on my shoulders—and, let people suppose what they may of you, they shall never know nothing" (chapter 53). Pip experiences the dispersal of those selves from the past that he wishes dead, to make way for a new self that may well be emerging through his disoriented laboring.

Pip, moved by a Carlylean "law of Perseverance," both desires and fears to quit Teufelsdröckh's "old house" of his self, to be "changed into a part of the vapour that [has] crept towards [him] but a little while before," like his "own warning ghost." The unresolved conflict is marked by his decision to come to the limekiln and by the curious dropping of the anonymous letter in the chambers shared with Herbert Pocket. He has left behind a sign that leads to his rescue. The loss of consciousness he experiences before his rescue is but another stage in the unreal progress that is to free him from the past and to prepare him for yet another form of being adumbrated by the remorse he feels not only about Magwitch but about Biddy and Joe. He has begun to anticipate the self he wills into being; he has started to impose upon the chaotic tale of his life an interpretation that will render it at once intelligible and endurable.

"Melted at heart," as Miss Havisham has melted into tears, Pip now lives out the logic of a self that has an acknowledged debt to Magwitch, so that he may become free of it. One hypothetical self has been figuratively consumed by the fire at Satis House, leaving Pip maimed and dependent on others. Another possible self, whose second father is Magwitch, will be surrendered to the waters of the Thames. On the night before the plan to spirit Magwitch out of England is implemented, the illness that has plagued Pip intensifies: "My burning arm throbbed, and my burning head throbbed, and I fancied I was beginning to wander. I counted up to high numbers, to make sure of myself, and repeated passages that I knew in prose and verse" (chapter 53). The self is no longer sure and though Pip will awaken the following morning to feel strong and well, it is, at best, only a temporary respite from a process of dissolution that goes on apace. Pip, with Pocket and Startop, who must row for him, moves along the debris-strewn river. The "rusty chain-cables, frayed hempen hawsers, and bobbing buoys, . . . [the] chips of wood and shaving," the general refuse of the river, reflect the chaos within Pip. The degree to which he unwillingly performs the final obligation to Magwitch is revealed in his curious inability to name him. Time and again the convict is only "he," rarely, if ever, Magwitch or Provis: Pip unwittingly consigns the convict to the realm of namelessness from which he has come.

Magwitch himself anticipates, more surely than Pip, what is to happen: "We can no more see to the bottom of the next few hours, than we can see to the bottom of this river what I catches hold of. Nor yet we can't no more hold their tide than I can hold this" (chapter 54). Magwitch seems to accept the fate that, within the submerged currents of the self, Pip wishes both for himself and the ex-convict. Their journey downstream occurs amidst signs of the impending doom of this version of

Pip's self. The shore reminds Pip of his own marsh country. A squat shoal-lighthouse on open piles, stands "crippled in the mud on stilts and crutches," while "an old landing-stage and an old roofless building" slip into the mud, just as the edifice of Pip's self undergoes its own collapse. The public-house in which the four rest has bedrooms from which "the air [is] as carefully excluded . . . as if air were fatal to life" (chapter 54). The Jack of the causeway wears a "bloated pair of shoes, . . . interesting relics that he [has] taken a few days ago from the feet of a drowned seaman washed ashore." The tavern, like Satis House, is a burial vault. The Jack is reminiscent of the bloated gaoler in La Force who introduces Charles Darnay to the kingdom of the living-dead; he prefigures Gaffer Hexam and Rogue Riderhood, those fishers of the Thames in *Our Mutual Friend*.

Pip's malaise, like the river's tides, must run its course. With the appearance of Compeyson in the four-oared galley, Pip is figuratively returned to the marshes, to the old triad of a shivering boy and two convicts, one of whom has been mauled: "I saw that the face disclosed was the face of the other convict of long ago. Still in the same moment, I saw the face tilt backward with a white terror on it that I shall never forget, and heard a great cry on board the steamer and a loud splash in the water, and felt the boat sink from under me" (chapter 54). The ark of the self founders with the sinking of the boat and the disappearance of the two convicts, who are really convicts no more, into the river. Only Magwitch returns from the depths after the fierce struggle with Compeyson whose disfigured body is later reclaimed. One specter from the past has been dispatched, soon to be followed by Magwitch. His repugnance to Magwitch has "all melted away," but Pip nevertheless feels it "unquestionably best that he should die." He wills the death of Magwitch, who remains the last connection to the past he has so deftly reconstructed. Pip finds it impossible to imagine a viable self able to accommodate itself to the riddles posed by the past. He can only will the annulment of time, a return to a new beginning. He remains loyal to Magwitch to the end, informing the dying man that his lost daughter is alive and a lady and that he loves her. But the connections between Magwitch, Molly, and Estella are never proved. They are willed, convincing to Pip, and to us, because they satisfy a profound need: they provide a sense of an ending, achieved by an act of the imagination.[20]

With no purpose and power left to him, Pip sinks into the realm of

delirium and dream, the final stage of his disease. He dreams of the river-
boat, metonymically associated with the riven self; of lighting a lamp,
"possessed by the idea that he was coming up the stairs"; of Miss Havisham consuming within an iron furnace; of the vapors of the limekiln.
He wants to dispel the past in his fear that it will return and that he will
be compelled to repeat it. At last, he wills the death of the selves he has,
in part, created, but from which he is now estranged. The two men who
appear to arrest him for debt hang in his memory by a single thread. The
onset of fever leads to a loss of reason and to the sense that time seems
interminable. He describes that time: "I confounded impossible exis-
tences with my own identity; . . . I was a brick in the house wall, and yet
entreating to be released from the giddy place where the builders had set
me; . . . I was a steel beam of a vast engine, clashing and whirling over
a gulf, and yet . . . I implored in my own person to have the engine
stopped, and my part in it hammered off" (chapter 57). Two tropes so
central to the novel again converge: the slender thread connecting Pip to
this De Quinceian fever will be sundered; the edifice of which he is an
unwilling part, a brick deprived of human agency, will be removed. He
has spoken to Estella of those "stones of which the strongest London
buildings are made" as not "more real, or more impossible to be displaced . . . than [her] presence and influence" have been to him (chapter 44). Here he wills the collapse of the self of which Estella has been
the figurative keystone. He wants no longer to be a mere thing, a beam
in the engine of the past, but to become his "own person." This passage
does not suggest Pip's acceptance of the past, but his denial of it. The
past remains an entangling web, a haunted labyrinth, from which he
wants to escape. And escape he does, as he awakens to a face looking
tenderly upon him, the face of Joe. He perceives Joe, "this gentle Christian man!" as the one feature in his life that does not change.

Pip is in the process of reconstituting a self based upon yet another
triad. Joe and Biddy are to replace both the two convicts on the marshes
and Miss Havisham and Estella. Pip will imagine a self modeled upon
Joe, decent, unimaginative, and enduring, but a self relieved of bondage
to the forge. Joe remains the bumbling, inept figure from whom Pip
once legitimately turned away. Unchanged, he is apart from the tides of
history that have engulfed Pip: "Exactly what he had been in my eyes [in
the past], he was in my eyes still; just as simply faithful, just as simply
right" (chapter 57). Within this passage lies a falsification of Pip's experi-

ence with Joe, hinted at by the ambiguities of the word *simply*. Joe was the man who could not protect Pip from the Tickler, the man who could only observe that "lies is lies." Even now, he wields a pen as if it were a crowbar or a sledge-hammer. Joe prefers not to hear Pip's late history: the entangled mysteries of the past are "onnecessary" subjects to him.

Pip turns to Joe, who annihilates time and simplifies the human condition. He becomes the child again, "as if [he] were still the small helpless creature to whom [Joe] had so abundantly given of the wealth of his great nature" (chapter 57). Pip recreates Joe in his imagination, falsifying the past in his desire to "believe that all [his] life since the days of the old kitchen was one of the mental troubles of the fever that was gone." Pip, a poet of the memory like David Copperfield before him, has behaved as timelessly as the unconscious itself in the service of the muse of personal history. But, in being true to his muse, whether Clio or Clio's mother, Mnemosyne, Pip has woven a history that appalls. The action of the knitting fingers of Estella and Molly connect the two, suggesting a web of the past that can only ensnare. Pip will always connect the mother and the daughter not only with the Fates, but with "a face rising out of [a] caldron," a dreadful likeness of Molly and Estella, with "no other natural resemblance to [them] than . . . derived from flowing hair": Clio or Mnemosyne has proved, for Pip, to be a Medusa whom he has been unable to slay. Pip betrays his muse, relinquishing the visionary capacity to detect significant repetitions and to connect them into a coherent whole. Like Victor Frankenstein, he recoils, not from Magwitch, but from his own imaginative achievement: "The imaginary student pursued by the misshapen creature he had impiously made, was not more wretched than I, pursued by the creature who had made me" (chapter 40). Pip writes of Magwitch here, but he is more truly speaking of his reconstruction of a past that seems to determine a self, or selves, from which he flees. He flees that self and its history, only to imagine another past, one that never was, which will be the foundation of a new self he wills into existence.

Pip returns to his native place and to the now "dear old forge" in his desire to annul the past once and for all. His dream of marrying Biddy involves his acceptance of her earnest, conservative values that deny the legitimacy of his former aspirations and also the mysteries of time, change, and personal history. Before he can escape the Blue Boar to act upon his plan, he meets Pumblechook, who accuses the figurative Telemachus of ingratitude. Already, there emerges a new way of imposing meaning upon his experience and of obscuring its darkest implications. Pip begins to see himself as the prodigal son, now chastened, returning home. On this delightful June day, he feels "like one who was toiling home barefoot from distant travel, and whose wanderings had lasted many years" (chapter 58). The mingled pain and pleasure David Copperfield feels on his return to Yarmouth, to find Emily and Ham engaged, suggests the sense of loss and relief Pip feels in discovering that Biddy and Joe are married. He need not discover the falseness of his vision of the past, nor be reminded of the differences between himself and that couple. They inhabit an ethical and psychological realm he now seeks to enter in his flight from the metaphysical mysteries of time and change so perplexing to the human spirit. As he once fabricated a self by looking into the faces of Miss Havisham and Estella, he does so again, seeking from Joe and Biddy the blessing that will consolidate the structure of a new self.

Pip emulates a reassuring simplicity of vision; he abandons his romantic questings, and the pilgrimage of being, to become the earnest Victorian in the house of Clarriker and Company, where they have "a good name, and [work] for [their] profits, and [do] very well." He wills the repetition of a past that never was in order to escape a past that has proved too threatening. He seeks to free himself from the other triangular constellations in his life, to become part of an idealized family of the imagination. Pip identifies with his namesake, the son of Joe and Biddy, even as he acts the role of an avuncular Pickwick. In his bachelorhood, he abjures the role of a father, so that he will not become part of his young namesake's past as Magwitch, Compeyson, and Miss Havisham were once part of *his* past. Yet, he takes the boy to the churchyard where he first became aware of the identity of things, setting him upon a certain tombstone there. The elder Pip may hope to deny Mircea Eliade's "terror of history" and the romantic imperative to create history as he creates a self.[21] He may seek refuge in illusory Being, itself a form of paralysis, to evade the process of Becoming. The burdens of self-creation and of imagining a historical context in which the self may act without repeating, consciously or unconsciously, the past prove too great. The inevitability of the repetition that makes one an unwilling plagiarist, "a mere memorial of the past," becomes inescapable: it paralyzes the imagination as the gorgon's head once paralyzed the St. Evrémonde château, turning it into a "stony business altogether." But Pip's former experiences, from which he is now permanently alienated, may nevertheless be repeated, with a difference, in the career of his namesake, the young Pip, who may find within himself the capacity to accept the implications of his talismanic name, become the figurative seed, and endure the vicissitudes of growth and change inherent in the life of the Faustian self: for "Man errs as long as he will strive."

Part Three

Dickens's Urban Gothic

Our Mutual Friend and
The Mystery of Edwin Drood

Chapter 6

It might be worth while, sometimes, to inquire
what Nature is, and how men work to change
her, and whether, in the enforced distortions so
produced, it is not natural to be unnatural.
—*Dombey and Son*

Labyrinthine Selves

Although *Great Expectations* intervened between the weekly serialization
of *A Tale of Two Cities* in 1859 and the appearance of the first monthly
number of *Our Mutual Friend* in May 1864, the thematic preoccupations
connecting the three novels are suggested by this entry in the Memorandum Book that Dickens kept from 1855 to 1865:

A man, and his wife—or daughter—or Niece. The man, a reprobate and ruffian;
the woman (or girl), with good in her, and with compunctions. He ⟨be⟩ believes
nothing, and defies everything; yet has suspicions always, that she is "praying

against" his evil schemes, and making them go wrong. He is very much opposed to this, and is always angrily harping on it. "(If wh) If she *must* pray, why can't she pray in their favor, instead of going against 'em? She's always ruining me— she always is—and calls that, Duty! There's a religious person! Calls it Duty to fly in my face! Calls it Duty to go sneaking against me!"[1]

This entry points to Jerry Cruncher, the grave robber, whose wife, with her "flopping tricks" prays against Jerry's prospering as an honest tradesman. Jerry, the self-styled Resurrection-Man, extends the euphemism to speak of his nocturnal activities as "fishing."[2] Jerry, as the Compleat Angler, anticipates the honest trade of a Gaffer Hexam who fishes for corpses in the waters of the Thames while his daughter, Lizzie, reluctantly maneuvers their boat as it floats on the river, "between Southwark Bridge which is of iron, and London Bridge which is of stone."[3] The comic relationship of Jerry and Mrs. Cruncher—a man, and his wife— becomes the somber one of Lizzie—a daughter—and her father. The polluted waters of the Thames, flowing between the bridges of iron and stone, return us to the St. Evrémonde château, a structure of stone, lead, and iron, engulfed by the elemental violence of the French Revolution. Dickens has returned to the pilgrimage of being, to the enduring paradox within the romantic conception of the self. The "untamed ontology" of the romantic self, as Michel Foucault observes, "bears [beings] for an instant towards a precarious form and yet is already secretly sapping them from within in order to destroy them. In relation to life, beings are no more than transitory figures, and the being that they maintain, during the brief period of their existence, is no more than their presumption, their will to survive."[4]

In his last novels Dickens, ever the Resurrection-Man, and ever alert to those unconscious repetitions to which the artist and his characters fall prey, returns to the exploration of obsolete forms of being, both social and personal, as embodied in those unyielding edifices, the St. Evrémonde château and the barred and shuttered Satis House.[5] Increasingly, the tendency of the self to become the victim of the gorgon's stare of the past, and of the stares of those Others embodying the past, leads Dickens to place at the heart of his novels characters who have become mere images, Kierkegaardian memorials of the past. Finally, the names of Bradley Headstone and John Jasper proclaim a condition at the center of nineteenth-century culture. The Nature of *Dombey and Son* acknowledged by the unwitting Mrs. Chick who claims that "It's a world of change," and by Mr. Morfin with his preoccupation with the dangers of habit, is the Nature of *Our Mutual Friend* and *The Mystery of Edwin Drood*. Those characters who legitimately rebel against dead social forms may, in their rebellion, adopt unchanging stances in defiance of Foucault's "fundamental force" that dooms not only obsolete institutions but individuality, "with its forms, limits, and needs" to a "precarious moment," and to dissolution (pp. 278–79). Dickens finds the rebel succumbs to a version of habit in himself that he, ironically, defies in social institutions: in the distortions so produced in the living self, it becomes natural to be unnatural.

The convulsive changes experienced by Victorian England—and the transformation of Staggs's Gardens by the railway in *Dombey and Son* is one such change—lead not to an acceptance of the reality of change, but to fear, to a refusal to acknowledge the fact for which Mrs. Chick's emblematic silkworm stands. Change, after all, *is* "a metaphysical sort of thing. We—we haven't leisure for it. We—we haven't courage." The factories and cities created by the disruptive transformations of an industrializing society serve only to perplex, and to obscure other, no less radical, forms of change. They isolate members of society, increasingly inhabitants of cities, from the contact with physical nature that provides a model, a trope, for imagining the process of change. Men and women find themselves peering into a mirror of their own making, perceiving a distorted image of humanity in the artifacts of culture.[6] In *A Tale of Two Cities* and *Great Expectations,* the dislocated self is increasingly objectified through edifices erected to deny both the medium of time and the imperatives of change. The London of the later novels is such an edifice writ large, peopled by characters alienated from a viable identity that makes action and change possible for the living self.

Dickens urbanizes the Gothic novel, transporting the haunted rooms of Chesney Wold, the St. Evrémonde château, and Satis House to the streets and buildings of London, now rendered unfamiliar to those most accustomed to them. Dickens's London, with its Gothic villains and its gallery of grotesques, all victims of Mr. Morfin's dreaded habit, has its antecedents in De Quincey's *Confessions,* in the haunted castle through which De Quincey, the hero in a Gothic romance, searches for Ann of Oxford Street: "If she lived, doubtless we must have been sometimes in search of each other, at the very same moment, through the mighty labyrinths of London; perhaps even within a few feet of each other—a bar-

rier no wider in a London street, often amounting in the end to a separation for eternity!"[7] De Quincey's rendering of the city is suggestive and
Dickens exploits it throughout his career, responding in his own way to
the historical London and to the metropolis of the imagination that is
his special domain. Eugene Wrayburn and Bradley Headstone will move
through the mighty labyrinths of London in search of Lizzie Hexam and
each other. John Jasper, the opium-addicted choirmaster of *Edwin Drood,*
will enter the urban labyrinth in quest of some illusory figure who inhabits his dreams. Jasper, no longer the conventional villain of Gothic
melodrama, suffers a form of dislocation rooted in his alienation from
Victorian society and from the elusive, mysterious self floating in the
depths of the mirrors into which Dickens's heroes inevitably gaze.

It is in *Our Mutual Friend,* through a figure like John Harmon, that
Dickens most dramatically exploits the theme of alienation. There is a
much quoted passage in the Memorandum Book that suggests the desperate condition of a Harmon and the bizarre stratagem to which he
resorts: "LEADING INCIDENT FOR A STORY. A man—young and eccentric?—feigns to be dead, and *is* dead to all intents and purposes external
to himself, and ⟨xx⟩ for years retains that singular view of life and character."[8] Harmon, "anathematised" in his youth by his father, flees England, to return fourteen years later, after his father's death. Disguised as
Julius Handford after an attack on his life, Harmon is literally and figuratively lost: he is a stranger in the city he has not seen for years, as Pip is
a stranger to London and Smithfield: like Charles Darnay, he is a stranger
to his own self that he is in the process of piecing together, first as Julius
Handford, then as John Rokesmith. His feigned death, a repetition of
the feigned deaths of *A Tale of Two Cities,* suggests the radical nature of
his situation: he must not simply acquiesce to the terms of the father's
will and repeat the past; he must, in creating a viable self, avoid a tendency to fragmentation through a series of potentially discontinuous
identities.

London becomes a mystery, perhaps permanently unintelligible, reflecting the labyrinthine mysteries of the self. Dickens's characters move
through its streets as does the orphaned, illiterate Jo: "It must be a
strange state to be like Jo! To shuffle through the streets, unfamiliar with
the shapes, and in utter darkness as to the meaning, of those mysterious symbols, so abundant over the shops, and at the corners of streets,
and on the doors, and in the windows! To see people read, and to see

people write, . . . and not to have the least idea of all that language—to be, to every scrap of it, stone blind and dumb!"[9] London, and the signs and tokens abounding there, may, like the self, be foreign even to those most habituated to it. The city never exists independently of the consciousness of each of its denizens. Dickens knows that a sudden wrenching of perspective may produce a sense of disorientation in the midst of the previously hospitable city streets. A character may awaken to a city, and a self, he has never before seen. In *Our Mutual Friend*, Fascination Fledgeby encounters the crippled Jenny Wren in Riah's rooftop garden. Ignorant of the world that he thinks he knows and controls, Fledgeby meets someone who has experienced London in a new way. He is deaf to Jenny's cry, "Come back and be dead, Come back and be dead!" He returns, unthinkingly, to the "close dark streets" in which "you hear the people who are alive, crying, and working, and calling to one another" (book 2, chapter 5). He descends into the narrow streets, the communal crypt of those Londoners caught in the stasis of death-in-life.

Fascination Fledgeby, "deaf, dumb, blind, and paralytic, to a million things, from habit," accepts his condition. Others in *Our Mutual Friend* do not. They may not achieve Jenny Wren's clarity of vision, with its inversion of conventional conceptions of life and death; but they resist, chafe, pursue dubious strategies for survival in a society whose hostility they vaguely sense. In Eugene Wrayburn and Mortimer Lightwood, Dickens captures the disorientation accompanying an emerging estrangement from one's society and oneself. Wrayburn first appears in the novel, buried alive in the back of his chair, at the Veneerings' preposterous dinner party. He has adopted a second self, languid and bitterly self-ironic, in response to a father who seems intent on choosing both a career and wife for him: "M.R.F. [My Respected Father] pre-arranged for myself that I was to be the barrister I am (with the slight addition of an enormous practice, which has not accrued), and also the married man I am not" (book 1, chapter 12). In response to the apparent coercion of the father, and to the world of the Veneerings, Wrayburn has adopted the role of the bored parasite and, like Lady Dedlock before him, embraces paralysis. He scorns conventional notions of energy because energetic commitment involves risk, especially to his carefully cultivated "second nature" of lassitude and indifference. He may echo Lightwood's claim that if *he* is shown "something really worth being energetic about," he will "show you energy" (book 1, chapter 3). But this is a ruse, a communal fiction the two sustain to hide from themselves the state of despair in which they contrive to live. At best, Wrayburn and Lightwood, like the corpses in the Thames, float with the stream. They preserve a specious sense of integrity by disowning, like Edith Granger in *Dombey and Son,* the masks they turn to society: yet the mask effectively conceals, from themselves and others, any genuine life they may still possess.

In Wrayburn and Lightwood, Dickens reaffirms the poetics of the self worked out within the personal history of David Copperfield. Once again, as in his other novels, characters offer their stories, almost their case histories, to those who will listen. Each character remains determined to have his story, his life, seen by that same light in which he has seen it. Often characters will think of themselves, and others, as characters in a novel. Eugene Wrayburn will speak of Mrs. Radcliffe's *The Mysteries of Udolpho* and will see himself as a character in a Gothic novel as he leads Bradley Headstone, with "Venetian mystery," through the streets of London. Both Wrayburn and Lightwood try to understand themselves through the stories they create to explain their ennui and their state of terrible alienation. Dickens has returned not only to David Copperfield, but to Dick Swiveller. But the pleasant fictions by which Swiveller sustains himself, with the aid of his friends, have been transformed to nightmare. The fictions of Wrayburn or Lightwood are neither pleasant nor life-sustaining. They are suspect and incomplete: they are symptomatic of the condition of their tellers. Their stories are those fictional anticipations of the stories Freud was to hear from patient after patient: "I would begin by getting the patient to tell me what was known to [him] and I would carefully note the points at which some train of thought remained obscure or some link in the causal chain seemed to be missing" (*SE,* 2:139). Because their stories are finally suspect, Wrayburn and Lightwood—urbane, witty, bored—drift toward paralysis; toward Edith Granger and Lady Dedlock and Mr. Dick, with his recurring allusion to King Charles the First. They will find themselves in an impasse, fixated upon their fathers, and the real or imagined past, alienated from the present and from a future walled off to them.

Within the urban labyrinth of *Our Mutual Friend,* man remains the novelist of himself, faced once again with the question whether he will be an original or a plagiarist. A John Harmon's fictional status gathers potentially bewildering levels of multiplicity: a fictional character in a novel, he is discussed, and will imagine himself, as if he were a fictional character within a still uncompleted narrative. At the Veneerings's dinner party, Mortimer Lightwood entertains Lady Tippins and the other guests with the story of John Harmon, the so-called man from "Somewhere," or "Nowhere." Lightwood is acutely aware that the true story he tells is inherently novelistic in structure: "We must now return, as the novelists say, and as we all wish they wouldn't, to the man from Somewhere" (book 1, chapter 2). As usual, Lightwood, emulating Wrayburn, seems ironic and detached, the perfect raconteur. But the story, with the father's Will whose terms seek to dictate John Harmon's life, fascinates Lightwood and Wrayburn. It reminds them of the stories they tell each other, of the power of the father, and of their own apparent helplessness in the face of that power.

At the beginning of *Our Mutual Friend*, neither Harmon, Wrayburn, nor Lightwood possesses a viable story by which to live. They have not yet appropriated to themselves their own stories, their own histories. And Harmon's life, his story, seems abruptly and permanently ended when Lightwood reads the contents of the note directed to him:

"This arrives in an extraordinarily opportune manner," says Mortimer then, looking with an altered face round the table: "this is the conclusion of the story of the identical man."

"Already married?" one guesses.

"Declines to marry?" another guesses.

"Codicil among the dust?" another guesses.

"Why, no," says Mortimer; "remarkable thing, you are all wrong. The story is completer and rather more exciting than I supposed. Man's drowned!" (Book 1, chapter 2).

The chapter, concluding in this tantalizing manner, like a serialized account, a novel in monthly parts, offers hypothetical endings, each logically possible within the context of what we know, to the story of John Harmon, as well as to the stories of Mortimer Lightwood and Eugene Wrayburn. The endings are suggested by others, by those either not fully aware of the implications of the story they have heard or indifferent to the legitimate aspirations of the story's hero. They are, in fact, those hypothetical endings, literal and figurative, that Harmon himself must ponder in his effort to become the hero of his own story. John Harmon, like David Copperfield before him, faces the same task, to create a plausible ending to his story and to his life. He must strive within the limits of those alternatives posed to him, not by a past that he has chosen, but by a past that has chosen him. Harmon, like David, must ascribe meaning to the past, and must choose to accept or reject the past he has only in part created if he is to gain possession of his story and his self.[10]

John Harmon's project within *Our Mutual Friend* mirrors Eugene Wrayburn's, as the story of Old John Harmon, and the terms of the Harmon Will, parallels the story, true or not, that Wrayburn tells Lightwood: "M.R.F. [has] always in the clearest manner provided (as he calls it) for his children by pre-arranging from the hour of the birth of each, and sometimes from an earlier period, what the devoted little victim's calling and course in life should be" (book 1, chapter 12). As yet another self-styled victim of that "natural destiny" mentioned by the Marquis St. Evrémonde, Wrayburn relinquishes his energy, his self, through a conscious act of will. He adopts a pose designed to free him from the son's need to rebel, while it protects him from society. In perfecting that second nature to which he becomes habituated, Wrayburn, another Sydney Carton, settles into a lassitude impeding the imperative to change. He becomes increasingly alienated from a vital, if elusive, self.

For Wrayburn, Lizzie Hexam comes to represent that "something really worth being energetic about" of which Lightwood has spoken. When the two accompany the Inspector to apprehend the accused Gaffer, Wrayburn is affected by the sight of Lizzie gazing at the fire: she seems "a deep rich piece of colour, with the brown flush of her cheek and the shining lustre of her hair, though sad and solitary [as she weeps] by the rising and the falling of the fire" (book 1, chapter 13). The incident is deeply sexual, and more than that. Lizzie shares in the life of the fire into which she gazes. And Wrayburn, in spite of his accustomed ennui, is shaken by a response to Lizzie that eludes his understanding. His manner more carelessly extravagant than usual, Wrayburn retreats into his habitual pose: "I am a ridiculous fellow. Everything is ridiculous" (book 1, chapter 13). But the posturing fails as Lightwood notices "a change of some sort, best expressed perhaps as an intensification of all that was wildest and most negligent and reckless in his friend" (book 1, chapter 13). Lightwood's observation echoes that of David Copperfield, who is alert to Steerforth's application to "some habitual strain of the fervent energy which, when roused, was so passionately roused within him." Steerforth has just returned to London from Yarmouth after successfully persuading Emily to run off with him. The Byronic energy of a Steerforth has become the suspect lassitude of a Eugene Wrayburn.

Steerforth, even in the days at Salem House, accepts the destiny that is his own erratic character. Wrayburn's anxiety lies in his confusion about his motives. The bored young gentleman should be able to prey upon someone of Lizzie's class without reflection: seduction is his class prerogative. But the drifting Wrayburn, fascinated and disturbed by Lizzie's vitality and integrity, struggles to transcend the stereotypes of his class. For him Lizzie becomes a disturbing call to action, and to life: a call to the disruption of the facade behind which an enfeebled self is languishing. In his efforts to understand his attitude toward Lizzie, Wrayburn seeks to understand himself. When he offers to provide a tutor for her, there is real urgency behind his self-deprecating manner, behind the pose of the "bad idle dog" who is now preparing "to be of some use to somebody" (book 2, chapter 2). Whatever design he entertains eludes him, for to know it, to articulate it, would involve either acquiescence to his former self, and the seduction of Lizzie, or the transformation of the habitual self into some new, and as yet unimaginable, form.

Lightwood and Wrayburn engage in a conversation about the elusive design on the evening that Wrayburn and Bradley Headstone at last come face to face. Wrayburn's uneasy ambivalence—which inclines him "to pursue such a subject," only to feel that it is "absurd, and that it tire[s] and embarrasse[s]" him (book 2, chapter 6)—becomes a fitting and necessary prelude to the first encounter between the two men who find themselves curiously attracted to Lizzie Hexam. For Wrayburn's counterpart in *Our Mutual Friend* becomes Bradley Headstone: Wrayburn will turn the man he contemptuously refers to as Schoolmaster into his Double, a haunting figure out of Gothic fictions. The two inhabit different social worlds. And Wrayburn's studied nonchalance and social insolence appear the antithesis of Headstone's habitual self-repression. But the two establish a curious bond whose basis is deeper than their attraction to Lizzie. Wrayburn and Headstone have both taken refuge in the stratagem of an Edith Granger or a James Carker: each believes in an inward self existing behind the facade each offers to the penetrating eyes of others. Each identifies that fictive or false self, not with the image in the mirror, but with his body. The true self in which Wrayburn and Headstone fitfully believe watches with ironic detachment, or hatred, the actions of the public self. But both selves remain fictions, at best, with which Wrayburn and Headstone confront society, even as they pretend the true self remains hidden from, and impervious to, the searching looks of others.[11]

Headstone, whose decent and conventional clothing is worn with a total "want of adaptation between him and it," becomes an unembodied self. As such, like Wrayburn, he gazes upon his own actions, yet does not participate directly in them. In a bizarre act of plagiarism, Headstone apes the values of the class to which he aspires. In the process he suppresses his inherent vitality without quite extinguishing it. Lizzie Hexam threatens the detached, inward self that is still susceptible to the sexual and imaginative depths within him. The schoolmaster, in need of others, lest his inner self wither away and die, is threatened with a loss of self-control as he opens himself up to the influence of another human being.

Headstone—Dickens originally toyed with the name "Deadstone"—has figuratively turned part of himself into a monument to his suppressed self.[12] Wrayburn, in his own way, is buried alive in his proto-Wildean stance. Each has created a bulwark behind which he hides from an alien world. But the self behind the bulwark becomes increasingly impoverished. Wrayburn and Headstone long for fulfilled lives through genuine relationships with others: yet each fears the exposure of his inner need. Headstone reacts uneasily when Charley Hexam speaks of his sister's habit of staring into the fire, "full of fancies." Wrayburn has become an "embodied conundrum" to himself. His perplexity intensifies as he wavers indecisively between seducing Lizzie Hexam and establishing her as his mistress, or courting her in a manner that acknowledges the value of her sexual and personal integrity.

The secret, sure perception passing between the two during their first encounter in the rooms shared by Wrayburn and Lightwood involves more than an acknowledgment of sexual rivalry. It reveals, at the same time, each man's dimly felt awareness that his second nature is crumbling under the pressure of the need he feels for Lizzie. Headstone can only envy and hate Wrayburn's apparent invulnerability, his class prerogative; he is tormented by an insolence and a placidity that drives him "well-nigh mad." Wrayburn, on his part, begins to look upon Headstone "as if he found him beginning to be rather an entertaining study" because Headstone exists as a version of himself: someone driven to despair or madness by an uncontrollable desire. Through that "curious monomaniac," as he calls Headstone, Wrayburn can study himself. It is the mark of Wrayburn's dislocation that he remains indifferent to Headstone's pain. Wrayburn has not, as he claims, ceased toying with that "troublesome conundrum long abandoned," the riddle posed by his self (book 2, chapter 6). Rather, he determines to experiment upon Headstone, to discover through him to what frenzied acts a commitment to Lizzie Hexam may lead. Impelled by forces beyond his conscious control, Wrayburn pursues the conundrum that is himself.

Out of their shared malaise emerges one of the remarkable achievements of *Our Mutual Friend:* that chase in which Wrayburn and Headstone participate as hunter and hunted, victim and victimizer. Their roles are not static. They shift and vary as each man tries to lay to rest forever that "unspeakable desire" to track out Matthew Arnold's "buried life" still existing within him. It stirs, it possesses an ambiguous life of its own. But it apparently cannot express itself through love, through a commitment to Lizzie Hexam. Rather, the buried self emerges in the ritual of the chase. Wrayburn's account of it reveals how each man invests it with meaning, however perverse:

"Then soberly and plainly, Mortimer, I goad the schoolmaster to madness. I make the schoolmaster so ridiculous, and so aware of being made ridiculous, that I see him chafe and fret at every pore when we cross one another. The amiable occupation has been the solace of my life. . . . I do it thus: I stroll out after dark, stroll a little way, look in at a window and furtively look out for the schoolmaster. Sooner or later, I perceive the schoolmaster on the watch. . . . Having made sure of his watching me, I tempt him on, all over London. One night I go east, another night north, in a few nights I go all round the compass. Sometimes, I walk; sometimes, I proceed in cabs, draining the pocket of the schoolmaster, who then follows in cabs. I study and get up abstruse No Thoroughfares in the course of the day. With Venetian mystery I seek those No Thoroughfares at night, glide into them by means of dark courts, tempt the schoolmaster to follow, turn suddenly, and catch him before he can retreat. Then we face one another, and I pass him as [if] unaware of his existence, and he undergoes grinding torments. . . . Night after night his disappointment is acute, but hope springs eternal in the scholastic breast, and he follows me again to-morrow. Thus I enjoy the pleasures of the chase, and derive great benefit from the healthful exercise." (Book 3, chapter 10).

These are the words of a man driven to a final act of desperation. Balked and confused by Lizzie's disappearance, Wrayburn lives out his despair in this Gothic novel of his own making. London, as in De Quincey's *Confessions,* becomes a haunted castle of labyrinthine mazes, subterranean cells, dungeons without means of egress. Wrayburn peoples it with Headstone and himself. Together they seem to be engaged in the eternal quest for the inviolable maiden of Gothic romance. In fact, they become the Gothic hero and his mysterious Double discovering their kinship to each other. Wrayburn's disorientation expresses itself in this compulsive patterning of his nocturnal existence: he lives out the nightmare that would otherwise disturb his sleep. In creating the labyrinth for Headstone, in seeking out so consciously the No Thoroughfare that permits him to goad Headstone to madness and revenge, Wrayburn constructs his own dead end. The artistry employed in his creation of his own Venetian mystery becomes ultimately self-destructive.

The high-point of the chase, for both men, occurs with their face-to-face encounter, in which Wrayburn refuses to acknowledge Headstone's existence. And Headstone, undergoing "grinding torments," acquiesces in the act. Wrayburn confirms Headstone's own sense that he is socially and ontologically a nothing. But, as he wields the Medusa's head of his own consciousness, turning Headstone more truly into stone, Wrayburn reveals the deadness at the center of his own being, his own potential nothingness. Behind the languid mask of the careless barrister there may be no authentic self at all: there may only be perversity, or a void. The chase reveals the plight of the romantic self in the intersubjective realm from which God has been exiled. In the words of J. Hillis Miller, "When God vanishes, man turns to interpersonal relations as the only remaining arena of the search for authentic selfhood. Only in his fellow men can he find any longer a presence in the world which might replace the lost divine presence."[13]

Both Wrayburn and Headstone seek to affirm their own existence in their pursuit of Lizzie: they wish her to acknowledge them, and reassure them of the presence of their inaccessible selves. But they pull back, with a sense of self so fragile that they fear the exposure of this fact to themselves and to others. In the chase the two act out the consequences of their failure. Wrayburn withholds that recognition by another that Headstone both needs and fears. He withholds himself from Lizzie and from Headstone. In his chosen isolation, he consolidates his sense of defeat: he will not participate in a dialectic acknowledging that one's own identity is necessarily grounded in the existence of the Other. Moreover, Lizzie's attraction for the two men lies not only in her own beauty and personal vitality, not even in the desire of each man for her, but in the desire each imagines the other feels for her. The autonomous self has collapsed. The self's desire is always based upon the imagined desire of another self. Desire becomes, in the analysis of René Girard, always "triangular." The self pursues an Other only because it imitates the desire for the Other by another self.[14] Such desire is always hauntingly Oedipal in its structure, a recreation of the family constellation. Headstone pursues Lizzie with Wrayburn in his mind. He says, "With Mr. Eugene Wrayburn in my mind, I have been set aside and I have been cast out" (book 2, chapter 15). It is the fate Headstone so assiduously courts. He will at last rise up against his nemesis and attack him only after he sees Lizzie and Wrayburn in a moment of ambiguous intimacy.

When Wrayburn and Headstone pass in the night, we see two paralyzed selves, each encountering its mirror image. The London they now inhabit, the London which is a trope for the self, is a version of those Gothic halls in Piranesi's *Dreams* that, according to De Quincey, "record the scenery of [Piranesi's] own visions during the delirium of a fever" (p. 330). The maze that Wrayburn, the novelist of himself, has created possesses a Minotaur at its center—a version of Wrayburn himself. His healthful exercise suggests that whatever dimension of himself he studies in Bradley Headstone is not to be denied. The recurring refusal to acknowledge Headstone, who embodies for Wrayburn the inert deadness at the center of his obsolete self, becomes a muted plea to Headstone to rise up against his oppressor and destroy him. The paralysis that both men experience wreaks its own havoc, leading to the fragmentation of the self. Wrayburn and Headstone are involved in a process of *self*-annihilation. The fragile and dishonest structure of their lives, expressed in Wrayburn's lassitude and Headstone's self-repression, has crumbled. The final refuge for each is the ease of death, and the chase is subtly devised, by both, to ensure it.[15]

This implicitly suicidal pact between the insulted and the injured leads to the explicit doubling of Headstone that has always been inherent in the precarious organization of his self. The "performance of his routine of educational tricks" becomes unbearable: "Under his daily restraint, it was his compensation, not his trouble, to give a glance towards his state at night, and to the freedom of its being indulged" (book 3, chapter ii). Headstone eagerly awaits a "perverse pleasure akin to that which a sick man sometimes has in irritating a wound upon his body." He consciously prepares for the moment when he will no longer acquiesce to being made the nightly sport of Wrayburn. Headstone becomes a haggard, disembodied head, suspended in air "like the spectre of one of the many heads erst hoisted upon neighbouring Temple Bar." The murder of Eugene Wrayburn will answer Wrayburn's own longing to die; and it will lead to Headstone's own inevitable execution. The moment in which, under the eyes of Rogue Riderhood, Headstone erases his name from the blackboard and ceases figuratively to exist has been long in the making. Headstone has been seeking dissolution and release before Riderhood appears to haunt him.

Dickens's own sure perception of the function of the chase is dramatized on one of those nights when Riderhood encounters Headstone on watch outside Wrayburn's chambers. Riderhood knows neither Wrayburn's name nor Headstone's: for him Wrayburn is the "T'other Governor" and Headstone the "T'otherest Governor." Riderhood's words are reminiscent of Jo's in *Bleak House* when the boy, confused about Esther's identity, whispers to Charley, "If she ain't the t'other one, she ain't the forrenner. Is there *three* of 'em then?" (chapter 31). For Riderhood, for us, the nameless two become one. Headstone's wraithlike face floats through the London streets or up the stairs to the door of Wrayburn's chambers: two heads become, as is so often the case in dreams, superimposed upon a single body. Headstone, like Sydney Carton, becomes a "Double of coarse deportment" to Wrayburn's Charles Darnay. They coexist in the same dream, the shared nightmare of their despair.

In his precisely rendered study of Wrayburn and Headstone, Dickens has shown two men engaged in a dance of death. Its horror and its power lie in the reality of the human waste involved. Eugene Wrayburn, like the Steerforth of whom he is a diminished echo, possesses the capacity to create a viable self. The paralysis that now torments him has been engendered by a society indifferent to the integrity of those within it. And Bradley Headstone, slow-witted as he seems to be, has, or had, an animal vitality within him that could have found expression in a life of physical exertion and challenge. In the tangled fates of the barrister and the schoolmaster we see Dickens's indictment of a society whose primary concern is "Dust," the pursuit of the filthy lucre of the pound in the barren landscape of the urban desert.

Within *The Mystery of Edwin Drood* the chase, the Gothic invention of Eugene Wrayburn, an incipient artist of the perverse, becomes internalized in the consciousness of John Jasper, the opium-addicted choirmaster. Wrayburn and Headstone, the T'other and the T'otherest, are fused into a single figure who reenacts an even more bizarre version of their shared malaise. In spite of its fragmentary nature, *Edwin Drood* reveals Dickens's continuing preoccupation with the situation of the romantic self divided between Eros and Thanatos, between the imperative to change and the desire to cling tenaciously to obsolete and deadly forms of being. Dickens offers a systematic critique of the fictive world of the novel and returns, once again, to the poetics of impasse, to a situation in which the romantic self is doubly alienated, from society and from some viable, if fictive, identity, making action and change possible.

The impasse explored within the chase becomes more fully realized in the experience of the tortured Jasper. Just as Wrayburn and Headstone come to live for the pleasures of the chase, Jasper lives for his expeditions to London or for those opium journeys in his own chambers when he "lights his pipe, and delivers himself to the Spectres it invokes at midnight."[16] Those specters are curiously akin to the ritual of the chase. As Jasper explains to the Princess Puffer, each opium dream involves "a hazardous and perilous journey, over abysses where a slip would be destruction" (chapter 23). The journey involves, always, an unsuspecting fellow-traveler who has no awareness that he *is* a fellow-traveler. It culminates in an act performed "hundreds of thousands of times," indeed, "millions and billions of times," an act that, when done in fact, seems hardly worth the doing. Yet, this obscure act that may involve the unwitting fellow-traveler serves, in the dream if not in life, as the necessary prelude to some kind of release, followed by "changes of colors and . . . great landscapes and glittering processions," the exotic dreamscape with which the novel begins. The fate, even the identity of the fellow-traveler who "went the journey, and never saw the road" is not revealed (chapter 23), one of those many riddles whose solutions were lost to us with the death of Dickens on 9 June 1870. But the dream and its structure recall the Venetian mystery so carefully orchestrated by Eugene Wrayburn. For the

chase, like Jasper's dream journey, ends in an act of violence and potential release: Headstone's attack upon Wrayburn. The time and the place
of Jasper's dream suggest just such a moment; the fellow-traveler seems
just such a potential victim.

Jasper's conscious decision to resort to opium and to indulge in the
reveries it produces is rooted in the same need for escape from himself
and his circumstances that has driven both Wrayburn and Headstone to
what Wrayburn calls their "healthful exercise." Jasper, early in the novel,
advises his nephew that he has "been taking opium for a pain—an agony—that sometimes overcomes [him]" (chapter 2). He tells the Princess Puffer, "Yes, I came on purpose. When I could not bear my life, I
came to get the relief, and I got it. It WAS one! It WAS one!" (chapter 23).
It is the relief so consciously sought out by Jasper that links him, as
much as the texture of the dream itself, to the self-destructive activities
of those trapped within the claustrophobic London of *Our Mutual
Friend*. But the fact that the dream journey *is* an internalization of the
chase is significant. Wrayburn and Headstone exist as distinct, in some
ways antithetical figures, united by a common despair; they are further
evidence of the degree to which Dickens relies upon and exploits the
Double relationship: in *Edwin Drood* Dickens concentrates upon a single
figure, whose solitary and isolated consciousness becomes the center of
the novel.

Doubles continue to appear in *The Mystery of Edwin Drood*; in many
ways the novel offers a proliferation of Double relationships unusual
even in Dickens's novels. But John Jasper, although he seeks out, and
even creates, his own counterpart, needs none. The fellow-traveler of his
dreams may be Edwin Drood or himself. No other character necessarily
exists to embody that part of himself with which Jasper, like Wrayburn
or Headstone, must contend. Yet, in *Edwin Drood,* self-division, which
the Double can so fully explore, especially as a form of extreme dislocation, has become almost the norm. The pressures of Victorian culture
compel Wrayburn, Lightwood, Headstone, and others to take refuge in
the fiction of a true inward self, detached from its public actions, yet
yoked to an alien self who inhabits, paradoxically, the same body. The
characters who inhabit the Cloisterham and London of *Edwin Drood*
seem, rather, to have accepted the psychological division urged upon
them by their milieu. John Jasper, the opium addict, rejects as inadequate the conventional ways by which others adapt to their world.

Jasper takes refuge neither in the pious calisthenics of the Reverend Septimus Crisparkle nor in a state of mind that at first seems unique to Miss Twinkleton, headmistress of the Nuns' House, but is, in fact, the psychic stratagem to which so many in the novel turn:

As, in some cases of drunkenness, and in others of animal magnetism, there are two states of consciousness which never clash, but each of which pursues its separate course as though it were continuous instead of broken (thus if I hide my watch when I am drunk, I must be drunk again before I can remember where), so Miss Twinkleton has two distinct and separate phases of being. Every night, the moment the young ladies have retired to rest, does Miss Twinkleton smarten up her curls a little, brighten up her eyes a little, and become a sprightly Miss Twinkleton whom the young ladies have never seen. (Chapter 3)

One of the sources of Jasper's discontent, the pain for which he has been taking opium, is his very inability to maintain Miss Twinkleton's two states of consciousness that seem to exist in total separation. Jasper suffers because these two states of consciousness have fused into a single, anguished awareness. Only the greatest act of will and his ambiguous devotion to his nephew permit him to maintain, for ever shorter periods of time, the separation between his two fragile selves. As the successor both to Bradley Headstone and Eugene Wrayburn, he shares their fate: once his self-command is weakened, each man yearns for the freedom yielded him by the night. However, most of the characters in *Edwin Drood,* like Miss Twinkleton, are protected from the violent collision between two fictive states of being, the conventional public self and the other, truer self to which even Miss Twinkleton harmlessly turns at night. They exist apparently without the need to achieve the dynamic integration of the romantic self. Within each character a dialogue of sorts, implicit or explicit, is established. The dialogue is sometimes objectified through the existence of another character representing one half of the divided self. Always the states of being interact, impinge upon each other. But for Jasper the interaction is more violent and sustained, in part because it is more clearly within him: and, finally, as in the cases of Wrayburn and Headstone, it proves uncontrollable.[17]

John Jasper, then, is never a "horrible wonder apart," as Rosa Bud comes to perceive him. His isolation and his suffering proclaim a twisted expression of his integrity; they are responses to a society that refuses to acknowledge the expression of the ambiguous, dynamic energy haunting Wrayburn and Lightwood in *Our Mutual Friend*. This romantic energy can be sublimated into art: as a choirmaster Jasper is an artist of sorts. But the sanctioned channels for human energies, amorphous and self-contradictory as they are, only heighten the frustration of Jasper, who is so acutely aware of the inadequacies of the society in which he finds himself. His musical art is as mechanical and dully habitual as his relationships with those around him. Forced to deny at least one half of himself, possessed of energies far more intense than those influencing the lives of all others but the Landlesses, Jasper turns to opium and the fantasies providing temporary relief from the paralysis of his life.

The opium dream with which the novel opens reveals at once the fragmented consciousness of Jasper and the ambiguities inherent in his situation:

An ancient English Cathedral Town? How can the ancient English Cathedral town be here! The well-known massive grey square tower of its old Cathedral? How can that be here! There is no spike of rusty iron in the air, between the eye and it, from any point of the real prospect. What IS the spike that intervenes, and who has set it up? Maybe, it is set up by the Sultan's orders for the impaling of a horde of Turkish robbers, one by one. It is so, for cymbals clash, and the Sultan goes by to his palace in long procession. Ten thousand scimitars flash in the sunlight, and thrice ten thousand dancing-girls strew flowers. Then, follow white elephants caparisoned in countless gorgeous colors, and infinite in number and attendants. Still, the Cathedral tower rises in the background, where it cannot be, and still no writhing figure is on the grim spike. (Chapter 1)

Within this highly erotic fantasy, Dickens initiates us into an awareness of the inevitable conflict between Miss Twinkleton's two states of consciousness, into the underworld of vitality upon which the Cathedral Town erects itself. And within it the two perhaps illusory halves of John Jasper are fantastically pieced together in a Blakean revelation, in an irrefutable marriage of Heaven and Hell. The generalized Eastern setting, with its Sultan and his harem, coexists with the intimidating massiveness of the grey tower of Cloisterham Cathedral—the emblem of that most representative of English institutions, the Anglican church and all the values for which it stands. Jasper, the dreamer, is caught and suspended between two worlds. The sinister spike, in reality a rusty spike upon a bedpost, is simultaneously a part of both worlds. It belongs to the world of the Sultan, an exotic realm where conventional restraints become meaningless: the Sultan is as savage in his defense of his harem as the Turkish robbers who seem intent upon ravishing the dancing girls swirling through the dream. But, as an instrument of punishment, the spike also suggests to the dreamer's consciousness that the world in which the tower belongs punishes, just as remorselessly, those who defy its mores and conventions. The massive tower has been erected to deny the legitimacy, even the existence, of impulses sustained by an energy quite different from the conventional energy repelling Lightwood and Wrayburn.

Within and beyond the context of this dream, John Jasper plays many clearly contradictory roles. He is at once the Sultan jealously guarding his female chattels from the robbers, eager to see them die one by one upon the spike. He is also the potential intruder, the writhing figure, soon to be impaled upon the waiting stake. The dream reflects Jasper's confusion about his relationships to society, to his nephew, Edwin Drood, and to himself. Jasper experiences that disorientation described by De Quincey in an account of one of his dreams in the *Confessions of an English Opium-Eater*. De Quincey speaks of the "unimaginable horror which these dreams of Oriental imagery, and mythological tortures" impressed upon him: "I brought together all creatures, birds, beasts, reptiles, all trees and plants, usages and appearances, that are found in all tropical regions, and assembled them together in China or Indostan" (p. 333). Both dreams make use of Eastern landscapes, both fix the dreamer in a condition of excruciating disorientation in which he is by turns "the idol . . . the priest . . . [the] worshipped . . . [the] sacrificed" (p. 333). For Jasper the disorientation is rooted in his attitudes toward Edwin Drood. In his dual role as Drood's legal guardian and his sexual rival, John Jasper is the father and the son, the Sultan and the Turkish renegade. He is guilty of that desire at which even the creatures encrusted with De Quincey's "Nilotic mud" might tremble.

The true nature of the relationship between the uncle and the nephew is almost casually defined in their chatty interchange in the early pages of the novel, concluding with Drood's whimsical outburst, "And some uncles, in large families, are even younger than their nephews. By George, I wish it was the case with us!" (chapter 2). The opium dream and Drood's comment define Jasper's personal and social predicaments. In his relationship with Drood, Jasper is torn by the conventional affection of an uncle for a nephew and by his hatred of the youth who would, in his own words, prefer to be older than his own uncle. Simultaneously, Jas-

per is at war with the society in which he finds himself. That bizarre and
elusive relationship between Eugene Wrayburn and Bradley Headstone,
with its muted Oedipal implications, recurs here. To rebel against society is always, figuratively, to rebel against the father, or someone who
replaces the father in the rebel's imagination. Bradley Headstone's determination not to strike until he sees Lizzie and Wrayburn together and
his vision of Wrayburn as a paternal specter come to haunt him, so close
to Wrayburn's vision of his own M. R. F., suggest the nature of Headstone's motives. Drood's whimsical desire to be older than "Jack" ironically coincides with one of the ways in which Jasper, in his fantasy, perceives *him*; for "Ned," as Jasper calls him, is the Sultan, the father, of the
opium dream, as well as the son seeking to displace the father. Dickens
has returned to the family constellation and to René Girard's triangular
desire: for Jasper, Drood has unwittingly become a figure to be envied
and hated, for envy invites the plagiarism of imitation, the capture of the
self by an Other.[18]

Out of the Oedipal center of the dream landscape, which serves to
disclose the multiplicity of his desires, emerges Jasper's need to punish
and be punished: he both fears and desires the stake. Jasper's rebellion
involves his rejection of the values of Cloisterham and his conscious pursuit of those fantasies he finds in the liberating influence of opium. But
he has already been led to a punishment more terrible than the physical
torture of the dream. The spike is embedded in Jasper's consciousness; it
produces a relentless sense of guilt and anxiety. Ironically, the title of
Bazzard's unproduced "tragedy," *The Thorn of Anxiety,* becomes a not-
so-comic parody of Jasper's situation. The thorn of anxiety exerts its
pressure upon Jasper; he writhes because of its existence.

The opium dream has revealed the extent to which Jasper's consciousness is no longer safely compartmentalized into autonomous and
discrete parts. He may flee the opium den and London itself with the
coming of the dawn, but he cannot leave behind the fantasies of his
dreams. Dickens is now consciously working with a romantic conception of the mind like that which De Quincey describes in his *Confessions*:
"A thousand accidents may, and will interpose a veil between our present
consciousness and the secret inscriptions on the mind; accidents of the
same sort will also rend away this veil; but alike, whether veiled or unveiled, the inscription remains for ever; just as the stars seem to withdraw before the common light of day, whereas, in fact, we all know that

it is the light which is drawn over them as a veil" (pp. 328–29). Those stars shining at night with such intensity, like the red glow of the Princess's opium pipe, continue to exert their influence, for "there is no such thing as *forgetting* possible to the mind." Jasper may return to the cathedral world of Cloisterham, but he brings with him dreams that no longer remain in another realm of experience. The veil of sunlight, a fragile illusion obscuring "the secret inscriptions on the mind"—the hieroglyphs of the self—waits only to be torn by the accidents of life, by the oppressive atmosphere of the cathedral town that denies the existence of the night and its stars and yet forever reminds us, and Jasper, of its enduring presence.

When he dons his sullied white robes, Jasper reenters the world that grates on his ever more irritable nerves. Once again he must cope with the obsequiousness of a Crisparkle; he must endure the enervating boredom of the Alternate Musical Wednesdays, an obligatory gesture to culture routinely made by Cloisterham. This is the mundane reality pressing upon him, compelling him to reveal his hopelessness to the surprised Drood: "I hate [my life]. The cramped monotony of my existence grinds me away by the grain" (chapter 2). Jasper's opium dreams reveal the confinement that he feels, his searing awareness that the art he pursues is neither a true vocation, nor an authentic expression of his private self. The gargoyles decorating the stalls, seats, and desks of the old cathedral at least provided release for the wretched monks. Victorian England denies Jasper even that outlet. In response to such a world a Eugene Wrayburn adopts, if unsuccessfully, a second nature of lassitude. For Jasper that is not enough. He furtively turns to opium and the fantasies it offers as a substitute for the open acknowledgment of the repressed energies of his life. He has been deprived of an integrated, fulfilled life that exists, at best, as a hypothetical norm in the novel. Jasper, in "carving [demons] out of [his] heart," has become, as his name and manner suggest, another living gargoyle, like James Carker whose suspect tastes set him apart in *Dombey and Son*.

Carker, in his subtle caricature of Mr. Dombey and the cultural values he accepts, fixes an obsessed gaze upon an Edith of his imagination, desiring her because Dombey desires her. John Jasper turns to his ambiguous love for Rosa Bud, Edwin Drood's fiancée. Drood's unfinished portrait of Rosa, endowed by him with a "beauty remarkable for a quite childish, almost babyish, touch of saucy discontent, comically conscious of itself" (chapter 2), presides over Jasper's chambers like the image of an impish, secular madonna. Dickens alludes to Matthew Lewis's *The Monk* and to Ambrosio's reverence of the portrait of Matilda in the role of the Virgin Mary. Ambrosio and Jasper share a common fate: they are reduced—one unconsciously, the other consciously—to the futile worship of the inviolable virgin of the imagination. Their entombment within dead and deadening institutions produces a form of isolation bordering upon romantic solipsism and an act of self-repression, leading, in Matthew Lewis's words, to a division between the "real and [the] acquired character." Thus "the different sentiments, with which Education and Nature had inspired him [Ambrosio], were combating in his bosom: It remained for his passions which as yet no opportunity had called into play, to decide the victory."[19]

Dickens's repetition of a situation so recognizably analogous to that in *The Monk* reveals once again his debt to the Gothic tradition. It also further illuminates the transformation of the Gothic, a rejection of the merely melodramatic. The change in language alone is significant. The passions of Matthew Lewis, and the eighteenth century, have become the Energy of Dickens's late novels. The words are not simply synonymous. *Passion* immediately suggests its traditional antithesis, *reason*; the psychic battle is essentially bipolar. We are in the realm of Doctor Johnson's *Rasselas,* in which the ascendancy of reason over passion is the norm. *Energy* is a romantic term, a possible rendering of the German *die Kraft* when Faust audaciously undertakes his interpretation of the word *Logos* in the Gospel according to John, moving from Mind to Energy to Deed. This elusive energy underlies the restless activity of the male, or female, Faust of the romantic movement.[20] Energy, the term to which Dickens, George Eliot, and other nineteenth-century novelists so often turn, suggests an amorphous reservoir of vitality, the source of consciousness itself. Such energy becomes the impelling force within the dynamic self, engaged in its pilgrimage of being in a realm of intersubjectivity. The unfinished portrait reveals that Rosa Bud is herself unfinished, responding always to others' perceptions of her, and that, for Drood and Jasper, she remains a creature of their imaginings, forever eluding their understanding. The Gothicism of the late eighteenth century merges with the psychological vision of Rousseau's *Confessions* and the nineteenth-century novel.

Dickens further transforms the Gothic by abandoning a central Gothic motif, the use of a Roman Catholic setting distant in time and place. Matthew Lewis chooses Madrid in the time of the Inquisition to obscure his implicit challenge to contemporary mores. In *The Mystery of Edwin Drood* the critique of conventional rationalism and bourgeois society is no longer disguised and intermittent. Dickens exploits the Gothic, not to veil the thrust of his critique, but to establish causal relations between the individual predicament and the environment. London is a Gothic castle haunted by incubi and grotesques of various kinds, suggesting the social and psychological terrors of Victorian society. Cloisterham becomes the analogue of the haunted castle, the monastery of the Gothic tradition. But it is the monastery transformed. There is no distinction between the suspect values of the cloister and the saner values of a secular society. Instead, the secular world becomes permeated with the conventional attitudes repressing and destroying Matthew Lewis's Ambrosio. And although the concern with repressed sexuality remains a significant issue in *Edwin Drood,* the novel encompasses, often indirectly and by implication, the full complexity of the individual's situation in nineteenth-century England: the quest for the unified self is the core of the novel. The spirit of Silas Wegg, in pursuit of his amputated leg, presides over both *Our Mutual Friend* and *Edwin Drood.* His anxious complaint to Mr. Venus is a credo of sorts for both novels: "I shouldn't like—I tell you openly I should *not* like . . . to be what I may call dispersed, a part of me here, and a part of me there, but should wish to collect myself like a genteel person" (book 1, chapter 7). It is a moment of high comedy and terrible seriousness. The dispersal of the self seems the inevitable fate for the inhabitants of London and Cloisterham.

At last, London, "the great black city [which casts] its shadow on the waters, [with] its dark bridges [spanning] them as death spans life" (chapter 22), fuses with the world of Cloisterham. The provincial cathedral town, in the green garden of the countryside, becomes an extension of the city of death. The cathedral itself is sepulchral, rising above the crypts beneath it. The town's inhabitants are strangely cut off from nature and from change: for them time has stopped. Although Cloisterham "was once possibly known to the Druids by another name, and certainly to the Romans by another," and to the Saxons and Normans by even other names, the townspeople "seem to suppose, with an inconsistency more strange than rare, that all its changes lie behind it, and that there are no more to come" (chapter 3). The reality of past change and the violence that has preceded the current peacefulness have disappeared from the collective consciousness of those in Cloisterham. For Dickens, the recognition of change is not designed to celebrate continuity, but to assert the need for the necessary change that the town of Cloisterham resists as if it were its natural destiny. This, in spite of the fact that daily "the Cloisterham children grow small salad in the dust of abbots and abbesses, and make dirt-pies of nuns and friars; while every ploughman in its outlying fields" grinds the bones of "once puissant Lord Treasurers, Archbishops, Bishops, and such-like" to make his bread (chapter 3). The past does not contribute as it should to the enduring life of the town, providing the dust in which to fertilize new forms of life. Instead, the past reinforces the oppressive respectability of the town. Its weight lies heavy upon the people of Cloisterham, imposing upon them the outmoded values of another era: "In a word, a city of another and a bygone time is Cloisterham." The town *is* the past. It impinges upon the present architecturally by incorporating its fragments into surviving buildings. But the past has also insinuated itself into the consciousness of its inhabitants through those "jumbled notions . . . incorporated into many of its citizens' minds"—as if the gorgon's head had surveyed the town and its inhabitants centuries ago.

The cathedral is the dominant landmark, the ultimate emblem of the sway of the past. But another landmark of bygone days exists to remind us that apparently long-abandoned practices are even now imposed upon unwitting victims. The Nuns' House, its name "derived from the legend of its conventual uses," now a Seminary for Young Ladies, serves functions similar to those it served in the past. The zealous abbess from the pages of *The Monk* has become the innocuous Miss Twinkleton. Her scrupulous observation of existing proprieties makes her an unconscious representative of values persisting from an age less enlightened than that of Victorian England. The Nuns' House is clearly a pale, but very real, reflection of a severer time: "Whether the nuns of yore . . . were ever walled up alive in odd angles and jutting gables of the building for having some ineradicable leaven of busy mother Nature in them which has kept the fermenting world alive ever since; these may be matters of interest to its haunting ghosts (if any), but constitute no item in Miss Twinkleton's half-yearly accounts" (chapter 3). Miss Twinkleton may forget the past and its relevance to the present, but Dickens cannot. John Jasper is the Ambrosio of *Edwin Drood:* he has taken "to carving demons" out of his own psyche. The girls of the Nuns' House are its trapped novitiates, direct descendants of Agnes in *The Monk*. Agnes, in her time, succumbs to that "ineradicable leaven of busy mother Nature" in her and, like the storied nuns of Cloisterham, is walled up alive amidst the decaying corpses in the vaults beneath the abbey of Saint Clare. The students of the Nuns' House remain figuratively buried alive, encircled by the chaste admonitions of a Miss Twinkleton, who inevitably refrains from the use of the all-too-suggestive word "bosoms," substituting in its place the far more delicate and genteel euphemism "hearts." Even as she reads aloud to Rosa Bud from the romantic novels fashionable in the thirties and forties, Miss Twinkleton bowdlerizes them in a way initially comic, but finally disturbing. The romantic drivel that she finds so offensive is no less untrue to human realities than the interpolated passages she creates to celebrate the "pious frauds" of a bourgeois conception of domestic bliss in a "suburban establishment," sanctioned by the consent of papa and the silver-haired rector (chapter 22). The sterility of Miss Twinkleton's, and society's, vision of marriage is as stifling as the religious asceticism of old. The domestic arrangement of which she speaks sentences even someone like Rosa to a version of the ancient punishment reserved for nuns who would not deny the vitality that keeps the fermenting world alive.

No one associated with Cloisterham escapes the influence of obsolete values and conventional expectations perpetuated through a communal inertia. Edwin Drood, with his condescending and proprietary attitude toward Rosa, and with his airy confidence in his ability "to wake up Egypt a little," epitomizes the conventional self. His predicament, to which he seems so oblivious, is similar to that of John Harmon and Eugene Wrayburn in *Our Mutual Friend*. All three must contend with fathers, living or dead, who try to control the lives of their sons. Rosa Bud has been willed to Drood, in the words of Bella Wilfer, "like a dozen of spoons, with everything cut and dried beforehand, like orange chips" (book 1, chapter 4). But Drood, Miss Twinkleton, and society as a whole acquiesce without question to the absurdity of the will that shapes, or distorts, both his life and Rosa's. Drood, young English gentleman that he is, accepts the role that society and a dead father have fashioned for him. He is not even stirred by the sense of uneasiness that Eugene Wrayburn

responds to in similar circumstances. He succumbs to the gorgon's spell
of conventional English society.

In this context, Jasper's revelation to Drood that he hates "the cramped
monotony of [his] existence" makes his accompanying warning particularly ambiguous. Drood should realize that "even a poor monotonous
chorister and grinder of music—in his niche—may be troubled with
some stray sort of ambition, aspiration, restlessness, dissatisfaction, what
shall we call it?" (chapter 2). Jasper relishes his own ironic use of the
word "niche." In repeating Drood's own phrase, Jasper implies that the
uncomprehending Drood, mouthing conventional platitudes, is implicitly responsible for *his* suffering. And, yet, his avowal of his discontent is to be taken as a warning. Jasper implies that even the confident
Drood may find himself forced to subdue himself to a career and a life
offering no satisfaction. Drood's youthful lack of imagination makes it
impossible for him to conceive that he, too, might awaken one day to a
sense of his life's meaninglessness. His uncle's suffering is his first exposure to a certain potentiality within himself.

Nor can Drood perceive that Jasper's "ambition, aspiration, restlessness, dissatisfaction" may pose a threat to his own life. Understandably,
he cannot imagine that he stands as an obstacle between his uncle and
Rosa Bud. The ambiguity of the warning is not the dissembling of a
merely melodramatic villain. It reveals Jasper's own confusion and disorientation, for his commitment to his nephew is genuine. The look that
Jasper ordinarily casts upon Drood, "a look of intentness—a look of
hungry, exacting, watchful, and yet devoted affection" is necessarily enigmatic. The "Jasper face," turned to Drood, is more than an allusion to
the gargoyle Jasper has become. The phrase points to the mask of stone
concealing Jasper's curious identification with the young man he envies
and despises, the youth who is at once son and father in his tortured
imaginings. He yearns to be in Drood's position, even as he senses the
inadequacies of Drood's unreflecting conventionality. The intensity of
his look, as it feeds upon Drood, suggests the complexity of Jasper's relationship to him and to himself.[21]

The diary that Jasper keeps is, as he admits to Crisparkle, "in fact, a
Diary of Ned's life too." What he records there are not simply the events
of his routine life or the conventional milestones in Drood's. The entries
reveal his internal struggle, his ongoing debate about himself and Drood:
they become a dialogue between the conventional self and its rebelling

counterpart. Jasper is full of love and concern for his "dear boy," now almost a man; he is, simultaneously, jealous, perhaps murderous, in his lust for Rosa Bud. When he warns Drood and is reassured to learn that Drood can't be warned, Jasper has not yet made the choice between his nephew and Rosa Bud. So, on one night of many such nights, John Jasper stands with a peculiar-looking pipe, filled with something that is *not* tobacco, and gazes into one of the two bedrooms in his set of chambers where "his nephew lies asleep, calm and untroubled." He contemplates the sleeping Drood, that avowedly "shallow, surface kind of fellow" who has not yet responded to the violation of his own integrity posed by his engagement to Rosa. Jasper passes from Drood's room to his own, from a shallow realm to the depths inhabited by specters which have yet to disturb Drood's sleep (chapter 5). He has discarded an obsolete part of himself and slipped into the kingdom of dreams incessantly whispering to him.

Appropriately, Dickens moves from this nocturnal scene to the daylight world and the Reverend Septimus Crisparkle performing his daily calisthenics. Cloisterham's world of walls, gates, and locks now has *its* Minotaur in the form of John Jasper. The oppressiveness of the cathedral town produces the need for the affirmation of some norm offering a compromise between the claims of human energy and the entrenched proscriptions of society. Crisparkle would seem to embody a viable accommodation between oppressive respectability and the fermenting vitality of the human spirit. But just as the city of London casts its shadows on the waters of the Thames, the past and present cast their shadows upon the life of the Minor Canon. Like so many characters in Dickens's novels who seem to be offered as moral and psychological touchstones, Crisparkle provides no real alternative to the predicament of Jasper. His association with the Anglican Church and his dependence on the patronage that has led to his present position compel us to take an ironic view of what he does and what he stands for. For Crisparkle's contented satisfaction with "his present Christian beat" is based all too clearly on his incapacity for entertaining an ironic vision of himself or others. Jasper, so acutely sensitive to the affectations of those around him, inevitably smiles when the ingenuous Crisparkle pointedly emphasizes that he is inquiring about the choirmaster's health at the express wishes of the Dean: he, at least, is aware of the Dean's hypocrisy and patronizing manner, if Crisparkle is not.

But it is primarily the exaggerated physical well-being and self-satisfaction of Crisparkle, and the ways in which they are achieved and at what cost, that Dickens knowingly dwells upon. To come upon Crisparkle in the midst of his morning exercises is to learn the nature of his limitations. We find Crisparkle, after "having broken the thin morning ice near Cloisterham Weir with his amiable head," in the act of "assisting his circulation by boxing at a looking-glass with great science and prowess" (chapter 6). While John Jasper grapples with his private demons, Septimus Crisparkle is free to feint and dodge before his own benevolent reflection. He is captive to the framed image of himself, offering no hint of the mysteries suggested by the mirror into which Esther Summerson looks after her illness or by the mirror in the Old Bailey with its watery depths. Crisparkle, not unlike the Veneerings and the Podsnaps, mirrored in the two-dimensional realm of the great looking-glass, dwells upon the surface of life. A certain naiveté, if not willed ignorance, is the source of his soft-hearted benevolence, his mental and physical health. The domestic arrangements in Minor Canon Corner, the nature of the tranquility reigning there, suggest Crisparkle's retreat from certain moral and psychological complexities. The Mrs. Crisparkle with whom he lives is, as Dickens rather too pointedly observes, the mother, not the wife, of the Reverend Septimus. As the old lady stands to say the Lord's Prayer before their breakfast, the Minor Canon also stands "with bent head to hear it, he being within five years of forty: much as he had stood to hear the same words from the same lips when he was within five months of four" (chapter 6).

Time has stopped for Septimus Crisparkle, much as it seems to have stopped for Cloisterham and Minor Canon Corner: "Swaggering fighting men had had their centuries of ramping and raving about Minor Canon Corner, and beaten serfs had had their centuries of drudging and dying there, and powerful monks had had their centuries of being sometimes useful and sometimes harmful there, and behold they were all gone out of Minor Canon Corner, and so much the better" (chapter 6). The passage reads like a burlesque of evolutionary platitudes, masking a corrosive irony. The old savagery, brutality, and energy appear to be gone, banished from the earth, and so much the better. Perhaps "one of the highest uses of their ever having been there" was to make way for a higher order of existence, for that comfortable world inhabited by the china shepherdess and her compliant son. The "blessed air of tranquillity," the "serenely romantic state of the mind," that is theirs to enjoy is the result of eras of violence and suffering. Implicitly, the passage asks why these two people—harmless, perhaps even generous and kind—should be the beneficiaries of those centuries of turbulence. They have not quelled the violence and engendered order; they have only inherited it. But the complexity of Dickens's vision lies finally in the reference to the past as "a sorrowful story that is all told, or a pathetic play that is played out" (chapter 6). The ramping, the raving, the drudging, the dying are not things of the past. John Jasper haunts the quiet of Cloisterham and Minor Canon Corner. The young Deputy, with the peculiar "object" Durdles has provided him as a channel for his energies, roams the streets of Cloisterham, as do other young present-day savages, victims of ignorance and neglect. As the Reverend Septimus Crisparkle benevolently walks his Christian beat, Cloisterham seethes with Jasper's frustrated passion and the malignant but justified resentment of ferocious boys like Deputy, who are destroyers for want of what Durdles calls an "enlightened object." The value of Crisparkle's benevolence and the validity of the conventional wisdom for which he stands are circumscribed by the reality of his limitations. The world of Minor Canon Corner becomes a fragile ark in a sea of dark and unacknowledged forces.

Dickens has created a figurative No Thoroughfare, like those in De Quincey's *Confessions* or in Wrayburn's chase, in which each of the major figures of the novel exists. The individual and the social predicament is one of acute paralysis, awaiting one of those De Quinceian accidents to rend the veil of apparent tranquility. With the appearance of Helena and Neville Landless the veil is torn: the exotic and savage Orient erupts upon the peaceful routine of Cloisterham. The world of Jasper's dreams manifests itself, embodied and undeniable, in the forms of the brother and sister, incongruous in the midst of the cathedral close and the monastery ruins, "much as if they were beautiful barbaric captives brought from some wild tropical dominion," as Crisparkle observes to himself. They pose a striking contrast to the shallowness of Drood, to the domesticated vitality of Crisparkle, and to the distorted energies of a Deputy or a Jasper. These splendid creatures, as yet untouched by the oppressive respectability of Cloisterham, possess in their untamed natures an elusive and indefinable vitality that the walls of the cathedral, the monastery, and the Nuns' House have been built to confine. Their presence in Cloisterham reveals that the psychic and physical qualities they possess cannot be walled in without destructive consequences for the individual and society. The dusky Landlesses, who are "slender, supple, quick of eye and limb; half shy, half defiant," suggest undifferentiated Energy itself, reasserting its priority, challenging the jumbled notions of a culture that has turned away from the issues the existence of such energy poses.

In a single stroke the brother and sister reassert the continuity between *Edwin Drood* and De Quincey's *Confessions*. For Dickens, the Landlesses and the Ceylon from which they come possess that aura of mystery, revelation, and potential terror echoing De Quincey's response to those Eastern images finally dominating his dreams. The Malay, real or imaginary, who appears at De Quincey's cottage in the Lake Region eventually represents everything that is alien and unEnglish in De Quincey himself, everything that is somehow taboo and to be denied at all costs. Within the *Confessions* the incident has far-reaching consequences. The Malay becomes the embodiment of De Quincey's guilt, the living expression of desires that, in the elaborate mythology of opium addiction, are unleashed through the agency of the drug. The Malay, by reappearing in his dreams, becomes the medium through whom De Quincey is initiated even further into a knowledge of the unspeakable:

The Malay has been a fearful enemy for months. I have been every night, through his means, transported into Asiatic scenes. I know not whether others share in my feelings on this point; but I have often thought that if I were compelled to forego England, and to live in China, and among Chinese manners and modes of life and scenery, I should go mad. The causes of my horror lie deep; and some of them must be common to others. Southern Asia, in general, is the seat of awful images and associations. (p. 332)

Through his identification with the Malay, De Quincey can express the horror, as well as the appeal, of those potentialities that southern Asia, as the cradle of the human race, holds for him. The feeling of abhorrence is intensified by the undeniable lure of "the ancient, monumental, cruel, and elaborate religions of Indostan" (p. 333). The barrier of terror protecting De Quincey from the savagery and fecundity of the Orient is far more fragile than he would like to admit.

The Ceylon from which Dickens brings the Landlesses—a Ceylon of the imagination—emerges from a De Quincean vision of the East, "the seat of awful images and associations," and of "a dim and reverential feeling." The Landlesses, like De Quincey's Malay, are from the cradle of the human race; they, too, are "antediluvian man renewed," dark but beautiful emissaries from a realm fermenting with life, savagery, and passion: "Man is a weed in those regions" (p. 333). There the recent invention, man, is swept aside, along with illusions of identity and individuality. The precarious self is inundated by the "fundamental force" of which Foucault writes, "one that is opposed to being in the same way as movement to immobility, as time to space, as the secret wish to the visible expression. Life is the root of all existence, and the non-living, nature in its inert form, is merely spent life; mere being is the non-being of life" (p. 278). Neville and Helena Landless, adumbrations of Foucault's "untamed ontology," come from a figurative realm proclaiming the enduring presence of those volatile, chaotic eras that only seem to be of the past. The Landlesses exist beyond English conceptions of identity, communicating by a mysterious process of intuition or telepathy transcending language: they defy prevailing conceptions of autonomous selfhood rooted in the language the people of London and Cloisterham unreflectingly speak.[22]

The Landlesses, mysterious and volatile, are harbingers of the life force in the midst of unambiguous death. They introduce alien and alternative forms of being into Cloisterham. They also act as catalytic agents, like the opium John Jasper smokes. Their presence tends to subvert the elaborate social and psychological barriers that have, so far, provided that illusory separation between Crisparkle's daylight world and the midnight world into which Jasper moves for refuge and release. With their appearance, Jasper's already disintegrating command of himself undergoes further erosion. He begins to communicate more explicitly and more urgently his repressed desires.

Rosa Bud is already troubled by Jasper's obsession with her. She is woman enough to have felt the desire he expresses through his music and his singing. However, she cannot understand that her fear is informed by some vaguely stirring response to Jasper within herself. On the night of the dinner party welcoming the Landlesses to Cloisterham, Rosa finds herself engaged in the inevitable performance required of a young lady at such a party. Jasper accompanies her on the piano: "The song went on. . . . As Jasper watched the pretty lips, and ever and again hinted the one note, as though it were a low whisper from himself, the voice became a little less steady, until all at once the singer broke into a burst of tears, and shrieked out, with her hands over her eyes: 'I can't

bear this! I am frightened! Take me away!'" (chapter 7). Of all those in
the drawing room only Helena, Rosa, and Jasper understand what lies
behind the girl's outcry. The intense eroticism of the proceedings, the
subtle violation of Rosa's person, as Jasper hints "the one note, as though
it were a low whisper from himself," has gone unnoticed by others. But
Helena, endowed with an awareness banned from the respectable par-
lors of respectable people, understands the implications of Jasper's attentiveness. While Edwin Drood blindly assumes that Jack's conscientious-
ness has intimidated Rosa, Helena senses the real basis of Rosa's fear.
And knowing it, possessing knowledge that Victorian society denies,
she would not be afraid of Jasper "under any circumstances."

In Helena Landless, Rosa finds her antithesis. She calls herself a "mite
of a thing," while Helena seems "womanly and handsome," with "resolution and power enough to crush" the less confident Rosa (chapter 7).
Her own remarks suggest that Rosa, wonderfully pretty and childish,
has willed her innocence, and her denial of her own ambiguous nature.
But Helena inhabits a different psychological realm. She has seen that
Jasper is obsessed with Rosa. Helena even pierces Rosa's self-delusion
that "He has made a slave of me with his looks" (chapter 7). The act of
compulsion, from Rosa's perspective, seems all on the part of Jasper; yet
Rosa's susceptibility to his presence, to his every gesture, reveals she is
not merely a slave to her music master, but an unconscious partner in an
intensely charged exchange. There is a certain thrill behind her confession that on this night, "It was as if he kissed me, and I couldn't bear it,
but cried out" (chapter 7). But in a society in which Miss Twinkleton
speaks of "the future wives and mothers of England" in a lowered voice,
lest the company be shocked by even a veiled allusion to certain facts,
Rosa has been denied the capacity to accept her own sexuality. She is
drawn to a Helena Landless who can ask, quite directly, "You do not
love him [Jasper]? . . . You know that he loves you?" (chapter 7), because she has not yet acquiesced to Cloisterham's pervasive inhibitions.
In embracing Helena, Rosa has turned to someone whose vision of her
situation must be different from her own. Helena's "wild black hair
[falls] down protectingly over [Rosa's] childish form." Hers is a vivid
beauty: "There was a slumbering gleam of fire in the intense dark eyes,
though they were then softened with compassion and admiration"
(chapter 7). Here, Rosa is lost in an embrace as potentially erotic as any
Jasper might offer.

But the evening is not over. The gates of the Nuns' House close upon Rosa and Helena, but the volatile forces that have been released have not yet played themselves out. As Rosa and Helena are brought together by the fascination that opposites hold for each other, Edwin Drood and Neville Landless are drawn together by the power of mutual contempt, even hatred. Drood has already been moved by the sensual intensity of the dark-complexioned Helena, just as Landless has responded to the fragile, childlike beauty of Rosa. Each seeks out, intuitively, an opposite to complement his own nature. Their unexpressed desires help to create the antagonism they feel for each other. It is intensified by the casual sense of superiority that Drood exudes as the anointed Westerner ready to bring the wonders of technology to Egypt, and as Rosa's fiancé with his infuriatingly proprietary attitude. Landless's own feeling of racial inferiority, his acute sensitivity to the most casual slight, adds the final measure of provocation. He lacks the easy ability to mask his emotions that Drood has inherited, much as he has inherited Rosa, without the knowledge that his mannerisms remain, at best, a fragile facade. Drood's genteel composure has so maddened Landless that only the sudden intervention of Jasper prevents a violent quarrel. He appears, as it were, out of the darkness, to lay a startling right hand on Drood's shoulder and to stand between the two, at once separating and joining them, as he places his left hand on the inner shoulder of Landless. In the darkness of the tranquil Cloisterham night John Jasper has encountered the externalized manifestation of his own warring states of mind.

The following scene in Jasper's chambers reveals the extent to which Jasper's private dreamworld now impinges more and more upon the world of conventional reality. Eugene Wrayburn finds in Bradley Headstone an "entertaining study" and incorporates the schoolmaster into a version of his own Gothic novel through the chase: John Jasper presides over the dramatic reenactment, before his very eyes, of the conflicts dominating his dreams. He casually calls attention to the unfinished portrait of Rosa Bud, hanging in its central place over the chimneypiece. This act, alone, rekindles the quarrel he has only recently interrupted. For on this evening Jasper has found an intriguing substitute for his usual means of escape. If he has, in fact, drugged the mulled wine he prepares, with "much mixing and compounding," he artfully creates the conditions under which all that has been so long repressed may be exposed without risk to himself. In the opium den of the Princess Puffer and in his own bedchamber, Jasper has repeatedly undertaken, in the company of an unsuspecting fellow-traveler, a perilous dream journey, "over abysses where a slip would be destruction." Jasper has before him, now, Drood and Landless, each a traveler, each a potential threat to the other. As a spectator, he momentarily possesses even the illusion of distance and self-command that enables Eugene Wrayburn to sleep so soundly after the healthful rigors of the chase.

As he goads Landless to renewed fury, Jasper participates in the envy and frustration behind it. He speaks of Drood's prospects, of the world before him, of the marriage that is his legacy, and then exposes his own resentment, carefully screened by his bantering manner: "You [Landless] and I have no prospect of stirring work and interest, or of change and excitement, or of domestic ease and love. You and I have no prospect . . . but the tedious, unchanging round of this dull place" (chapter 8). Under other circumstances Jasper has revealed his sense of alienation and frustration to Drood; he has seemed to understand that his nephew might well find himself in a niche like his own. But now he is free, under the aegis of Landless's presence, to express obliquely an envy of his nephew that has become inextricably bound to his own discontent. Drood justifiably protests that his situation is not as comfortable, as free of constraints, as it seems: both he and Rosa have begun to perceive the absurdity of their engagement, the element of coercion behind the benevolence of two dead fathers and the unthinking acquiescence of society. But Drood's emerging awareness of the violation of his integrity by the will lies beyond the comprehension of either Landless or Jasper. Neither can understand Drood's apparent lack of commitment, his maddening indifference to the tempting "golden fruit that hangs ripe on the tree for him" (chapter 8). Drood's pose, so akin to the adopted languor of Eugene Wrayburn, is his muted protest to the circumstances into which he has been born. But his air of patronage and indifference as he speaks of the unfinished portrait of Rosa as a "joke, sir, a mere joke," is enough to madden Landless, and Jasper. Jasper has identified himself with Landless: both are dark, alien young men, with no prospects, and are taunted by Drood's easy self-assurance. The man who stands before them is no longer simply a sexual rival. He represents a state of consciousness that the two both envy and abhor, for to embrace it involves their estrangement from themselves.

Jasper's self-possession throughout the intensifying quarrel resembles the passivity of the dreamer who observes the landscape and the flow of events passing before him. But, like the dreamer, Jasper participates in all that happens. His consciousness is the ultimate ground of the scene: all the characters are versions of his multifaceted self. Drood's patronizing words express a certain temptation for Jasper, the lure of an illusory autonomy and invulnerability. But in his response to Drood's annihilating condescension—"in the part of the world I come from, you would be called to account for it" (chapter 8)—Landless expresses Jasper's own sense of foreignness. The two belong to the same part of the world, a figurative Ceylon like De Quincey's southern Asia, that seat of awful images and associations. Drood's contemptuous answer reveals he has acquiesced more than he knows to the conventional world: "Only there? . . . A long way off, I believe? Yes; I see! That part of the world is at a safe distance" (chapter 8). But that part of the world is in Jasper's chambers this night, in defiance of the walls of Cloisterham and the social conventions designed to exclude it.[23]

Drood's claim that Landless is no judge of white men is the final thrust. Like Wrayburn's calculated denial of Headstone's existence, Drood's comment exiles Landless, as well as the dark Jasper, from the civilized island world of England, from that socially defined reality challenged by the two men. Drood's racism is only another version of the enduring attempt of society to shut out alternative visions of reality. At this point, only Jasper's intervention prevents a struggle between two modes of being. The nightmare has almost worked itself out to its logical conclusion, but Jasper's intercession imposes, once again, the barriers separating not only Landless and Drood, but the conflicting parts of Jasper's own consciousness. The two apparently distinct states of mind reassert their primacy. Landless finds himself in the dark, standing "with a bare head in the midst of a blood-red whirl, waiting to be struggled with, and to struggle to the death" (chapter 8). But the time, place, and fellow-traveler of Jasper's endlessly repeated dream journey are not yet at hand. At this moment Jasper is not prepared for the struggle to the death either with Drood or with himself. The crisis has not come; the choice between who is to live and who is to die, if only figuratively, is still to be made. And Jasper, speaking to Crisparkle of the events of the evening, reveals more completely than he realizes his own confusion and

anxiety: "I shall never know peace of mind when there is danger of those
two coming together with no one else to interfere" (chapter 8). The two
parts of the divided self are held, literally and figuratively, at arms' length
by an interceding agent. For the moment Jasper himself is the agent.
Even in his desperation he cannot as yet contemplate the destruction
of the nephew who is like a son to him, because he is a part of himself.
But that separation of the two bedrooms, reflecting the artificial com-
partmentalizing of Jasper's psyche, has run its course as a strategem for
survival.

His urgent need to integrate, if possible, his fragmented consciousness impels Jasper to turn to Septimus Crisparkle and to accept his
offer to effect a reconciliation between Landless and Drood. Crisparkle,
far more than Drood, remains the embodiment of conventional consciousness in the novel. Behind his gentle benevolence, he remains unrelenting in his determination to transform alien modes of being into ac-
ceptable and recognizable forms. In persuading Landless, and Helena,
to acquiesce to the idea of the proposed party, Crisparkle defends the
socially sanctioned, if anachronistic, betrothal of Drood and Rosa. He
asks Landless to deny his own feelings and his own nature, calling his
interest in Rosa a mere infatuation, a "fancy of the moment." He cons-
cientiously performs his duty, which is to deny not only the validity but
the existence of the Landlesses' world, their Ceylon, and to assert the
claims of Cloisterham. He speaks for a competing reality, a socially constructed reality, designed to alter consciousness itself. He succeeds, at
best, in drawing the veil of conventional consciousness over the volatile
energies of the brother and sister, once so like "beautiful barbaric captives . . . from some wild tropical dominion."[24]

The novel moves toward Christmas Eve and the violent storm that is
to disrupt the aura of tranquility in which Cloisterham takes refuge.
There are omens indicating that some final eruption of long suppressed
forces is imminent. Crisparkle's efforts to interpose a "veil between our
present consciousness and the secret inscriptions on the mind" fail. The
"obscuring daylight" of which De Quincey writes in his *Confessions* will
withdraw to reveal the ineradicable nature of those inscriptions. Under
the aegis of the red light burning steadily in his gatehouse chambers, the
forces within John Jasper defy his habitual constraint on that Christmas
Eve. In the midst of the turbulent darkness of the storm, the steady
burning of the lamp takes on a sinister significance. Jasper presides over

the violence thundering along the empty streets at midnight, "rattling at all the latches, and tearing at all the shutters, as if warning the people to get up and fly with it" (chapter 14). He is, figuratively, the source, if not the master, of "this tangible part of the darkness [that] madly whirls about." For the same red light has glowed throughout Jasper's curious midnight ramble with Durdles and the confrontation with Deputy. It has burned during all the lonely vigils when Jasper has delivered himself to his midnight specters. Its reflection has appeared in the cupped hands of the Princess Puffer as she nurses the red spark of light emanating from the bowl of the opium pipe. The red light unifies Jasper's existence: it becomes the spark of consciousness.

On this most un-Dickensian of Christmas Eves the storm whose ground is Jasper's consciousness assaults the most prominent emblems of the conventional world of Cloisterham. On the Christmas morning following the storm, "it is then seen that the hands of the Cathedral clock are torn off; that lead from the roof has been stripped away . . . ; and that some stones have been displaced upon the summit of the great tower" (chapter 14). The storm defies for the moment the gorgon spell that holds the cathedral town in thrall. It reveals, as the French Revolution in its elemental assault upon the St. Evrémonde château has revealed, a timeless dimension beyond merely human coordinates and the need for fundamental change within a society whose paralysis denies the existence of that realm. But the stone tower remains; the hands of the clock will be replaced. As in Jasper's recurring dream, the tower seems indestructible. With the return of day, the obscuring veil of light returns. The storm, "like a wounded monster," finally drops, sinks, and dies. The Minotaur has had its moment of ambiguous freedom. Now linear time and the values of a petrified society reassert themselves, as they always do: the primacy of inertia prevails.

The storm has manifested the violence behind John Jasper's self-conscious façade, the presence of the figurative Ceylon behind the pastoral landscape of rural England. It also obscures forever those events occurring while it rages on. The vexing impenetrability of events remains an inherent part of the fascination of The Mystery of Edwin Drood. For Jasper, like De Quincey, might well claim adherence to "the doctrine of the true church on the subject of opium: of which church I acknowledge myself to be the only member—the alpha and the omega" (p. 299). But as a communicant in a church that inverts the values of a Christianity he only routinely observes, Jasper writhes in the power of a god beyond his control. He cannot know whether the ritual he performs has culminated only in his erotic, narcissistic visions or in an act of perverse religious devotion, the sacrificial murder of Drood, and necessarily, of part of himself. Nor can we.

Jasper's behavior after the disappearance of his dear boy is intelligible only within this context of pure ambiguity. In the last chapter of the fragment as we have it, "The Dawn Again," Jasper returns to the opium den of the Princess Puffer. For months he has been preparing his own opium in spite of the hag's proud claim that only she has "the real receipt for mixing it." The possibility exists that the effects of the drug upon Jasper's consciousness have become unpredictable. The glowing red lamp visible during the storm suggests that he has once again taken refuge in his visionary world before Drood's return from the river bank: he has prepared himself to meet the fellow-traveler of the dream journey. But the complexity of Jasper's psychological situation becomes as labyrinthine as the novel itself. If a murder has been committed, it may have been assimilated into the journey Jasper has relived millions and billions of times. But the murder may only be a dream, a dream taking on the appearance of reality. Jasper's ravings in the presence of the Princess only reveal his total disorientation. The "it" which "comes to be real at last," but which "is so short that it seems unreal for the first time" (chapter 23), need not be the act itself. Dickens offers no clues as to whether it is a real or a visionary murder that has failed to satisfy Jasper. There is only Jasper's conviction that the enigmatic "it" must have occurred because his dreams now offer "no struggle, no consciousness of peril, no entreaty," because some ill-defined "*that*" has appeared for the first time in the panorama of the dreamscape (chapter 23).

In either case, the confused and shaken Jasper moves more than ever under the sway of conflicting and elusive motivations. The disappearance of Drood is a wrenching blow to the uncle who has taken an almost womanish interest in him. If Edwin Drood *is* dead, Jasper must struggle with the remorse overwhelming him, for he has lived through Drood in spite of his envy and resentment of him. At the same time, on some level of his wracked consciousness, his jealousy of Drood—at once a father and a son to him—asserts itself, and he is tormented by an excruciating guilt. But it cannot be directed toward himself. In his diary Jasper has evaded the full impact of his own feelings by concentrating upon the tableau of violence, involving Drood and Landless, that he has so artfully contrived. Once again his guilt is displaced onto Landless, who conveniently embodies the creative and destructive potentialities of his repressed self. The mechanisms of the dreamworld usurp the order of reality. Innocent or guilty of the enigmatic act itself, John Jasper will pursue a murderer because he must: he stalks himself in the form of Neville Landless. Like Oedipus, he proclaims judgment on himself. Deputy's defiant challenge, "I'll blind yer, s'elp me! I'll stone yer eyes out, s'elp me! If I don't have yer eyesight, bellows me!" (chapter 12), suggests the validity of the analogy.

   With the dragging of the river and the futile search along the riverbanks, the novel returns to familiar motifs in earlier novels and to the recurring theme of death-by-water: "All the livelong day, the search went on. . . . Even at night, the river was specked with lanterns, and lurid with fires; far-off creeks, into which the tide washed as it changed, had their knots of watchers, listening to the lapping of the stream, and looking out for any burden it might bear; . . . but no trace of Edwin Drood revisited the light of the sun" (chapter 15). The quintessential Dickens ritual has begun anew. The living may recoil from the dead, with that "innate shrinking of dust with the breath of life in it, from dust out of which the breath of life has passed" (chapter 12), but they struggle to retain their hope that an individual can defy death's power. As those who watch and yearn for Rogue Riderhood's return to life become a part of his solitary struggle in *Our Mutual Friend,* so the inhabitants of Cloisterham participate in the search for Drood. They listen and they gaze with the same rapt suspense possessing those who gather at the foot of Eugene Wrayburn's sickbed after he has been attacked by Bradley Headstone: "This frequent rising of a drowning man from the deep, to sink again, was dreadful to the beholders" (book 4, chapter 10). The watchers at the bedside are held there by that almost involuntary denial of the reality of death that makes life possible.

   The fate of Edwin Drood is never clearly adumbrated within the novel. He has, like John Harmon who refuses to acquire Bella Wilfer as part of his inheritance, defied a dead father when he releases Rosa from her engagement to him. Drood has not acquiesced to outmoded notions, however benevolent. He may be poised for a change that will release him from his habitual acceptance of prevailing values. Like Har-

mon and Wrayburn before him, he chooses life. But we cannot know if
he is dead or alive, ready to undergo further transformations. As his fate
must remain a matter of speculation, so must John Jasper's. He, too, is
one of the avid searchers, cruising the river in barge and boat, or "tramp-
ing amidst mud and stakes and jagged stones in low-lying places." The
foreign, muddy world of the Thames calls to him, also. He returns to his
gatehouse, "unkempt and disordered, bedaubed with mud that [has]
dried upon him, and with much of his clothing torn to rags" (chapter
15). He has returned from the potent mud of the river, which is the antithesis to the sterile dust of Cloisterham and the grit of London. He
becomes a recurring Dickens figure descending into the depths—like
Steerforth, Sydney Carton, and Bradley Headstone—perhaps never to
return alive, but to die in the violence of a storm off Yarmouth, or under
the ooze and scum behind one of the gates of a Plashwater Weir Mill
Lock; or to undergo the metamorphoses experienced by John Harmon
and Eugene Wrayburn. Jasper has made his own descent into the regions of the godlike river. His return from it suggests that he has been
granted the opportunity to accept or to deny the potentiality for change
within him: on some level of his consciousness, he must choose whether
or not to reinvent himself.

It is in this state of exhaustion and disorientation that Jasper must
encounter the calculated insensitivity of Mr. Grewgious as he persists in
his slow, provoking revelation of the broken engagement. The solicitor's
callousness suggests that he is already suspicious of Jasper. He remorselessly puts Jasper to the test and watches the "ghastly figure throw back
its head, clutch its hair with its hands, and turn with a writhing action
from him," until at last Jasper utters his shriek of horror and is reduced
to "nothing but a heap of torn and miry clothes upon the floor" (chapter 15). Jasper undergoes a process of total disintegration, collapsing into
the abyss of his self. His identity, fragile and confused as it is, has been
defined by the bizarre triangle uniting Rosa, Drood, and himself, just as
James Carker has defined himself in his relationship to Mr. Dombey and
Edith; just as Bradley Headstone has defined himself in *his* relationship
to Eugene Wrayburn and Lizzie Hexam. With the disappearance of
Drood and with the breaking of his engagement to Rosa, the entire edifice—so inverted, fantastic, and self-destructive—collapses. With the
loss of those relationships upon which his existence depends, Jasper becomes a nullity, a heap of clothes upon the floor, and no more. What the

unmoved, and unmoving, Grewgious gazes upon is the remnant of Jasper's extinguished self, like the "mutilated fragments" of James Carker who has uttered a shriek of terror just as the fiery engine of Death beats him down and spins him "round and round, and [strikes] him limb from limb" before the eyes of the pursuing Dombey.

In *Our Mutual Friend,* the failure of the attack upon Wrayburn and the marriage of Wrayburn and Lizzie lead to Bradley Headstone's willed self-extinction. When he erases his name from the blackboard, he accepts his own dissolution and prepares for the suicidal struggle with Rogue Riderhood, at best a poor substitute for the one he sought to have with Wrayburn. But the closing chapters of *Edwin Drood* as we possess them constitute, in part, Jasper's attempt to reconstruct an identity. It is not, as it might have been, a Carlylean rebirth. Jasper, caught in a No Thoroughfare at least partially of his own making, chooses stasis, not change. He seeks to recapture a state of being not unlike the one he has known for so long: he becomes, in Kierkegaard's words, a mere memorial of the past. That multifaceted but fixated role he has forged for himself has made him its captive. He enacts the process of which Freud writes in "Analysis Terminable and Interminable" as the romantic self responds to the principle of inertia and the compulsion to repeat the past: "The adult's ego . . . continues to defend itself against dangers which no longer exist in reality; indeed, it finds itself compelled to seek out those situations in reality which can serve as an *approximate substitute* for the original danger, so as to be able to justify, in relation to them, its maintaining its *habitual modes of reaction*" (*SE*, 23 : 238, emphasis mine). Jasper succumbs to those habitual modes of reaction that so perplex Dickens's Mr. Morfin, and Freud. Unerringly, he begins to reconstruct another version of the fantasy that has sustained and tormented him. Drood may long ago have ceased to be the rival separating him from Rosa Bud. There may be a part of Jasper withholding itself from any commitment to the girl. In the old fantasy, Drood has conveniently played the dual role of father and son; Rosa has become both mother and betrothed maiden, doubly tempting, doubly inviolable, because of her contradictory status in the choirmaster's distorted scheme of things.

With the recovery of Edwin Drood's watch and shirt-pin, evidence of sorts that he is dead, Jasper begins to weave anew the old fantasy by which he has contrived to live. The diary that was to have been destroyed upon the New Year, and that Jasper has called a record of "Ned's life" as well as of his own, has a new use. In its pages he returns to a form of the obsolete fiction that has already failed him, seeking in it a new reason for living, and yet another person to become the object of his obsessive attention: "I now swear, and record the oath on this page, ... That I will fasten the crime of the murder of my dear dead boy, upon the murderer. And That I devote myself to his destruction" (chapter 16). Jasper has had to conceal, even from himself, the complex nature of his absorption in Drood, his dear dead boy. But he experiences no such constraints in the case of Neville Landless, who can be loathed without remorse, without guilt. And by fastening his attention upon Landless as the suspected murderer of Drood and an apparent rival for Rosa Bud's love, Jasper need not forego the dream journey and the exquisite thrill of destroying the fellow-traveler, the prelude to a moment of erotic release. Unlike Bradley Headstone, who works on, obsessed with the idea that the "instrument might have been better, the spot and the hour might have been better," Jasper acts to create yet another opportunity to strike. He begins to fashion another time, another place, another fellow-traveler. But, in pursuing Neville Landless in his waking hours as in his dreams, Jasper pursues not another rival for Rosa's love, but himself.

When he finds Rosa in the garden of the Nuns' House, Jasper, as in the opening of the novel, is once again in the process of piecing together his scattered consciousness into its habitual structure. In the midst of summer and renewed life, he obeys his old impulses by forcing himself upon Rosa. The course of action he pursues terrifies the girl, causing her to recoil in repugnance. Rosa's love, apparently, is no longer what Jasper seeks. He finds other emotions more pleasing, and less immediately threatening, however sterile and self-destructive they may prove to be. He now prefers the illusory pleasures of the dreamworld, as James Carker fed upon the portrait reminding him of Edith Dombey, as Bradley Headstone came to relish the masochistic pleasures of the chase. Jasper's words and actions frustrate any possibility of satisfaction within the context of reality; and they protect him from the rejection that he would find intolerable. He will be driven back into the world of opium, away from the living. But the fantasy, with the Sultan and the dancing girls, relies on images incorporated into the dream landscape, static images of real persons. Jasper has returned to the enduring triangle, to the dreamlike figures fixed in yet another dance of death: he is lodged forever in the niche of his own bizarre version of the family constellation.

Behind Jasper's melodramatic words and gestures in his interview with Rosa lies this psychological reality. He leans casually upon the sundial, another emblem of that multifaceted time he is trying to deny, and engages in a remarkable *tour de force*. He directs his performance both at anyone who might glance out from the windows and at Rosa, who finds herself once more in his power, compelled by the intensity of his voice to listen, transfixed, to a confused torrent of love and hate: "In the distasteful work of the day, in the wakeful misery of the night, girded by sordid realities, or wandering through Paradises and Hells of visions into which I rushed, carrying your image in my arms, I loved you madly" (chapter 19). The melodramatic cadences of the speech obscure the insinuations with which it is charged. If, in loving Rosa, Jasper has betrayed his nephew and his guardian, so has Rosa in her failure to love Drood in quite the right way. If, through his patronizing indifference, Drood has proved unworthy of her, Rosa has been found to be unworthy of the Paradises and Hells into which Jasper has rushed, for her sake. The suppressed guilt that Jasper feels is to be shared by Rosa: both her repugnance for Jasper and her rejection of Drood are used to make her a secret partner in whatever crimes Jasper has committed or has dreamed of committing. And Rosa, however appalled, must respond to this man, apparently in spite of herself: "Her panting breathing comes and goes as if it would choke her; but with a repressive hand upon her bosom, she remains" (chapter 19).

The conventionalized language, the predictable gestures of the Gothic villain, and the inevitable responses of the fair virgin in this scene cannot dissipate the intensity of the energy produced in their confrontation. Rosa is reduced, through the pressure of literary convention and through the demands of her genteel education, to calling Jasper "a bad, bad man." Her words reveal the futility of Jasper's attempt to incorporate her into the visionary Paradises and Hells of which he speaks. Rosa may unwittingly respond to Jasper's intensity as she has done that night at the piano: she may not deny altogether her own sexuality. But she is not Helena Landless. The disparity between Rosa's bland timidity and the eroticism of Jasper's dreams reveals that she has no place in such dreams: she has not known the intensity of such feelings as Jasper's. She has become aware of the absurdity of her engagement to Edwin Drood. But she remains a stranger to Jasper's capacity for frustration and dissatisfaction, and to the ambiguous refuge offered by perversity. For her Jasper necessarily remains a "horrible wonder apart": her ignorance is the seal of her socially sanctioned innocence. Inevitably, the living Rosa Bud has ceased to be the object of Jasper's obsession: through the "Paradises and Hells of [the] visions" into which he rushes, he carries, in his arms, only her image. Jasper longs now for the exotic, sensual dancing-girls of his dreams. He may feed upon Rosa's hatred and exultingly claim that Rosa is "more beautiful in anger than in repose," that he wants not her love but her enchanting rage and scorn. But even this has ceased to be true. Rosa is now only the occasion for his fevered reveries. Her abhorrence becomes the sought-for check to action: it protects Jasper from experiencing the emptiness of his vision of her; it thrusts him more deeply into the realm of his own consciousness.

Edwin Drood's disappearance eliminates the obstacle to the realization of his desires, the obstacle upon which Jasper has relied. Now he reinvents the eternal triangle that informs his dreams and constitutes his habitual, unchanging self. Within the fantasy he weaves, Rosa Bud will remain the inviolable object, at once desired and hated for her inviolability. Neville Landless will replace Drood as Sultan *and* Turkish robber, to become the necessary barrier to the consummation of Jasper's desires. Jasper hopes to fix Rosa in her former role by threatening Landless's life. He offers to relinquish his vindictive pursuit of Landless and henceforth to have no object but Rosa. But the girl cannot submit to such coercion. The savage intensity of Jasper's words insures her moral revulsion: "There is my past and my present wasted life. There is the desolation of my heart and my soul. There is my peace; there is my despair. Stamp them into the dust, so that you take me, were it even mortally hating me!" (chapter 19). This is not a proposal. It is a perverse design to fix Jasper and Rosa in an eternal limbo of frustrated desire. The scene is a far darker version of the one in which Bradley Headstone proposes to Lizzie Hexam in *Our Mutual Friend*. Headstone sees Wrayburn as a real rival whom he cannot hope to defeat. Jasper creates a fictive rival in the form of Neville Landless. Both men succeed in driving the women they love into flight. In Headstone's case this leads to the suicidal chase. In Jasper's, it effects his final isolation from everything, from everyone, around him. The revulsion he has so artfully, compulsively, aroused in Rosa is a reflection of his own self-abhorrence: he has become the outcast, the De Quincean pariah, he has long felt himself to be.

John Jasper has arrived at the No Thoroughfare he has, from the start, been seeking. The windows of the Nuns' House, looking out upon the garden, become mirrors as well as windows. Jasper is acutely aware of them as such. He says to Rosa, "I do not forget how many windows command a view of us. . . . I will not touch you again, I will come no nearer to you than I am. Sit down, and there will be no mighty wonder in your music-master's leaning idly against a pedestal and speaking with you, remembering all that has happened and our shares in it" (chapter 19). The windows protect both Rosa and Jasper. They become his pretext for his immobility, his pose of idleness, which precludes touching the real Rosa. Jasper's self fragments, divides; he becomes paralytically animated by the need to reconstruct the fantasy within his own consciousness, even as he avoids acting upon it. The garden becomes a hall of mirrors of his own devising. The intensity of his voice, the workings of his features and hands, yoked to his attitude of studied ease, reveal the completeness of his self-division. He revels in this moment of pure stasis, even as it exposes the untenable nature of his situation: he cannot survive in this condition of isolation, with a self lacking the integration that is the hypothetical goal of the romantic process of self-creation. Nevertheless, the condition of isolation, division, and stasis remains Jasper's bizarre object. He is aware of his consummate performance, of the incongruity of a ferocity masked by his languid posture. His is an artistic achievement, however inverted and life-denying. He smiles and "folds his hands upon the sun-dial . . . so that his talk would seem from the windows (faces occasionally come and go there) to be of the airiest and playfullest" (chapter 19). But the faces see only what Jasper wishes them to see: they do not exist independently of his consciousness. Jasper has eluded the intersubjective reality of his own nature. He feels no need to touch, to encounter, others who might refute his conception of himself. He feels no need to act, for action would threaten his belief that he *is* the face reflected in the mirror of his imagination. His self-consciousness has led, inevitably, to the playing of a role within a role. He assumes he is the master of each part he performs. In fact, he has become, like James Carker and Bradley Headstone before him, a disembodied self for whom there are no authentic gestures, but only further means of disguising an illusory real self hidden behind impenetrable layers of posturing: no more than the faces in the windows can Jasper penetrate to the center, perhaps to the empty center, of his labyrinthine self.

The novel has come full circle; to some extent it has never left the opium den of the opening pages. The spike that fused the world of the Town with that of the Sultan reappears in the form of the sundial upon which Jasper has impaled himself. He has not transcended his situation; he still writhes upon the thorn of anxiety. He has failed to come to terms with the conventional time of the cathedral clock and the eternal fecundity of Ceylon. He has made a futile gesture, in defiance of the imperatives of the romantic self, to perpetuate an impasse. He is fixed, in De Quincey's words, at the summit: he is the idol and the priest, the worshipped and the worshipper. He shrinks from the reciprocity of relationships with living Others who are in time. His only object in life has become his dreams and himself. Failing to imbed Rosa Bud into the narcissistic mosaic that is his precarious identity, he has, nevertheless, fixed himself there. In the season of growth and maturation, with its natural movement toward the harvest, Jasper has chosen to deny his own participation in the process of change. He leaves the garden of the Nuns' House "with no greater show of agitation than is visible in the effigy of Mr. Sapsea's father opposite" (chapter 19). He has fulfilled the prophecy inherent in his name: he has become an effigy of himself, a mere monument to the past, turned to stone not by Rosa Bud, as Edith Dombey once cast her Medusa spell upon James Carker and herself, but by the image of himself within the mirror of his own consciousness.

John Jasper, potentially a romantic rebel in revolt against an oppressive society, has sought an impasse that, ironically, mirrors the inertia of the society he has rejected. Through Jasper, the voice of discontent becomes coherently articulated. His confession to Edwin Drood that he hates the cramped monotony of his existence is the cry of a suffering and cornered human being whose alienation from his society and himself is a mark of his humanity.[25] Jasper, apparently beyond the pale of human sympathy and comprehension, reveals the extent to which romantic energy, the impetus to change, may be twisted and inverted. Although fragmentary, *The Mystery of Edwin Drood* presents a study in social and personal impasse, a society and its various inhabitants succumbing to Mr. Morfin's habit, to the compulsion to repeat life-denying forms of being. Jasper becomes a living effigy to an obsolete self. Cloisterham, and the massive tower of its storied cathedral, becomes a monument to the irrelevant values of an obsolete past. Like France under the Bourbons in *A Tale of Two Cities,* the world of Cloisterham is paralytically animated by what Freud calls, in *Beyond the Pleasure Principle,* "the inertia inherent in organic life" (*SE*, 18:36). Dickens, following Carlyle and anticipating Freud, imagines the fate of society and the individual through the figurative language of biology, Foucault's "science of life." Where there is life there is also its dialectic opposite, "the *conservative* nature of living substance," (*SE*, 18:36), the tendency "towards the restoration of an earlier state of things." According to Freud, "The elementary living entity would from its very beginning have had no wish to change; if conditions remained the same, it would do no more than constantly repeat the same course of life" (*SE*, 18:38).

The gorgon's head has once surveyed the St. Evrémonde château, making it a stony business altogether. It has, as effectively, surveyed the cathedral, the town, and the people who pass daily through its streets: "A drowsy city, Cloisterham, whose inhabitants seem to suppose, with an inconsistency more strange than rare, that all its changes lie behind it, and that there are no more to come" (chapter 3). The gloomy cathedral becomes a sepulcher for the volatile energies of a Helena and a Neville Landless and of the figurative Ceylon from which they come. For in its tropical landscape Ceylon reveals the existence of a domain beyond the pastoral, ordered landscape of the domesticated English countryside. Ceylon, suggesting the "untamed ontology" of which Foucault writes in *The Order of Things,* discloses a primitive force bearing beings "for an instant towards a precarious form and yet . . . already secretly sapping them from within in order to destroy them. In relation to life, beings are no more than transitory figures, and the being that they maintain, during the brief period of their existence, is no more than their presumption, their will to survive" (p. 278).

In the effort to deny the existence of those primitive forces for which the Landlesses stand, and to which Jasper is initially drawn, the world of Cloisterham erects its cathedral, implicitly denying the existence of volatile, ambiguous energies that might sweep over and inundate its precious, and precarious, forms of being, both social and personal. Ironically, the cathedral, and the system of values for which it stands, not only denies the existence of the figurative Ceylon, it finally denies the less threatening world of nature beyond its sepulchral interior. Mr. Grewgious, looking into the cathedral on an autumn afternoon, can only sigh, "It's like looking down the throat of Old Time" (chapter 9). The cathedral, sign of a bankrupt Christianity and of repressive, life-denying institutions, is always distinguished from "the free outer air, the river, the green pastures, and the brown arable lands, the teeming hills and dales . . . reddened by the sunset" (chapter 9). The cathedral still stands, still holds sway. It subdues the "sea of music" that "rose high, and beat its life out, and lashed the roof, and surged among the arches, and pierced the heights of the great tower." The resurgent sea of sound, of human aspiration, presses rhythmically, persistently, against unyielding cathedral walls. There is a question of how long the walls can defy time and the cycles of the seasons before calling forth the more elemental forces of De Quincey's Southern Asia, the "part of the earth most swarming with human life; the great *officina gentium*": in the midst of such a world man is but a weed (p. 333). The novel opens upon an autumnal day presaging winter and death. It ends, in its fragmentary form, upon a summer day on which the sun shines, trees wave in the balmy air, birds sing, and "scents from gardens, woods, and fields—or, rather, from the one great garden of the whole cultivated island in its yielding time— penetrate into the Cathedral, subdue its earthy odour, and preach the Resurrection and the Life" (chapter 23). The island pulsates with harbingers of life. But the society and its inhabitants, including John Jasper, seem deaf, dumb, blind, and paralytic not only to the domain of Ceylon, but to the call of the English countryside.

Metamorphosis is checked, stasis is triumphant in the town through which a Stony Durdles appropriately rambles. John Jasper, ambiguous figure that he remains, has become a definitive study in romantic discontent. The cathedral town of the opium dream dissolves into the rusty spike on the bedstead in a sordid opium den; the spike resolves itself into the thorn of anxiety embedded in Jasper's consciousness. The Faustian, the Byronic, questing of a Steerforth, with *its* ambiguities, has come to this—confinement within the dull place of Cloisterham, which offers "no prospect of stirring work and interest, . . . of change and excitement." The romantic career of unceasing self-creation has come to a halt. Jasper's moral and psychological isolation, his solipsistic withdrawal into the world of dreams, expresses his awareness of the dislocation within conventional society and his inability to generate a humanly viable response to that society.

For John Jasper, the Resurrection and the Life preached by the whole cultivated island have become unimaginable illusions. He must writhe upon the spike of which he has dreamt, impaled there both by a conventional world hostile to a vision of Nature alien to its own and by his own habitual seeking out of that triangular constellation constituting his identity. He reeks of the taint of the eternal scapegoat, a role he compulsively pursues. If his words are oracular, if Deputy is a diminutive Tiresias to Jasper's Oedipus, the blight that has fallen upon the garden of England will pass only with the destruction of its apparent cause. But Jasper is never a source, a cause. His suffering, and his perversity, are symptomatic of a far too narrow vision of the human situation and of a rejection of the need for change in the name of a spent culture.

But Dickens remains, as ever, the Resurrection-Man, insistently seeking ways to resolve the impasse he has so surely explored. He cannot imaginatively abandon the possibility of change, the hope for social and personal regeneration. From the beginning the promise of regeneration has been offered in *The Mystery of Edwin Drood*. In the first chapter Jasper returns from the opium den to participate in the evening service that begins when the "intoned words, 'WHEN THE WICKED MAN—' rise among groins of arches and beams of roof, awakening muttered thunder" (chapter 1). The verse is from Ezekiel 18:27: "Again, when the wicked *man* turneth away from his wickedness that he hath committed, and doeth that which is lawful and right, he shall save his soul alive." [26] The Christian perspective explicit in the allusion, with its ethical and religious dimensions, stands in tension with the subversive, and ultimately romantic, vision of the Gothic. The lure of ritual pervades the novel, as the incantatory language of the search for the body of Edwin Drood reveals. Even references to the cycles of the seasons possess a Carlylean insistence, an attempt to resolve through the magic of language alone what may prove to be beyond resolution: the perplexing encounter between Faust and Mephistopheles, Eros and Thanatos, the impetus to change and the tendency to inertia. In *A Tale of Two Cities* and *Our Mutual Friend,* those novels so obviously joined within his imagination, Dickens has resorted, yet again, to the ritual of the Double, to the sacrifice of one part of a fixated self undergoing disintegration, so that another, potentially healthy part might survive and experience the mystery of change. Sydney Carton, the "Double of coarse deportment," dies so that Charles Darnay might live. In *Our Mutual Friend,* the pose that has become Eugene Wrayburn's second nature achieves an autonomy threatening to obliterate the inner, true self in which Wrayburn chooses to believe. As the T'otherest, as the most prominent of the fixated selves in the novel, it is Bradley Headstone, Wrayburn's Double, who will die to save Wrayburn, much as the drowning of George Radfoot in the waters of the Thames ritualistically saves the endangered John Harmon. As his state of paralysis and despair passes, Wrayburn is free to reinvent himself. He escapes from the straightjacket of his acquired self just as Headstone escapes, if only in death, from his respectable suit of clothes and his respectable life.

Sydney Carton, Bradley Headstone, and John Jasper are repetitions of each other, connected by the shadowy nature of their unacknowledged past lives and by the vaguely Oedipal nature of their situations. Through the ritual of the Double, Dickens has begun to seek out new departures in an attempt to resolve imaginatively the dilemma posed by the romantic self. He has explored the condition of that recent invention, man, and he, too, perhaps anticipates, with profound relief, that a "figure not yet two centuries old, a new wrinkle in our knowledge, . . . will disappear again as soon as that knowledge has discovered a new form" (p. xxiii). Carton and Headstone function primarily as the personal Doubles of Darnay and Wrayburn. Jasper, nominally the villain of the urban Gothic world of Dickens's last novels, becomes the universal Double of *The Mystery of Edwin Drood,* the shadow side of a society in paralysis: he embodies the tendency to inertia within each character and within the society itself. Dickens returns to the death of Old Foulon and the destruction of the St. Evrémonde château; to the humiliation of Pumblechook, his mouth stuffed "full of flowering annuals," and the fall of Satis House; to the ritual of regeneration through which, in not altogether Christian terms, the dying body of society and the paralytically animated selves of the citizens of that society are returned to the medium of time, to the reality of change, and to life. In his urbanization of the Gothic, Dickens captures forms of social and personal impasse, imposed or chosen, which deny the untamed ontology informing romantic conceptions of the self and the pilgrimage of being. In his recourse to ritual, he seeks to dispel the shadows of those ancient edifices—the St. Evrémonde château, Satis House, and Cloisterham Cathedral—that float upon the waters of time and change: they are those stony institutions, social and personal, resisting change, attempting "to keep themselves in existence after the time of their usefulness has passed," seeking out "those situations in reality which can serve as an approximate substitute for [an] original danger, so as to be able to justify, in relation to them, [their] maintaining [their] habitual modes of reaction" (*SE*, 23 : 237–38). Ultimately, Dickens tries to imagine a form of life, unshadowed by the threat of impasse, to succeed that of the recent invention, man, and annul the romantic imperative to the unceasing creation both of history and the self.

Conclusion

> What thou hast inherited from thy fathers,
> acquire it to make it thine.
> —Goethe, *Faust:* Freud, *Totem and Taboo*

Patriarchal Musings

In the context of the current obsession with origins and beginnings, *Our Mutual Friend* stands as an extended musing upon fathers and sons, upon what Walter Jackson Bate has called the burden of the past and Harold Bloom has identified as the anxiety of influence. This burden and this anxiety pervade *Our Mutual Friend*, generating the somber tone that Henry James could attribute only to the final exhaustion of the Inimitable's imagination: "*Our Mutual Friend* is, to our perception, the poorest of Mr. Dickens's works. And it is poor with the poverty not of momentary embarrassment, but of permanent exhaustion. It is wanting in inspiration."[1]

Yet, *Our Mutual Friend* continues to enjoy a spirited life of its own, while inspiring some of the great English-speaking writers of the twentieth century. A novel about fathers and sons fittingly becomes the precursor to certain enduring works of fiction and poetry. We know, of course, that the title of "The Waste Land" was once "He Do the Police in Different Voices," an appropriation of Betty Higden's words describing Sloppy's skill as a reader of police reports.[2] The unreal city of "The Waste Land" is the city of *Bleak House* and of *Our Mutual Friend;* its disoriented and sullen denizens are the inhabitants of the literal and figurative London of Dickens's novels. The Thames of Dickens's London flows through "The Waste Land": the theme of "Death by Water" informs the structure of Dickens's later novels and Eliot's poem.

The search for drowned corpses and the macabre discussions of Silas Wegg and Mr. Venus about the human anatomy and the dispersal of bodily parts have their echoes in *Ulysses,* in the drowned body in Dublin Bay, never to be recovered, and in Joyce's use of bodily organs as an organizing principle within his novel. Even Stephen Dedalus's not-so-whimsical speculations upon Shakespeare and *Hamlet,* and, by implication, upon the problem of literary influence, curiously repeat the more mundane predicaments of Eugene Wrayburn and John Harmon, each of whom wrestles with a ghostly father, one living and one dead, who poses the inevitable threat to the son's psychic survival.[3]

In *Sons and Lovers,* Paul Morel and Baxter Dawes, when they finally grapple in the darkness, reenact a version of the chase in *Our Mutual Friend* and bring to mind the moment when Bradley Headstone, goaded to madness, attacks Eugene Wrayburn and abandons his mutilated body to the waters of the Thames. Just as Headstone waits until he sees Lizzie Hexam and Wrayburn in a moment of ambiguous intimacy, Dawes engages Morel in battle only after he has passed the young man and Clara in the darkness: "One evening, as Paul and she were walking along Woodborough Road, they met Dawes. Morel knew something about the bearing of the man approaching, but he was absorbed in his thinking at the moment, so that only his artist's eye watched the form of the stranger."[4] But it is more than Morel's artist's eye or his desire to talk to Clara that causes him to turn to Clara and to put his hand on her shoulder, speaking to her as Dawes passes, almost touching Morel. At that moment, "The young man glanced, saw the dark brown eyes burning, full of hate and yet tired" (p. 361). Morel invites the attack that occurs a few nights afterwards just as Wrayburn invites Headstone's attack. And when the two men do battle, Dawes, like Headstone before him, is moved as much by despair as by hate, and love.

There is within *Our Mutual Friend* a creative potency to which James Joyce, D. H. Lawrence, and T. S. Eliot responded. What Henry James saw as Dickens's imaginative exhaustion is a reaching out for new modes of characterization, an attempt, perhaps, to break with the conventions of his own novels and to escape from the cul-de-sac to which his depiction of the romantic self has led. The insistent return in Dickens's novels to the infantile family constellation,[5] to the Oedipal situation, is a recurring encounter with the plight of the romantic self, ontologically alone and impelled to create an identity by confronting a real or imaginary family of the past. There are inevitable Oedipal overtones to Ortega's description of the pilgrimage of being: "The experiments already made with life narrow man's future. If we do not know what he is going to be, we know what he is not going to be. Man lives in view of the past."[6] It is the father who literally and figuratively embodies the experiments already made with life. If man, the eternal son, lives in view of the past, he lives in view of the father, of those structures of life the father sanctions and seeks to perpetuate. In the Oedipal situation, Dickens captures the need to reject or to modify the past, and to create new forms of life. He also explores the burden of personal identity, the difficulty of rejecting a past that is not an abstraction but a living or dead parent, whose will demands the perpetuation of experiments whose time, ironically, is past. The quest for personal identity leads, with seeming inevitability, to parricide, literal or figurative. This is the burden of the past, the anxiety of influence from which, in *Our Mutual Friend,* sons—and daughters—flee.

In his novels Dickens's persistent concern with names and with memory is a means of exploring further the issue of personal identity; of defining the predicament, sometimes harrowing, arising from the possession of a name, that hieroglyphic sign demanding decipherment. Pleasant Riderhood, daughter of Rogue Riderhood—like David Copperfield, Esther Summerson, and Philip Pirrip before her—must puzzle over the meaning of her name: "Why christened Pleasant, the late Mrs. Riderhood might possibly have been able at some time to explain, and possibly not. Her daughter had no information on that point. Pleasant she found herself, and she couldn't help it. She had not been consulted on the question, any more than on the question of her coming into these terrestrial parts to want a name."[7] No Dickens character is consulted on that question. Each is a child of contingency, a chance person, whose name seems arbitrarily imposed, an enigmatic talisman like the "arbitrary characters" of which David speaks in his encounter with the mysteries of stenography. Yet the name is binding. A parent's choice of a name is never purely arbitrary; it is always charged with meaning, conscious and unconscious, for the one who chooses it. In naming the child, the father—and occasionally the mother—seeks to dictate the child's identity. The parent who names the son or daughter anticipates the child's hypothetical future, already determined to control it. The child is born into a context, given not chosen, a context signified by a name. He or she chooses to accept and to perpetuate the context, the past, or to reject it, and to formulate something new. Namelessness is never a viable alternative, for in that direction lie dissolution and death. Instead, the child—and for Dickens it is commonly the son—must rename himself or confer upon the arbitrary sign with which he must live his own meaning. Philip Pirrip, through an act of mispronunciation, names himself. It is the first, tentative step in freeing himself from his past. But once he accepts the promise of great expectations by agreeing to retain his name, Pip, he abandons his freedom. Pip must learn the identity of his benefactor or benefactress, for only then can he understand what his name means for that shadowy personage: is it a talisman by which he may live or does it consign him to some unforeseen future that is a dreadful repetition of the past? It is necessary never to forget that "Pip" means one thing for Abel Magwitch and something quite different for Miss Havisham. Pip, no less than Oedipus, knows himself only when he knows truly the origin of his now legal name.

But the obsession with one's name, with its origin and its meaning, remains an obsession with personal identity, with the romantic self. To be so obsessed is to follow in the steps of Jean-Jacques Rousseau who, in proclaiming his uniqueness, confronts the reality of the dead mother and the living father whose influence manifests itself in the familial situations Rousseau, ever the young Orestes, seeks out in *The Confessions*. His celebration of personal identity involves the imperative to create himself through an encounter with the father and his values, an encounter with both a personal and a social past. In *The Confessions* a narrative conception of a self struggling against repetitions symptomatic of fixation rather than of coherent growth offers a model of self-creation, one followed by David Copperfield in *his* confessions. For Rousseau and for the fictive David, the program they follow is always endangered. In revealing his masochistic pleasure in being beaten by Mlle. Lambercier, Rousseau returns to a crystallizing experience that determines his "tastes and desires, . . . passions, [and] very self for the rest of [his] life." He writes: "Now I have made the first and most painful step in the dark and miry maze of my confessions. It is the ridiculous and the shameful, not one's criminal actions, that it is hardest to confess. But henceforth I am certain of myself; after what I have just had the courage to say, nothing else will defeat me."[8] But Rousseau can never be assured that his narrative will be altogether accurate and complete. The passing reference to the maze, to Daedalus, to Theseus, and the Minotaur, reveals Rousseau's awareness that, in writing his confessions, he is in the process of creating a maze in which he may become lost; or his awareness that at the center of the maze there resides a fabulous creature, himself, too horrible to gaze upon directly. In committing himself to the fabrication of personal history, Rousseau knows that he may lose his way in the labyrinth of the self he is in the process of creating: he may, like the worm of which Esther Summerson speaks, in describing her illness, be "ever turned . . . by some obstruction" in a garden path. Or, he may strike to the center to discover a terrifying absence, a void.

In *Our Mutual Friend,* Eugene Wrayburn and Mortimer Lightwood respond to the story of John Harmon because, as I have said, they see in it, appropriately or not, a version of the story they tell themselves. Perhaps their stories are mazes, intricate Gothic structures, in which they are lost; a series of turnings in which they evade an encounter with a father other than the one of the imagination. We never meet the man Wrayburn ironically refers to, in abbreviated form, as M.R.F., My Respected Father. We never know if Wrayburn's depiction of a willful father has been true, or if it is a fiction to justify his own lassitude. Wrayburn's impasse, from which his passion for Lizzie Hexam apparently frees him, lies in his inability to take up the burden of personal history, to create a viable narrative of his life in which the father's nature is accurately defined so that he, the son, may respond effectively to it.

John Harmon's own story, so airily told by Lightwood to the Veneer-ings and their guests, involves a confrontation with Old John Harmon and his values, values he seeks to impose upon his son so that, in the words of Leopold Bloom, the son will obey him in the grave. The mar-velous ambiguity about whose grave, or niche, is never resolved in *Ulys-ses,* while *Our Mutual Friend* drains the ambiguity out of a complex sit-uation. All of this has occurred in Dickens before, but there is a telling difference in *Our Mutual Friend.* The mystery to be unravelled in Dick-ens's last completed novel is in the present, no longer in the past. There is no need to reconstruct an obscured past as there is in *David Copper-field, Bleak House,* and *Great Expectations.* The richly textured past of a struggling hero or heroine—of a David Copperfield, an Esther Sum-merson, or a Pip—is missing. *Our Mutual Friend* reveals a tendency, not only within its central characters, but within Dickens's imagination, a movement away from personal history. Dickens offers a stereotypical, a potentially archetypal, past far closer to that of Charles Darnay in *A Tale of Two Cities.* The burdensome past exists as a given in *Our Mutual Friend,* its particular outlines sketched in broadly, if at all. The fate of Bradley Headstone, who has denied his obscure origins so completely that he exists without an acknowledged mother or father, suggests that a failure to incorporate the past into the present leads inevitably to death. Even this failure is treated emblematically: to die by drowning in the embrace of a Rogue Riderhood is, perhaps, to succumb not to a re-pressed amorphous energy, after all, but to the denied father—and the past—for whom Riderhood stands. The ghost of King Hamlet haunts the pages of *Great Expectations* and of *Our Mutual Friend,* until he saun-ters off stage, with his hat on one side, in the form of Eugene Wray-burn's M.R.F., who turns out to be a "much younger cavalier" than Wrayburn himself.

Surely, George Radfoot, the sailor, in his plan to dispose of John Harmon and to impersonate him, enacts Harmon's own inclination to acquiesce to the terms of his father's Will, to claim both the Harmon fortune and the bride of his father's choosing: and, thus, *to be claimed* by the past. Harmon, wearing a dead man's clothes and armed with a dead man's knife, reveals to Rogue Riderhood a rusty clasp-knife that sug-gests the murderous will of the dead father as much as the dead Rad-foot's murderous intentions. It is one part of Harmon's fragile, multifaceted self—a "heavy horrid unintelligible something," that is sundered from him after a "downward slide through something like a tube" into the waters of the Thames (book 2, chapter 13).

The loss of the dreadful burden of the past in the form of Radfoot's body—later to be found mutilated in the river—anticipates Headstone's attack upon Wrayburn and the mutilated body to which Lizzie Hexam restores life by pulling it from the blood-streaked river. There are Christian dimensions to the immersion of Harmon and Wrayburn in the Thames. But Radfoot's rusty knife and, on a comic level, Silas Wegg's lively wooden member suggest other myths and other rituals to which Dickens alludes. Christian revelation becomes, at best, a privileged myth competing with pagan myths whose similarities reveal a universal, secular experience explored with ruthless thoroughness in *The Golden Bough*. The mutilation, literal in the case of Wrayburn, figurative in the case of Harmon, can be read as a non-Christian myth, the story of Osiris: the dismemberment of Osiris's body and its reconstitution through the action of Isis is a story reenacted by Wrayburn and Lizzie Hexam, by Harmon and Bella Wilfer. For Dickens, the consolidation of the new self in each case seems unshadowed by the absence of the member for which Isis had to fashion an image as a substitute. Only Silas Wegg, the "mudworm," and his wooden leg, with its wildly comic implications, remind us of the darker side of the Osiris legend. And Wegg finds himself, "with his wooden leg in a highly unaccommodating state," unceremoniously deposited by Sloppy in a scavenger's cart. The prodigious splash of the mud-worm provides a wry reminder of Dickens's imaginative association of the Thames with the Nile, of the absurd Wegg with Osiris.

During his fall into the Thames, John Harmon undergoes a process of fragmentation so radical that he momentarily ceases to be: "There was no such thing as I, within my knowledge" (book 2, chapter 13). He then responds to his own name ringing in his consciousness and becomes, in turn, the disoriented Julius Handford, the secretive John Rokesmith, and, ultimately, a revitalized John Harmon. The serious counterpart to the absurd Wegg, Harmon faces the danger of psychic dispersal; he collects himself, like a genteel person, around the center that is his name and recreates himself anew through an accommodation to a past that he artfully dodges as he transforms the terms of his father's Will.

Within *Our Mutual Friend*, the impetus to ritual pervades the lives of its characters. Five of the male figures in the novel fall, plunge, or are hurled into the Thames: Gaffer Hexam is "baptized unto Death"; Rogue Riderhood's boat is figuratively dismembered by a steamer, and Riderhood nearly drowns; John Harmon and Eugene Wrayburn are consigned to the waters as dead, only to return to life mysteriously transformed; Bradley Headstone and Riderhood are found, drowned, under the ooze and scum, near a gate of Plashwater Weir Mill Lock. This is repetition with a vengeance, the repetition of ceremony and of ritual. The five male characters in *Our Mutual Friend*, much like the varied speakers in "The Waste Land," are repeating what Robert Langbaum has called "an ancient drama with ancient meanings."[9] They are unwittingly engaged in an endeavor to escape a no longer viable personal identity, to create an archetypal self for which a name, signifying one's individuality, has been rendered irrelevant. Moved by unacknowledged forces within themselves, they seek a return to the archaic consciousness of Mircea Eliade's *The Myth of the Eternal Return*, for which "no importance [is accorded] to personal memories," to the romantic imperative to create personal history in time.[10] Dickens's characters in *Our Mutual Friend*, no less than the spectral figures of "The Waste Land," are, "in spite of themselves," as Langbaum claims, "living their buried *life*; but they do this . . . through *unconsciously* making rituals even when they think they have abolished all rituals."[11]

John Harmon and Eugene Wrayburn are pursuing a single, archetypal identity through those ritualistic acts, based upon the myth of Osiris, that Dickens has them perform. They break the specular image in the glass that confines them to an inadequate conception of self: for the specular image confirms and perpetuates a sense of isolation; it threatens to congeal into an habitual pose denying the ontological need, and the capacity, for change. In the mirror of the river, Harmon and Wrayburn perceive the hieroglyphic image of the self that, like the name each bears, always threatens to fix the individual in time, to transform him into a Kierkegaardian epitaph to the past.[12] Like a Demetrius and a Lysander in *A Midsummer Night's Dream*, like the characters in D. H. Lawrence's mature novels and novellas—*The Man Who Died* comes immediately to mind—the names they bear become emptied of significance. The self-creating repetition of romanticism and of David Copperfield's personal history gives way to the repetition of archaic ritual. The triumph of the impersonal self occurs as the celebrants imitate, unwittingly, a heroic or a divine model. Mircea Eliade calls this a "'primitive' ontological conception":

An object or an act becomes real only insofar as it imitates or repeats an archetype [the action of a hero or of a god]. Thus, reality is acquired solely through repetition or participation; everything which lacks an exemplary model is "meaningless,". . . [and] lacks reality . . . . the man of a traditional culture sees himself as real only to the extent that he ceases to be himself (for a modern observer) and is satisfied with imitating and repeating the gestures of another. In other words, he sees himself as real, . . . as "truly himself," only, and precisely, insofar as he ceases to be so.[13]

So much for Jean-Jacques Rousseau; so much for David Copperfield. So much for the claims of Ortega's Goethean existentialism in which man, always the novelist of himself, creates a conception of life, an identity, a self.[14]

The Thames becomes the great mirror of *Our Mutual Friend,* the glass whose depths seem as mysterious and as inaccessible as those spoken of in *A Tale of Two Cities:* "No more can I look into the depths of this unfathomable water, wherein, as momentary lights glanced into it, I have had glimpses of buried treasure and other things submerged. . . . It was appointed that the water should be locked in an eternal frost, when the light was playing on its surface, and I stood in ignorance on the shore."[15] The city lights shine upon the surface and the mudflats of the Thames before John Harmon's plunge into its murky waters; moonlight plays upon the ripples before Eugene Wrayburn is attacked by Bradley Headstone and left to drown near the mill town upstream from London. As he tries to reconstruct the events of the night of his near-death, Harmon remembers the room to which Radfoot led him: "The room overlooked the river, or a dock, or a creek, and the tide was out. . . . I drew back the curtain (a dark-brown curtain), and, looking out, knew by the kind of reflection below, of the few neighbouring lights, that they were reflected in tidal mud" (book 2, chapter 13). And Wrayburn, struggling with his desire, his conscience, and his thoughts of how M.R.F. might respond to his marriage to Lizzie, pauses by the water's edge:

The rippling of the river seemed to cause a correspondent stir in his uneasy reflections. He would have laid them asleep if he could, but they were in movement, like the stream, and all tending one way with a strong current. As the ripple under the moon broke unexpectedly now and then, and palely flashed in a new shape and with a new sound, so parts of his thoughts started, unbidden, from the rest, and revealed their wickedness. (Book 4, chapter 6).

The river and the mind are explicitly fused. The surface of each reflects shapes fitful, obscure, tantalizing. To be plunged into the waters is to break through the image playing on the surface and to gain access to its depths, not through introspection, but through an immersion into the depths of the self. To break through the image is to shatter the reflection of the body constituting the boundaries of the individual self, is to annihilate the hieroglyphic shape adumbrating the power of the name as sign.

John Harmon and Eugene Wrayburn live with the talismanic names conferred upon them by their respective fathers. They live with the specular image of themselves reflected in the literal glass and in the figurative glass of the Thames. And they become, as Maurice Merleau-Ponty observes, the captives of that image:

At the same time that the image of oneself makes possible the knowledge of oneself, it makes possible a sort of alienation. I am no longer what I felt myself, immediately, to be; I am that image of myself that is offered by the mirror. To use [Jacques] Lacan's terms, I am "captured, caught up" by my spatial image. Thereupon I leave the reality of my lived *me* in order to refer myself constantly to the ideal, fictitious, or imaginary *me*, of which the specular image is the first outline.[16]

Harmon and Wrayburn break through the specular image, the reflection on the river's surface, shattering its outline. Their alienation from the "lived me" has proved intolerable. But the "lived me" Dickens tentatively contemplates in *Our Mutual Friend* is no longer the authentic self of romanticism and existentialism: it is the archetypal self of archaic consciousness. Individuality, the "recent invention," disappears as Romantic Becoming accedes to the yearning for Being in a gesture that denies the significance of linear time and personal history. In *Our Mutual Friend,* Dickens explores, however darkly, an archetypal selfhood for which the repetition of earlier deeds becomes the highest form of reality, rather than its denial. Repetition in ritual, whether pagan or Christian, involves what Mircea Eliade calls the abolition of history, the very history that was discovered—or created—during the Enlightenment and the romantic era which followed.[17]

Our Mutual Friend is not a definitive dramatization of the quest for archaic modes of consciousness. The romantic ontology of self retains its primacy in Dickens's imagination. He will return to the plight of the romantic self in the figure of John Jasper, fascinated by the impasse Jasper reaches, uncertain of the appropriate imaginative course for dealing with the poetics of impasse. *The Mystery of Edwin Drood* might well have ended, had Dickens lived to complete it, with yet another display of Dickensian legerdemain, a willed rather than an imaginatively satisfying dénouement. But within *Our Mutual Friend* there appears the nostalgia attributed by Mircea Eliade both to James Joyce and to T. S. Eliot, the desire for the abolition of time as an escape from the terror of history, from events no longer redeemed by "transhistorical" or "metahistorical" significance. The burden of the romantic self, the felt need to render history, personal and social, as meaningful in purely secular terms may prove intolerable as it does for Pip in *Great Expectations*. Dickens, in *Our Mutual Friend,* responds movingly to the yearning that will so powerfully influence Joyce, Lawrence, and Eliot both before and after the inexplicable horrors of the Great War:

Perhaps the old mirror was never yet made by human hands, which, if all the images it had in its time reflected could pass across its surface again, would fail to reveal some scene of horror or distress. But the great serene mirror of the river seemed *as if* it might have reproduced all it had ever reflected between those placid banks, and brought nothing to the light save what was peaceful, pastoral, and blooming. (Book 3, chapter 9, emphasis mine)

No human figure is reflected in the "old mirror" of the Thames, for Dickens seeks, if only momentarily, the annihilation of that image upon which the personal self is constructed. Here Dickens explores, as his successors continued to explore, the possibility of a meaning beyond the limits of personal consciousness and of a realm beyond linear time. The potentially heterodox nature of the explanation should not be dismissed, for the consolation offered by a release from time need not be conventionally Christian.

But, the longing for something beyond the scenes of horror and distress is significantly qualified by the words *as if*. To long for a release from time itself is not necessarily to achieve imaginatively the release desired. John Harmon and Eugene Wrayburn return from the river, from the depths of the self. They assume again the names by which they have lived, having redefined the mysterious signs under which they were born. The specular image consolidates itself once more upon the surface of the watery glass, while strong currents flow beneath it. Each plays the role that may entrap him into another habitual response to the inner currents of his feelings and to the perplexing world about him. Personal identity is precariously reestablished. The pilgrimage of being is undertaken once again. But the surface events of the pilgrimage may be more illusory than ever. As the fairy realm impels the actions of all the mortal lovers in *A Midsummer Night's Dream,* the timeless depths of an impersonal, archetypal self may now impel Harmon and Wrayburn, as such a self informs the questings of Eliot's Tiresias in "The Waste Land."

Such a vision of archetypal selfhood is never fully realized in *Our Mutual Friend.* Dickens remains perplexed by the paradoxes he has posed to himself and to his characters. To be nameless is to die, as Bradley Headstone's fate reveals. The denial of a particularized past, embodied in the father, and of the meanings latent in personal history leads only to the fate of being lived *by* that history: for Hans Loewald, following Freud in his use of the figurative language of psychology, the id and the superego become tropes for a complex past not integrated into the present, into conscious life: "The past comprises the inherited, innate potential of our genes, the historical, cultural, moral tradition transmitted to us by our elders, and finally that primordial form of mentation, called unconscious or id, and the 'contents' of our lives that are experienced in this primordial form at the earliest level. This past is to be acquired, appropriated, made ours, in the creative development of the future." [18] Fixated upon an unappropriated past, the ego—in Dickens's and in Hans Loewald's words—becomes frozen, rigid, isolated from others and alienated from the present and the future, from the opportunity to weave its history and to fashion an evolving self within the context of that history. [19]

"What thou hast inherited from thy fathers, acquire it to make it thine." The lines from *Faust,* appearing both in *Totem and Taboo* and in *An Outline of Psycho-Analysis,* stand as an appropriate epigraph for *Our Mutual Friend* and an apt motto for those characters in the novel who must struggle with a past—real or imagined, acknowledged or repressed—in order to make it theirs. Only then may they skirt the fate upon which Leopold Bloom broods in his dour observation, "We obey them in the grave." But Freud's acknowledgment of his multifaceted past in the lines quoted from *Faust* also serves as a credo for those artists who follow Dickens and who, consciously or not, perceive in *Our Mutual Friend* part of their historical, cultural, moral tradition. These artists, more thoroughly disenchanted with the romantic self and more skeptical of the efficacy of the pursuit of personal history than Dickens, seek new ways, or old ones, of conceiving the nature and the life of the self. *Our Mutual Friend* becomes a patriarchal text in the best sense: it offers itself to James Joyce, to D. H. Lawrence, and to T. S. Eliot not as an imperious document imposing itself upon its heirs but as a paternal influence to be appropriated and transformed. Within its pages the novel offers a model of its own influence: it becomes another Golden Dustman to its various sons. Their fascination with ritual and with myth transforms what is embryonic in *Our Mutual Friend* into works of art in the service of new, if never to be fully realized, conceptions of the problematic self. The artist exists *in* time. But so, too, do those conceptions of self informing the artist's work. We are left, in the end, with Mrs. Chick's dubious philosophizing: "It's a world of change. . . . Why, my gracious me, what is there that does *not* change! Even the silkworm, who I am sure might be supposed not to trouble itself about such subjects, changes into all sorts of unexpected things continually." It is the human fate to be troubled about such subjects and never to acquire enduring explanations for the mystery of change, for such explanations inevitably alter into all sorts of unexpected things continually. The desire to annul the tyranny and the terror of history may generate nostalgia for the archaic consciousness of traditional man. Or the disillusioned romantic may flirt with nihilism, the deconstruction of the text a displacement for the deconstruction, the annihilation, of the self.

For those for whom neither the archetypal nor the deconstructed self provides a viable paradigm of human life, there may well, for the moment, remain only the alternative of personal history and the self as a necessary fiction. In the romantic self—as imagined by Rousseau, by Goethe, by Dickens, and by Freud—there exists a refusal to annul the problematics of the past, the present, and the future. The vision of the self as a process evolving within the context of an imagined history, a self for which stasis is figurative death, confers a harrowing freedom. The romantic self strives to create its own center, ontological and ethical. The appeal of an archetypal identity lies in the release it apparently grants from the burden of the individual and the social past. But as the deconstructionists, following Nietzsche, would observe, the archetypal self is only another kind of fiction, a trope by which the individual tries to live. We are faced with a choice between fictions. But the fiction of the archetypal consciousness all too often threatens to harden into myth, as Frank Kermode has defined myth in *The Sense of an Ending:* "Myth operates within the diagrams of ritual, which presupposes total and adequate explanations of things as they are and were; it is a sequence of radically unchangeable gestures. Fictions are for finding things out, and they change as the needs of sense-making change. Myths are the agents of stability, fictions the agents of change. Myths call for absolute, fictions for conditional assent."[20] Kermode is discussing those explanations— scientific, philosophical, and religious—that human beings use to render their lives and their universe intelligible. But it is now possible to see that he has offered, implicitly, a definition of the romantic self. For the romantic self is a fiction for finding things out; it changes as the needs of sense making change; it calls for conditional assent. It is not radically discontinuous, but moves around an evolving center. This is the self David Copperfield creates in his odyssey of consciousness. It is the darkly elusive self for which Esther Summerson looks in the depths of her mirror. It is the self from which Charles Darnay and Pip retreat. Already, within *A Tale of Two Cities* and *Great Expectations,* there appear adumbrations of the ritualistic mode of *Our Mutual Friend* in which Dickens imaginatively grasps for the archetypal self. In *The Mystery of Edwin Drood,* he returns to the tortured, particularized consciousness of John Jasper, trapped within a society committed to the denial of time and change. But with its incantatory language, as the searchers look for the body of Edwin Drood, the novel seems to be sweeping Dickens once again toward the ritualistic gestures of *Our Mutual Friend.* The danger for Dickens, and for others, exists in the lure of the archetypal, in the failure to recognize that the archetypal identity is but another imaginative construct conjured up to dispel the terrors of personal and social history and to deny the need of the individual to make sense of the past, the present, and the future by creating history. Ironically, the deconstructionist, armed against such errors, often manages to abolish time too, and achieves this by abolishing the self.[21]

Both the pursuit of archetypal consciousness and the determination to pierce all forms of affirmation as fictions invite "a sequence of radically unchangeable gestures." The archetypal self of which Eliade writes becomes "real only to the extent that [the individual] ceases to be himself (for a modern observer) and is satisfied with imitating and repeating the gestures of another." The deconstructing self may well become a perpetual Artful Dodger, ritualistically deconstructing every text, every self, it encounters. The creation of personal and social history, the imperative posed by the romantic self, offers an alternative to the abolition of time; it offers a context, calling for conditional assent, in which the individual may embrace a chosen destiny as a moral agent. Such a vision protects from the compulsion to repeat and infuses the individual life with meaning.[22]

In the creation of history the Father or the Mother is never merely symbolic, the function of a place within the grammar of society. The parents have lived a particularized past rich with those meanings conferred upon it by father and by son, by mother and by daughter. The child must appropriate and, if necessary, transform the family of the imagination, not only to avoid the fixation that a Dickens and a Freud find so destructive to the life of the self, but to imagine new forms of being, both personal and social, to redeem the ills of the past. It is precisely this heightened awareness of the self as creator of itself that proves intolerable and impels artists, and others, to imagine alternatives to the romantic self. This is the plight of those who find themselves, as Matthew Arnold found himself, "Wandering between two worlds, one dead, / The other powerless to be born." Arnold speaks not only of traditional Christianity, but of that romantic vision he can no longer embrace. But such a condition itself threatens paralysis and alienation from the present and the future. Perhaps it is no longer a question of waiting for a truth to be delivered to the world, but rather of choosing, with conditional assent, a trope by which to live.

Notes

Introduction

1 Michel Foucault, *The Order of Things: An Archaeology of the Human Sciences* (New York: Pantheon Books, 1970), p. xxiii. All further references to this work appear in the text.

2 Frank Kermode, *The Sense of an Ending: Studies in the Theory of Fiction* (New York: Oxford University Press, 1967), p. 167.

3 Ibid., p. 39.

4 Ibid., p. 42.

5 Sigmund Freud, *Beyond the Pleasure Principle,* in vol. 18 of *The Standard Edition of the Complete Psychological Works of Sigmund Freud,* general ed. James

Strachey, 24 vols. (London: Hogarth Press, 1953–74), p. 60, emphasis mine. All further references in this book to works in the *Standard Edition* will be followed by the abbreviation *SE,* volume number, and page number in parentheses.

6 Friedrich Nietzsche, *Beyond Good and Evil: Prelude to a Philosophy of the Future,* trans. Walter Kaufmann (New York: Vintage Books, 1966), p. 16.

7 See Nietzsche, *Beyond Good and Evil,* p. 16.

8 Some critics would argue that Michel Foucault's deconstructive tendencies make history impossible. I would argue, following Frank Lentricchia, that Foucault makes history both *possible* and *necessary* while reminding us that history should not be Platonized and "that knowledge, however we may define it, is received through a situated human consciousness . . . this is in itself no excuse to give up the labors of research or the rigors of historical self-examination and yield to the fashionable and casual historical despair of contemporary criticism." See Lentricchia, *After the New Criticism* (Chicago: University of Chicago Press, 1980), p. 207.

9 David Hume, "Of Personal Identity," in *A Treatise of Human Nature,* ed. L. A. Selby-Bigge (Oxford: Clarendon Press, 1888), p. 251. All further references to this work appear in the text.

10 Jean-Jacques Rousseau, *The Confessions,* trans. J. M. Cohen (Baltimore: Penguin Books, 1954), p. 17. All further references to this work appear in the text.

11 See Lionel Trilling, *Sincerity and Authenticity* (Cambridge, Mass.: Harvard University Press, 1972). I have been influenced by *Sincerity and Authenticity,* and shall return to it in discussing *The Mystery of Edwin Drood.*

12 My discussion of Rousseau's *The Confessions* has been influenced by René Girard's *Deceit, Desire, and the Novel: Self and Other in Literary Structure,* trans. Yvonne Freccero (Baltimore: Johns Hopkins University Press, 1965). See p. 66: "Men of triangular desire no longer believe [in God] but are unable to get along without transcendency."

13 See J. Hillis Miller, "Ariadne's Thread: Repetition and the Narrative Line," *Critical Inquiry,* 3 (1976): 57–77.

14 Thomas De Quincey, *Confessions of an English Opium-Eater together with Selections from the Autobiography of Thomas De Quincey,* ed. Edward Sackville-West (London: Cresset Press, 1950), pp. 328–29. This is the 1822 edition of the *Confessions.*

15 Paul Ricoeur, *Freud and Philosophy: An Essay on Interpretation,* trans. Denis Savage (New Haven: Yale University Press, 1970), p. 412.

16 Steven Marcus, "Freud and Dora: Story, History, Case History," in *Representations: Essays on Literature and Society* (New York: Random House, 1975), pp. 276–77. I shall return to Marcus's important essay, particularly in my discussion of *David Copperfield.*

17 Marcus, "Freud and Dora," p. 278.

18 Ernest Jones, *The Life and Work of Sigmund Freud,* vol. 1 (New York: Basic Books, 1953), p. 174.

19 See John Forster, *The Life of Charles Dickens,* ed. J. W. T. Ley (London: Cecil Palmer, 1928), p. 525.

20 Charles Dickens, *David Copperfield,* ed. Nina Burgis, The Clarendon Dickens (Oxford: Clarendon Press, 1981), chapter 2. All further references to this edition appear in the text.

21 José Ortega y Gasset, "History as a System," trans. William C. Atkinson, in *History as a System and Other Essays Toward a Philosophy of History,* ed. Helene Weyl (New York: W. W. Norton, 1961), p. 203.

22 Robert Langbaum, *The Mysteries of Identity: A Theme in Modern Literature* (New York: Oxford University Press, 1977), p. 13. In my discussion of the romantic self in this Introduction I am indebted to Langbaum's discussion of similar issues.

23 Maurice Merleau-Ponty, "Cézanne's Doubt," in *Sense and Non-Sense,* trans. Hubert L. Dreyfus and Patricia Allen Dreyfus (Evanston: Northwestern University Press, 1964), p. 25.

24 See Frank Kermode, *Romantic Image* (London: Routledge and Kegan Paul, 1957).

25 Charles Dickens, *Dombey and Son,* ed. Alan Horsman, The Clarendon Dickens (Oxford: Clarendon Press, 1974), chapter 29. All further references to this edition appear in the text.

26 Steven Marcus, *Dickens: from Pickwick to Dombey* (New York: Basic Books, 1965), p. 164.

27 Foucault's discussion of this historical transition can be clarified and supplemented by the following works: Peter L. Berger and Thomas Luckmann, *The Social Construction of Reality: A Treatise in the Sociology of Knowledge* (Garden City, N.Y.: Anchor Books, 1967); François Jacob, *The Logic of Living Systems: A History of Heredity,* trans. Betty E. Spillmann (London: Allen Lane, 1974); Thomas S. Kuhn, *The Structure of Scientific Revolutions* (Chicago: University of Chicago Press, 1962).

28 José Ortega y Gasset, "In Search of Goethe from Within," trans. Willard R. Trask, in *The Dehumanization of Art and Other Essays on Art, Culture, and Literature* (Princeton: Princeton University Press, 1968), p. 146.

29 Ortega, "History as a System," p. 213.

30 Charles Dickens, *Bleak House,* eds. George Ford and Sylvère Monod (New York: W. W. Norton, 1977), chapter 7. All further references to this edition appear in the text.

31 Ortega, "History as a System," p. 216.

32 Søren Kierkegaard, *Repetition: An Essay in Experimental Psychology,* trans.

Walter Lowrie (1941; reprint, New York: Harper and Row, Harper Torchbook, 1964), p. 35.

33 Thomas Carlyle, *Sartor Resartus,* ed. Charles Frederick Harrold (New York: Odyssey Press, 1937), p. 192. All further references to this edition appear in the text.

34 Johann Wolfgang von Goethe, *Faust,* trans. Walter Kaufmann (Garden City, N.Y.: Doubleday, 1961), p. 161, lines 1338–41; 1349–52.

35 Charles Dickens, *Our Mutual Friend,* The Oxford Illustrated Dickens (London: Oxford University Press, 1952), book 1, chapter 7. All further references to this edition appear in the text.

36 Ortega, "History as a System," p. 215.

37 For discussions of Carlyle and of Carlyle and Dickens, see Albert J. LaValley, *Carlyle and the Idea of the Modern* (New Haven: Yale University Press, 1968), pp. 69–118, and Michael Goldberg, *Carlyle and Dickens* (Athens: University of Georgia Press, 1972).

38 In this Introduction I have sought to elaborate upon the following observation by Alexander Welsh in *The City of Dickens* (Oxford: Clarendon Press, 1971), p. 135: "Romantic consideration carries Dickens far along the road toward *The Interpretation of Dreams* and ideas of personality prevalent in the twentieth century." See also Lionel Trilling, "Freud and Literature," in *The Liberal Imagination: Essays on Literature and Society* (New York: Viking Press, 1951), p. 35: "For psychoanalysis is one of the culminations of the Romanticist literature of the nineteenth century."

Chapter 1

1 Charles Dickens, *Dombey and Son,* ed. Alan Horsman, The Clarendon Dickens (Oxford: Clarendon Press, 1974), chapter 10. All further references to this edition appear in the text.

2 Madeline House and Graham Storey, eds., *The Letters of Charles Dickens,* The Pilgrim Edition, vol. 4, ed. Kathleen Tillotson (Oxford: Clarendon Press, 1977), pp. 618–19.

3 See J. Hillis Miller, "Introduction," *The Disappearance of God: Five Nineteenth-Century Writers* (Cambridge, Mass.: Belknap Press, 1963), pp. 1–16. See also J. Hillis Miller, "The Ontological Basis of Form," in *The Form of Victorian Fiction* (Notre Dame: University of Notre Dame Press, 1968), p. 31: "The situation which [most Victorian novelists] confront with increasing clarity in their novels may most properly be defined not as the disappearance of God, but as the death of God, that shocking event announced most explicitly in paragraph 125 of Friedrich Nietzsche's *The Joyful Wisdom.*"

4 Charles Dickens, *Little Dorrit,* ed. Harvey Peter Sucksmith, The Clarendon

Dickens (Oxford: Clarendon Press, 1979), book 2, chapter 1. All further references to this edition appear in the text.

5 Charles Dickens, *A Tale of Two Cities,* The Oxford Illustrated Dickens (London: Oxford University Press, 1949), book 1, chapter 3. All further references to this edition appear in the text.

6 Jean-Jacques Rousseau, *The Confessions,* trans. J. M. Cohen (Baltimore: Penguin Books, 1954), p. 17.

7 Thomas Carlyle, *Sartor Resartus,* ed. Charles Frederick Harrold (New York: Odyssey Press, 1937), pp. 162–63.

8 Roland Barthes, *Roland Barthes by Roland Barthes,* trans. Richard Howard (New York: Hill and Wang, 1977), [p. 36]. See also Jacques Lacan, "The Mirror Stage as Formative of the Function of the I as Revealed in Psychoanalytic Experience," in *Écrits: A Selection,* trans. Alan Sheridan (New York: W. W. Norton, 1977), pp. 1–7. For a discussion of mirrors in Dickens's novels, see Fred Kaplan, *Dickens and Mesmerism: The Hidden Springs of Fiction* (Princeton: Princeton University Press, 1975).

9 See Maurice Merleau-Ponty, "The Child's Relations with Others," trans. William Cobb, in *The Primacy of Perception and Other Essays on Phenomenological Psychology, the Philosophy of Art, History and Politics,* ed. James M. Edie (Evanston: Northwestern University Press, 1964), p. 146: "It is the simple fact that I live in the facial expressions of the other, as I feel him living in mine." See also D. W. Winnicott, "Mirror-role of Mother and Family in Child Development," in *Playing and Reality* (New York: Basic Books, 1971), pp. 111–18. My specific debt to Merleau-Ponty's essay will be clear in my discussion of *Dombey and Son* and the other Dickens novels I consider.

10 My discussion of *Dombey and Son* has been influenced by H. M. Daleski, "*Dombey and Son,*" in *Dickens and the Art of Analogy* (New York: Schocken Books, 1970), pp. 116–55; Susan R. Horton, *Interpreting Interpreting: Interpreting Dickens' Dombey* (Baltimore: Johns Hopkins University Press, 1979); Steven Marcus, "The Changing World," in *Dickens: from Pickwick to Dombey* (New York: Basic Books, 1965), pp. 293–357; and J. Hillis Miller, *Charles Dickens: The World of His Novels* (Cambridge, Mass.: Harvard University Press, 1965), pp. 143–50.

11 Merleau-Ponty discusses this subject throughout the essay "The Child's Relations with Others." I have made use of his phrase "specular image" in this and later chapters. Merleau-Ponty discusses the acquisition of a self on p. 120 of his essay: "The objectification of the body intervenes to establish a sort of wall between me and the other: a partition. Henceforth it will prevent me from confusing myself with what the other thinks, and especially with what he thinks of me; just as I will no longer confuse him with my thoughts, and especially my thoughts about him."

12 Charles Dickens, *Bleak House,* eds. George Ford and Sylvère Monod (New York: W. W. Norton, 1977), chapter 3. All further references to this edition appear in the text.

13 See Merleau-Ponty, "The Child's Relations with Others," pp. 136–37: "I leave the reality of my lived *me* in order to refer myself constantly to the ideal, fictitious, or imaginary *me,* of which the specular image [in the mirror] is the first outline. . . . I am torn from myself, and the image in the mirror prepares me for another still more serious alienation. . . . this alienation of the immediate *me,* its 'confiscation' for the benefit of the *me* that is visible in the mirror, already outlines what will be the 'confiscation' of the subject by the others who look at him [or her]."

14 My discussion of this episode has been influenced by Jacques Lacan, *The Language of the Self: The Function of Language in Psychoanalysis,* trans. Anthony Wilden (Baltimore: Johns Hopkins University Press, 1968). See also Merleau-Ponty, "The Child's Relations with Others," p. 139: "I understand all the more easily that what is in the mirror is my image for being able to represent to myself the other's viewpoint on me; and, inversely, I understand all the more the experience the other can have of me for seeing myself in the mirror in the aspect I offer him."

15 See Merleau-Ponty, "The Child's Relations with Others," p. 137.

16 My discussion of Dickens's use of the gorgon motif is influenced by Sigmund Freud, "Medusa's Head," *SE,* 18 : 273–74, and by R. D. Laing's interpretation of the Medusa's head in *The Divided Self: An Existential Study in Sanity and Madness* (New York: Pantheon Books, 1962).

17 See Merleau-Ponty, "The Child's Relations with Others," pp. 140–41: "If we suppose that the conquest of the image is only one aspect in the total continuum made up of all the lived relations with others and the world, it becomes easier to understand how this continuum, once at work, functions as though autonomously and how at the same time, participating in all the contingencies of our relations with others, it is susceptible to degradations and setbacks."

18 Robert Langbaum, *The Mysteries of Identity: A Theme in Modern Literature* (New York: Oxford University Press, 1977), p. 11. The passage from which Langbaum quotes appears in Erik H. Erikson, "Foundations in Observation," in *Identity: Youth and Crisis* (New York: W. W. Norton, 1968), p. 46: Erikson states his reservations about the psychoanalytic "overdifferentiation between the isolated individual forever projecting his infantile family constellation on the 'outer world,' and the 'individual-in-the-mass,' submerged in what Freud calls an 'indistinct aggregate' of men. Yet that a man could ever be psychologically alone; that a man, 'alone,' is essentially different from the same man in a group; . . . these and similar stereotypes demand careful revision."

19 See René Girard, "'Triangular' Desire," in *Deceit, Desire, and the Novel: Self and Other in Literary Structure,* trans. Yvonne Freccero (Baltimore: Johns Hopkins University Press, 1965), pp. 1–52.

20 See *Charles Dickens' Book of Memoranda,* ed. Fred Kaplan (New York: New York Public Library, 1981). This is a facsimile edition of the original notebook in the Henry W. and Albert A. Berg Collection of The New York Public Library (Astor, Lenox, and Tilden Foundations). The notebook, begun in January 1855, seems not to have been continued after 1865. The passage I quote from the originally unpaginated notebook is entry number 112, as numbered by Professor Kaplan.

21 Charles Dickens, *The Mystery of Edwin Drood,* ed. Margaret Cardwell, The Clarendon Dickens (Oxford: Clarendon Press, 1972), chapter 19.

Chapter 2

1 Charles Dickens, *David Copperfield,* ed. Nina Burgis, The Clarendon Dickens (Oxford: Clarendon Press, 1981), chapter 1. All further references to this edition appear in the text.

2 Jean-Jacques Rousseau, *The Confessions,* trans. J. M. Cohen (Baltimore: Penguin Books, 1954), p. 144. All further references to this edition appear in the text.

3 See Nina Burgis's discussion of the relationship between the autobiographical fragment and *David Copperfield* in her Introduction to the Clarendon edition of the novel, pp. xv–xxvi.

4 See Garrett Stewart's discussion of "The Pivotal Swiveller" in *Dickens and the Trials of the Imagination* (Cambridge, Mass.: Harvard University Press, 1974), pp 89–113.

5 Charles Dickens, *The Old Curiosity Shop,* The Oxford Illustrated Dickens (London: Oxford University Press, 1951), chapter 7. All further references to this edition appear in the text.

6 For a discussion of autobiography see James Olney, *Metaphors of Self: The Meaning of Autobiography* (Princeton: Princeton University Press, 1972); *Autobiography: Essays Theoretical and Critical,* ed. James Olney (Princeton: Princeton University Press, 1980), especially Georges Gusdorf, "Conditions and Limits of Autobiography," trans. James Olney, pp. 28–48, and Michael Sprinker, "Fictions of the Self: The End of Autobiography," pp. 321–42; William C. Spengemann, *The Forms of Autobiography: Episodes in the History of a Literary Genre* (New Haven: Yale University Press, 1980), pp. 119–32.

7 See Steven Marcus, "Freud and Dora: Story, History, Case History," in *Representations: Essays on Literature and Society* (New York: Random House, 1975), p. 278. Although I shall return to Marcus's essay in my discussion of *David*

Copperfield, I am also indebted to ideas explored by Jacques Lacan in *The Language of the Self: The Function of Language in Psychoanalysis,* trans. Anthony Wilden (Baltimore: Johns Hopkins University Press, 1968), and to Anthony Wilden's indispensable commentary on Lacan.

8 Thomas S. Szasz, *The Myth of Mental Illness* (New York: Dell, 1961), p. 136.

9 See Szasz, *Myth of Mental Illness,* p. 301: "Indeed, it may be said that one of the aims of the analytic process is to induce the patient to relinquish his indirect ('symptomatic,' 'transference') communications and to substitute for them direct messages framed in the straightforward idiom of ordinary English." And see Garrett Stewart's differing interpretation of Mr. Dick in *Dickens and the Trials of the Imagination,* pp. 180–81. For other discussions of *David Copperfield,* see Avrom Fleishman, *"David Copperfield:* Experiments in Autobiography," in *Figures of Autobiography: The Language of Self-Writing in Victorian and Modern England* (Berkeley: University of California Press, 1983), pp. 201–18; and Dianne F. Sadoff, "Language Engenders," in *Monsters of Affection: Dickens, Eliot and Bronte on Fatherhood* (Baltimore: Johns Hopkins University Press, 1982), pp. 38–51.

10 The discussion of Mr. Dick's Memorial may also be seen as Dickens's allusion to *David Copperfield* as an autobiographical novel dealing indirectly with Dickens's own life. The autobiography Dickens never completed has been transformed into *novelistic* fiction, removed yet another step from Dickens's autobiographical fragment, his life as he once chose to remember it. Dickens plays upon the name of the martyred King, Charles the First, which obsesses Mr. Dick. Both names allude to the autobiographical origins of the novel and to Charles Dickens's own concern about the power of the past to dominate the present. See Albert D. Hutter, "Psychoanalysis and Biography: Dickens' Experience at Warren's Blacking," *Hartford Studies in Literature,* 8 (1976): 23–37.

11 See Q. D. Leavis, "Dickens and Tolstoy: The Case for a Serious View of *David Copperfield,*" in *Dickens the Novelist* (New York: Pantheon Books, 1970), pp. 34–117.

12 See René Girard, "'Triangular' Desire," in *Deceit, Desire, and the Novel: Self and Other in Literary Structure,* trans. Yvonne Freccero (Baltimore: Johns Hopkins University Press, 1965), p. 15: "In the nineteenth century spontaneity becomes a universal dogma, succeeding imitation. Stendhal warns us at every step that we must not be fooled by these individualisms professed with fanfare, for they merely hide a new form of imitation."

13 See Maurice Merleau-Ponty, "The Child's Relations with Others," trans. William Cobb, in *The Primacy of Perception and Other Essays on Phenomenological Psychology, the Philosophy of Art, History and Politics,* ed. James M. Edie (Evanston: Northwestern University Press, 1964), pp. 102–3: "Ambivalence consists

in having two alternative images of the same object, the same person, without making any effort to connect them or to notice that in reality they relate to the same object and the same person. . . . As opposed to ambivalence, ambiguity is an adult phenomenon, a phenomenon of maturity. . . . It consists in admitting that the same being who is good and generous can also be annoying and imperfect. Ambiguity is ambivalence that one dares to look at face to face." For more traditional psychoanalytic discussions of the Double see Sigmund Freud, "The 'Uncanny,'" *SE,* 17 : 217–56; Otto Rank, *The Double: A Psychoanalytic Study,* trans. and ed. Harry Tucker, Jr. (Chapel Hill: University of North Carolina Press, 1971); and Robert Rogers, *A Psychoanalytic Study of the Double in Literature* (Detroit: Wayne State University Press, 1970).

14 For discussions dealing in various ways with the Double and the nature of the self, see Patrick Brantlinger, "Romances, Novels, and Psychoanalysis," *Criticism,* 17 (1975): 15–40; and Norman O. Brown, "Boundary," in *Love's Body* (New York: Random House, 1966), pp. 141–61.

15 See Mark Spilka's discussion of *David Copperfield* in *Dickens and Kafka: A Mutual Interpretation* (Bloomington: Indiana University Press, 1963), pp. 175–95.

16 Charles Dickens, *Bleak House,* eds. George Ford and Sylvère Monod (New York: W. W. Norton, 1977), chapter 16. All further references to this edition appear in the text.

17 J. Hillis Miller, Introduction to *Bleak House,* by Charles Dickens (Baltimore: Penguin, 1971), p. 11.

18 See Merleau-Ponty, "The Child's Relations with Others," pp. 113–41. For another discussion of *David Copperfield* and the "Tempest" episode, see Barry Westburg, *The Confessional Fictions of Charles Dickens* (Dekalb: Northern Illinois University Press, 1977), pp. 33–114. Barry Westburg's discussion of *David Copperfield,* like mine, is indebted to the writings of Merleau-Ponty.

19 Marcus, "Freud and Dora," p. 278.

20 See Maurice Merleau-Ponty, "Cézanne's Doubt," in *Sense and Non-Sense,* trans. Hubert L. Dreyfus and Patricia Allen Dreyfus (Evanston: Northwestern University Press, 1964), p. 25: "Psychoanalysis does not make freedom impossible; it teaches us to think of this freedom concretely, as a creative repetition of ourselves, always, in retrospect, faithful to ourselves."

21 See Marcus, "Freud and Dora," pp. 278–79. Marcus speaks of a narrative tradition culminating in the great bourgeois novels of the nineteenth century: "Indeed, we must see Freud's writings—and method—as themselves part of this culmination, and at the same moment, along with the great modernist novels of the first half of the twentieth century, as the beginning of the end of that tradition and its authority." My debt to Steven Marcus, throughout my discussion of *David Copperfield,* should now be clear.

Chapter 3

1 Charles Dickens, *Bleak House,* eds. George Ford and Sylvère Monod (New York: W. W. Norton, 1977), chapter 15. All further references to this edition appear in the text.

2 See Judith Wilt, "Confusion and Consciousness in Dickens's Esther," *Nineteenth-Century Fiction,* 32 (1977): 285–309, for another essay dealing with the issue of being and nonbeing in *Bleak House* and with the problem of self-creation.

3 See Leonard G. Wilson, *Charles Lyell: The Years to 1841: The Revolution in Geology* (New Haven: Yale University Press, 1972), p. 94.

4 See Barry Westburg, *The Confessional Fictions of Charles Dickens* (Dekalb: Northern Illinois University Press, 1977), p. 52: "The claustral nature of the city corresponds to the repetitious consciousness of the hero. London is like a mind that can never forget."

5 See William Axton, "Esther's Nicknames: A Study in Relevance," *Dickensian,* 62 (1966): 158–63, for a discussion of the implications of Esther's nicknames.

6 See Alex Zwerdling, "Esther Summerson Rehabilitated," *PMLA,* 88 (1973): 429–39. My own discussion of Esther's alienation from herself is, once again, influenced by Maurice Merleau-Ponty, "The Child's Relations with Others," trans. William Cobb, in *The Primacy of Perception and Other Essays on Phenomenological Psychology, the Philosophy of Art, History and Politics,* ed. James M. Edie (Evanston: Northwestern University Press, 1964), p. 136: "I am torn from myself, and the image in the mirror prepares me for another still more serious alienation, which will be the alienation by others."

7 My discussion of this episode and of those that follow is influenced by Maurice Merleau-Ponty, "The Child's Relations with Others"; by Jacques Lacan, "The Mirror Stage as Formative of the Function of the I as Revealed in Psychoanalytic Experience," in *Écrits: A Selection,* trans. Alan Sheridan (New York: W. W. Norton, 1977), pp. 1–7; and by D. W. Winnicott, "Mirror-role of Mother and Family in Child Development," in *Playing and Reality* (New York: Basic Books, 1971), pp. 111–18.

8 Charles Dickens, *A Tale of Two Cities,* The Oxford Illustrated Dickens (London: Oxford University Press, 1949), book 2, chapter 2.

9 Once again, in my discussion of the Double, I am indebted to the following works: Otto Rank, *The Double: A Psychoanalytic Study,* trans. and ed. Harry Tucker, Jr. (Chapel Hill: University of North Carolina Press, 1971); Robert Rogers, *A Psychoanalytic Study of the Double in Literature* (Detroit: Wayne State University Press, 1970); and Ralph Tymms, *Doubles in Literary Psychology* (Cambridge: Bowes and Bowes, 1949).

10 For a reading of this episode that parallels mine, see Robert Newsom, *Dickens on the Romantic Side of Familiar Things: Bleak House and the Novel Tradition* (New York: Columbia University Press, 1977).

11 See J. Hillis Miller, Introduction to *Bleak House*, by Charles Dickens (Baltimore: Penguin Books, 1971), pp. 11–34.

12 My reading of this part of *Bleak House* has been influenced by Rollo May, "Contributions of Existential Psychotherapy," in *Existence: A New Dimension in Psychiatry and Psychology*, eds. Rollo May, Ernest Angel, and Henri F. Ellenberger (New York: Basic Books, 1958), and particularly by the case history of a woman who confronts the problem of her own illegitimacy on p. 43:

I remember walking that day under the elevated tracks in a slum area, feeling the thought, "I am an illegitimate child." I recall the sweat pouring forth in my anguish in trying to accept that fact. Then I understood what it must feel like to accept, "I am a Negro in the midst of privileged whites," or "I am blind in the midst of people who see." Later on that night I woke up and it came to me this way, "I accept the fact that I am an illegitimate child." But "I am not a child anymore." So it is, "I am illegitimate." That is not so either: "I was born illegitimate." Then what is left? What is left is this, "I Am." This act of contact and acceptance with "I am," once gotten hold of, gave me (what I think was for me the first time) the experience "Since I Am, I have the right to be."

13 I have not tried to deconstruct entirely the self with which Esther lives. For an essay on *Bleak House* influenced by the writings of Jacques Derrida, see Michael Ragussis, "The Ghostly Signs of *Bleak House*," *Nineteenth-Century Fiction*, 34 (1979): 253–80.

14 See Winnicott, *Playing and Reality*, pp. 111–18.

15 For important and suggestive discussions of the novel, see J. Hillis Miller, "*Bleak House*," in *Charles Dickens: The World of His Novels* (Cambridge, Mass.: Harvard University Press, 1965), pp. 160–224; and H. M. Daleski, "*Bleak House*," in *Dickens and the Art of Analogy* (New York: Schocken Books, 1970), pp. 156–90.

Chapter 4

1 See Robert Louis Brannan, ed., *Under the Management of Mr. Charles Dickens: His Production of "The Frozen Deep"* (Ithaca: Cornell University Press, 1966); and Philip Collins, "A Tale of Two Novels: *A Tale of Two Cities* and *Great Expectations* in Dickens' Career," *Dickens Studies Annual*, 2 (1972): 336–51.

2 Maurice Merleau-Ponty, "Cézanne's Doubt," in *Sense and Non-Sense*, trans. Hubert L. Dreyfus and Patricia Allen Dreyfus (Evanston: Northwestern University Press, 1964), p. 25.

3 See Mircea Eliade, *The Myth of the Eternal Return, or, Cosmos and History,* trans. Willard R. Trask (Princeton: Princeton University Press, 1971), p. 159. See also p. 162: Modern man lives with "a despair provoked . . . by his presence in a historical universe in which almost the whole of mankind lives prey to a continual terror (even if not always conscious of it)."

4 Georg Lukács, *The Historical Novel,* trans. Hannah and Stanley Mitchell (London: Merlin Press, 1962), p. 243. See also Michael Goldberg, *Carlyle and Dickens* (Athens: University of Georgia Press, 1972), pp. 100–128.

5 For a similar reading, see Albert D. Hutter, "Nation and Generation in *A Tale of Two Cities,*" *PMLA,* 93 (1978): 448–62.

6 See Erik H. Erikson, "Foundations in Observation," in *Identity: Youth and Crisis* (New York: W. W. Norton, 1968), p. 46.

7 Charles Dickens, *A Tale of Two Cities,* The Oxford Illustrated Dickens (London: Oxford University Press, 1949), book 2, chapter 9. All further references to this edition appear in the text.

8 See John T. Irwin, *Doubling and Incest/Repetition and Revenge: A Speculative Reading of Faulkner* (Baltimore: Johns Hopkins University Press, 1975), p. 105. Irwin is discussing dynastic ambitions in William Faulkner's *Absalom, Absalom!:* "Sutpen's revenge requires that he found a dynasty, for the proof that he has succeeded in becoming the father will finally be achieved only when he bequeaths his authority and power to his son as an inheritance (a gift, not a right)."

9 I would like to acknowledge my debt, at this point, to Steven Marcus's discussion of *Barnaby Rudge,* "Sons and Fathers," in *Dickens: from Pickwick to Dombey* (New York: Basic Books, 1965), pp. 169–212; and to Taylor Stoehr's discussion of Dickens's style in general and of *A Tale of Two Cities* in particular in *Dickens: The Dreamer's Stance* (Ithaca: Cornell University Press, 1965), pp. 1–33 and pp. 195–203.

10 See Michel Foucault's discussion of the execution of "Damiens the regicide" in *Discipline and Punish: The Birth of the Prison,* trans. Alan Sheridan (New York: Pantheon Books, 1977), pp. 3–31.

11 This part of my discussion of *A Tale of Two Cities* has been influenced by V. E. von Gebsattel, "The World of the Compulsive," trans. Sylvia Koppel and Ernest Angel, in *Existence: A New Dimension in Psychiatry and Psychology,* eds. Rollo May, Ernest Angel, and Henri F. Ellenberger (New York: Basic Books, 1958), p. 177: "We see that an action can be completely executed, in the sense that it has served to implement a purpose, without being completed—or indeed, having occurred at all—in terms of its life-historical meaning. Although it is done, it is as if it had not been done. The person, as a living being moving ahead in time, does not enter into the objective performance of his

action, and therefrom arises—after the completion of the action—doubt as
to the reality of its occurrence."

12 See Otto Rank, *The Double: A Psychoanalytic Study,* trans. and ed. Harry
Tucker, Jr. (Chapel Hill: University of North Carolina Press, 1971), and Rob-
ert Rogers, *A Psychoanalytic Study of The Double in Literature* (Detroit: Wayne
State University Press, 1970).

13 For a more traditional psychoanalytic discussion of *A Tale of Two Cities,* see
Leonard Manheim, "A Tale of Two Characters: A Study in Multiple Projection," *Dickens Studies Annual,* 1 (1970): 225–37.

14 See Irwin, *Doubling and Incest,* p. 113: "Is there no virgin space in which one
can be first, in which one can have authority through originality?"

15 Charles Dickens, *David Copperfield,* ed. Nina Burgis, The Clarendon Dickens
(Oxford: Clarendon Press, 1981), chapter 23. All further references to this edition appear in the text.

16 See Alexander Welsh, "The Bride From Heaven," in *The City of Dickens* (Oxford: Clarendon Press, 1971), pp. 141–79.

17 See René Girard, "'Triangular' Desire," in *Deceit, Desire, and the Novel: Self
and Other in Literary Structure,* trans. Yvonne Freccero (Baltimore: Johns
Hopkins University Press, 1965), pp. 1–52; and pp. 186–87, n. 1: "From a
Freudian viewpoint, the original triangle of desire is, of course, the Oedipal
triangle. The story of 'mediated' desire is the story of this Oedipal desire, of
its essential permanence beyond its ever changing objects. . . . One of the
tasks facing criticism is the establishment of a genuine dialogue with Freud."

18 See Stoehr, *Dickens: The Dreamer's Stance,* pp. 21–25.

19 Ibid., pp. 197–8.

20 Otto Rank, "The Double as Immortal Self," in *Beyond Psychology* (1941; reprint, New York: Dover Publications, 1958), p. 92.

21 Rank, "The Double as Immortal Self," pp. 91 and 96.

22 See Irwin's discussion of Abraham and Isaac, God the Father and Jesus the
Son, in *Doubling and Incest,* pp. 125–35.

23 See Irwin, *Doubling and Incest,* p. 117: "The primal affront that the son suffers
at the hands of the father and for which the son seeks revenge . . . is the very
fact of being a son."

Chapter 5

1 Charles Dickens, *Great Expectations,* The Oxford Illustrated Dickens (London: Oxford University Press, 1953), chapter 1. All further references to this
edition appear in the text.

2 For recent discussions of *Great Expectations* that deal with issues of the self,

see Dianne F. Sadoff, "Charles Dickens: Authors of Being," in *Monsters of Affection: Dickens, Eliot and Bronte on Fatherhood* (Baltimore: Johns Hopkins University Press, 1982), pp. 10–64; Barry Westburg, "*Great Expectations* and the Fictions of the Future" and "'A Cobweb Meant Expectations': Pip and the Act of Confession," in *The Confessional Fictions of Charles Dickens* (Dekalb: Northern Illinois University Press, 1977), pp. 115–77.

3 For examples of classic ethical readings of *Great Expectations,* see Humphry House, "G. B. S. on *Great Expectations,*" in *All in Due Time* (London: Rupert Hart-Davis, 1955), pp. 201–20; and G. Robert Stange, "Expectations Well Lost: Dickens' Fable for His Time," *College English,* 16 (October 1954): 9–17. For a more recent reading in this vein, see H. M. Daleski, "*Great Expectations,*" in *Dickens and the Art of Analogy* (New York: Schocken Books, 1970), pp. 237–69.

4 See René Girard on the snob in his chapter, "Men Become Gods in the Eyes of Each Other," in *Deceit, Desire, and the Novel: Self and Other in Literary Structure,* trans. Yvonne Freccero (Baltimore: Johns Hopkins University Press, 1965), pp. 53–82. The phrase "ontological sickness" occurs on p. 97.

5 See Maurice Merleau-Ponty, "The Child's Relations with Others," trans. William Cobb, in *The Primacy of Perception and Other Essays on Phenomenological Psychology, the Philosophy of Art, History and Politics,* ed. James M. Edie (Evanston: Northwestern University Press, 1964), p. 136: "At the same time that the image of oneself makes possible the knowledge of oneself, it makes possible a sort of alienation. I am no longer what I felt myself, immediately, to be; I am that image of myself that is offered by the mirror." See also Robert Garis's "Dickens's Civilization and its Discontents," in *The Dickens Theatre: A Reassessment of the Novels* (Oxford: Clarendon Press, 1965), pp. 191–225.

6 See Q. D. Leavis's discussion of the legitimacy of Pip's dissatisfaction with a life at the forge, "How We Must Read *Great Expectations,*" in *Dickens the Novelist* (New York: Pantheon, 1970), pp. 277–331.

7 See Girard, *Deceit, Desire, and the Novel,* p. 107: "The indifferent person always seems to possess that radiant self-mastery which we all seek. He seems to live in a closed circuit, enjoying his own being, in a state of happiness which nothing can disturb. He is God."

8 See Ortega y Gasset, "History as a System," trans. William C. Atkinson, in *History as a System and Other Essays Toward a Philosophy of History,* ed. Helene Weyl (New York: W. W. Norton, 1961), p. 215.

9 My discussion of the relationships of Pip and Estella to their respective pasts has been influenced significantly by Peter Brooks's essay "Repetition, Repression, and Return: *Great Expectations* and the Study of Plot," *New Literary History,* 11 (1980): 503–26.

10 For a discussion of the attack on Mrs. Joe and on Pip's relationship to Orlick

see Julian Moynahan, "The Hero's Guilt: The Case of *Great Expectations*," *Essays in Criticism*, 10 (Jan. 1960): 60–79. For the significance of repetitions see Maurice Merleau-Ponty, "Cézanne's Doubt," in *Sense and Non-Sense*, trans. Hubert L. Dreyfus and Patricia Allen Dreyfus (Evanston: Northwestern University Press, 1964), pp. 9–25; and J. Hillis Miller, "Two Forms of Repetition," in *Fiction and Repetition: Seven English Novels* (Cambridge: Mass.: Harvard University Press, 1982), pp. 1–21.

11 My discussion of Pip's response to Jaggers's appearance at the Three Jolly Bargemen is influenced not only by Peter Brooks's essay "Repetition, Repression, and Return," but by the case history of "Miss Lucy R." (*SE*, 2:106–24) and by this exchange between Freud and his patient: "'But if you knew you loved your employer why didn't you tell me?'—'I didn't know—or rather I *didn't want to know*. I *wanted* to drive it out of my head and not think of it again; and *I believe latterly I have succeeded*'" (*SE*, 2:117, emphasis mine).

12 See Merleau-Ponty, "Cézanne's Doubt," pp. 24–25; and see Miller, "Two Forms of Repetition."

13 Girard, *Deceit, Desire, and the Novel*, p. 38.

14 For a similar and fuller reading of this episode, see Brooks, "Repetition, Repression, and Return," 513–14.

15 See Thomas De Quincey, *Confessions of an English Opium-Eater together with Selections from the Autobiography of Thomas De Quincey*, ed. Edward Sackville-West (London: Cresset Press, 1950), pp. 328–29. All further references to this edition appear in the text.

16 See Harold Bloom, "The Internalization of the Quest-Romance," in *Romanticism and Consciousness: Essays in Criticism*, ed. Harold Bloom (New York: W. W. Norton, 1970), pp. 3–24.

17 Once again see R. D. Laing's discussion of the Medusa's head in *The Divided Self: An Existential Study in Sanity and Madness* (New York: Pantheon Books, 1962).

18 See Hans W. Loewald, *Psychoanalysis and the History of the Individual* (New Haven: Yale University Press, 1978), pp. 21–22: "To own up to our own history, to be responsible for our unconscious . . . means, to bring unconscious forms of experiencing into the context and onto the level of the more mature, more lucid life of the adult mind. . . . What is possible is to engage in the task of actively reorganizing, reworking, creatively transforming those early experiences which . . . first gave meaning to our lives. The more we know what it is that we are working with, the better we are able to weave our history."

19 Steven Marcus, "Freud and Dora: Story, History, Case History," in *Representations: Essays on Literature and Society* (New York: Random House, 1975), p. 278.

20 See Brooks's discussion of these episodes in "Repetition, Repression, and Return," 511–23, for a different reading.
21 See Mircea Eliade, "The Terror of History," in *The Myth of the Eternal Return, or, Cosmos and History,* trans. Willard R. Trask (Princeton: Princeton
   University Press, 1971), pp. 141–62.

Chapter 6

1 *Charles Dickens' Book of Memoranda,* ed. Fred Kaplan (New York: New York
  Public Library, 1981): the passage I quote from the unpaginated notebook is
  entry number 70, as numbered by Professor Kaplan.
2 Charles Dickens, *A Tale of Two Cities,* The Oxford Illustrated Dickens (London: Oxford University Press, 1949), book 2, chapter 14. All further references to this edition appear in the text.
3 Charles Dickens, *Our Mutual Friend,* The Oxford Illustrated Dickens (London: Oxford University Press, 1952), book 1, chapter 1. All further references
  to this edition appear in the text.
4 Michel Foucault, *The Order of Things: An Archaeology of the Human Sciences*
  (New York: Pantheon Books, 1970), p. 278. All further references to this work
  appear in the text.
5 The phrase "unconscious repetitions" occurs in an often cited letter to John
  Forster written by Dickens in October 1860 as he began work on *Great Expectations:* "The book will be written in the first person throughout, and during
  these first three weekly numbers you will find the hero to be a boy-child, like
  David. . . . To be quite sure I had fallen into no unconscious repetitions, I
  read David Copperfield again the other day, and was affected by it to a degree
  you would hardly believe." The letter appears in vol. 3 of *The Letters of Charles
  Dickens,* ed. Walter Dexter, The Nonesuch Dickens (Bloomsbury, Eng.: Nonesuch Press, 1938), p. 186.
6 See J. Hillis Miller, "Introduction," in *The Disappearance of God: Five Nineteenth-Century Writers* (Cambridge, Mass.: Belknap Press, 1963), p. 5: "The
  industrialization and urbanization of man means the progressive transformation of the world. Everything is changed from its natural state into something
  useful or meaningful to man. Everywhere the world mirrors back to man his
  own image, and nowhere can he make vivifying contact with what is not
  human."
7 Thomas De Quincey, *Confessions of an English Opium-Eater together with Selections from the Autobiography of Thomas De Quincey,* ed. Edward Sackville-West
  (London: Cresset Press, 1950), p. 289. All further references to this edition
  appear in the text.

8 *Dickens' Book of Memoranda*, entry number 92.

9 Charles Dickens, *Bleak House*, eds. George Ford and Sylvère Monod (New York: W. W. Norton, 1977), chapter 16. All further references to this edition appear in the text.

10 Once again, see Steven Marcus, "Freud and Dora: Story, History, Case History," in *Representations: Essays on Literature and Society* (New York: Random House, 1975), pp. 247–310.

11 My discussion is indebted to R. D. Laing's concepts of ontological insecurity and the unembodied self explored in *The Divided Self: An Existential Study in Sanity and Madness* (New York: Pantheon Books, 1962); and to René Girard, *Deceit, Desire, and the Novel: Self and Other in Literary Structure*, trans. Yvonne Freccero (Baltimore: Johns Hopkins University Press, 1965).

12 See Ernest M. Boll, "The Plotting of *Our Mutual Friend*," *Modern Philology*, 42 (1944): 96–122. The essay includes a reproduction of Dickens's working notes for the novel.

13 J. Hillis Miller, *The Form of Victorian Fiction* (Notre Dame: University of Notre Dame Press, 1968), p. 33.

14 See Girard, "'Triangular' Desire," in *Deceit, Desire, and the Novel*, p. 16.

15 See Christopher Herbert, "De Quincey and Dickens," *Victorian Studies*, 17 (March 1974): 247–63, for another discussion of the two authors.

16 Charles Dickens, *The Mystery of Edwin Drood*, ed. Margaret Cardwell, The Clarendon Dickens (Oxford: Clarendon Press, 1972), chapter 5. All further references to this edition appear in the text.

17 Critics discussing Miss Twinkleton's "two states of consciousness" ordinarily point to Wilkie Collins's *The Moonstone*, published in serial form in *All the Year Round* from January to August 1868 as an influence upon Dickens. In the novel, Ezra Jennings, a De Quincean pariah and proto-psychoanalyst, cites the works of De Quincey, Sir John Elliotson, and W. B. Carpenter to convince Franklin Blake of the existence of two forms of consciousness. For a fascinating discussion of *The Moonstone* see Albert D. Hutter, "Dreams, Transformations, and Literature: The Implications of Detective Fiction," *Victorian Studies*, 19 (December 1975): 181–209. For a discussion of Dickens and animal magnetism see Fred Kaplan, *Dickens and Mesmerism: The Hidden Springs of Fiction* (Princeton: Princeton University Press, 1975).

18 See Girard, *Deceit, Desire, and the Novel*, pp. 10–11: "Only someone who prevents us from satisfying a desire which he himself has inspired in us is truly an object of hatred. The person who hates first hates himself for the secret admiration concealed by his hatred. In an effort to hide this desperate admiration from others, and from himself, he no longer wants to see in his mediator anything but an obstacle."

19 Matthew Lewis, *The Monk: A Romance,* ed. Howard Anderson (London: Oxford University Press, 1973), pp. 237–38. See Peter Brooks's essay, "Virtue and Terror: *The Monk,*" *English Literary History,* 40 (1973): 249–63.

20 I am quoting, in part, from Walter Kaufmann's translation of Goethe's *Faust* (Garden City, N.Y.: Doubleday, 1961). Kaufmann translates *die Tat* as "act," while others translate it as "deed," and I follow them. The phrase "restless activity" occurs in line 1759 of Part One of *Faust.*

21 See Girard, *Deceit, Desire, and the Novel,* pp. 186–87, n. 1: "The story of 'mediated' desire is the story of this Oedipal desire, of its essential permanence beyond its ever changing objects. . . . The Self discovers that the Other, who has become the hated Double, is really identical to himself in those very features which make him appear most hateful."

22 See Friedrich Nietzsche, *Beyond Good and Evil: Prelude to a Philosophy of the Future,* trans. Walter Kaufmann (New York: Vintage Books, 1966), pp. 27–28: "It is highly probable that philosophers within the domain of the Ural-Altaic languages (where the concept of the subject is least developed) look otherwise 'into the world,' and will be found on paths of thought different from those of the Indo-Germanic peoples and the Muslims: the spell of certain grammatical functions is ultimately also the spell of *physiological* valuations and racial conditions." Nietzsche writes as a philologist, a student of languages; De Quincey and Dickens write of a figuratively alien realm, intuitively anticipating Nietzsche.

23 For a long discussion of the Western vision of the Orient see Edward W. Said, *Orientalism* (New York: Pantheon Books, 1978).

24 This paragraph is indebted to Peter L. Berger and Thomas Luckmann, *The Social Construction of Reality: A Treatise in the Sociology of Knowledge* (Garden City, N.Y.: Anchor Books, 1967); and to J. H. van den Berg, *The Changing Nature of Man: Introduction to a Historical Psychology,* trans. H. F. Croes (New York: W. W. Norton, 1961), pp. 224–25: "For where would we be if we granted any individual a right to have a world of his own? A world in which everything looks different, a world in which things have another substantiality? Soon there would be more and more people who would demand the same right. Things must retain their stability, they are the condition of our understanding. Even more than that, they are understanding itself. . . . No one is allowed to take it away from us, not even [a] patient [under analysis]. If he were, our common existence would fall to pieces."

25 Much of this discussion of *Edwin Drood* was written with Lionel Trilling's *Sincerity and Authenticity* (Cambridge, Mass.: Harvard University Press, 1972) in mind. I have clearly been responding to his discussion of R. D. Laing in the final chapter of his book. I only want to emphasize that I have tried not to confuse fictionalized madness with the madness of real and suffering human

beings. I am not arguing *for* madness as the only authentic response to modern culture, nor am I claiming that there can be civilization without its discontents. But there is a need for remembering that madness, in fiction and in life, may well be intelligible as a commentary upon the ways in which a culture has failed the individual. For Trilling's own discussion of this issue, see his "Freud: Within and Beyond Culture," in *Beyond Culture: Essays on Literature and Learning* (New York: Viking Press, 1965), pp. 89–118.

26 See Richard M. Baker, *The Drood Murder Case: Five Studies in Dickens's Edwin Drood* (Berkeley: University of California Press, 1951), p. 43.

Conclusion

1 Henry James, "The Limitations of Dickens," in *The Dickens Critics*, ed. George H. Ford and Lauriat Lane, Jr. (Ithaca: Cornell University Press, 1961), p. 48. The review of *Our Mutual Friend* first appeared in *The Nation* in 1865.

2 See T. S. Eliot, *The Waste Land: A Facsimile and Transcript of the Original Drafts Including the Annotations of Ezra Pound*, ed. Valerie Eliot (New York: Harcourt Brace Jovanovich, 1971).

3 See Jackson I. Cope, "Joyce's Waste Land," in *The Genres of the Irish Literary Revival*, ed. Ronald Schleifer (Norman, Okla.: Pilgrim Books, 1980), pp. 93–120.

4 D. H. Lawrence, *Sons and Lovers* (New York: Viking Press, 1958), p. 361. All further references to this work appear in the text.

5 Erik H. Erikson, "Foundations in Observation," in *Identity: Youth and Crisis* (New York: W. W. Norton, 1968), p. 46.

6 José Ortega y Gasset, "History as a System," trans. William C. Atkinson, in *History as a System and Other Essays Toward a Philosophy of History*, ed. Helene Weyl (New York: W. W. Norton, 1961), p. 217.

7 Charles Dickens, *Our Mutual Friend*, The Oxford Illustrated Dickens (London: Oxford University Press, 1952), book 2, chapter 12. All further references to this edition appear in the text.

8 Jean-Jacques Rousseau, *The Confessions*, trans. J. M. Cohen (Baltimore: Penguin Books, 1954), pp. 26 and 28.

9 Robert Langbaum, *The Mysteries of Identity: A Theme in Modern Literature* (New York: Oxford University Press, 1977), p. 93.

10 Mircea Eliade, *The Myth of the Eternal Return; or, Cosmos and History*, trans. Willard R. Trask (Princeton: Princeton University Press, 1971), p. 47.

11 Langbaum, *Mysteries of Identity*, p. 89, emphasis mine.

12 See John T. Irwin, *American Hieroglyphics: The Symbol of the Egyptian Hieroglyphics in the American Renaissance* (New Haven: Yale University Press, 1980), for his Lacanian interpretation of the Narcissus myth in which

Narcissus's encounter with his shadow becomes the origin of "man" and language.

13 Eliade, *Myth of the Eternal Return,* p. 34.

14 See Ortega, "History as a System," p. 203.

15 Charles Dickens, *A Tale of Two Cities,* The Oxford Illustrated Dickens (London: Oxford University Press, 1949), book 1, chapter 3.

16 Maurice Merleau-Ponty, "The Child's Relations with Others," trans. William Cobb, in *The Primacy of Perception and Other Essays on Phenomenological Psychology, the Philosophy of Art, History and Politics,* ed. James M. Edie (Evanston: Northwestern University Press, 1964), p. 136. Merleau-Ponty's discussion of the specular image, with its Lacanian aspects, is echoed by Roland Barthes in the passage I have quoted from *Roland Barthes by Roland Barthes,* trans. Richard Howard (New York: Hill and Wang, 1977), [p. 36]: *"You are the only one who can never see yourself except as an image: you never see your eyes unless they are dulled by the gaze they rest upon the mirror or the lens . . . : even and especially for your own body, you are condemned to the repertoire of its images."*

17 See Eliade, *Myth of the Eternal Return,* p. 53. I am also drawing upon Stephen Toulmin and June Goodfield, *The Discovery of Time* (London: Hutchinson, 1965).

18 Hans W. Loewald, *Psychoanalysis and the History of the Individual* (New Haven: Yale University Press, 1978), pp. 24–25.

19 See Loewald, *Psychoanalysis and the History of the Individual,* p. 22.

20 Frank Kermode, *The Sense of an Ending: Studies in the Theory of Fiction* (New York: Oxford University Press, 1967), p. 39. My reading of Dickens's novels throughout this book is indebted to Professor Kermode's *Romantic Image* (London: Routledge and Kegan Paul, 1957) and to *The Sense of an Ending.* The fusion of Kermode and Freud is my own doing, though Kermode's *The Genesis of Secrecy: On the Interpretation of Narrative* (Cambridge, Mass.: Harvard University Press, 1979) begins and ends with references to *The Interpretation of Dreams.*

21 See Colin MacCabe, *James Joyce and the Revolution of the Word* (New York: Barnes and Noble, 1979), p. 4: "Literary criticism depends on a theory of the subject in order to carry out its task of interpretation." All recent debate about the status of the text becomes a debate about the status of the subject.

22 I have written this conclusion with two discussions of the fate of the self in mind: see Leo Bersani, *A Future for Astyanax: Character and Desire in Literature* (Boston: Little, Brown, 1976); and J. Hillis Miller, "Stevens' Rock and Criticism as Cure," *Georgia Review,* 30 (1976): 5–31, 330–48.

Index

Wrayburn, Eugene, in *Our Mutual
Friend*, 27, 29, 56–57, 131, 133, 142,
190–207, 211, 215, 219–21, 225–27,
230, 235–36, 239–40, 242–49

Wren, Jenny, in *Our Mutual Friend*,
191

Zwerdling, Alex, 262n.6